Chosen for Reasons Unknown

A Holocaust Survivor's Journey

By Murray Ebner

Library of Congress Control Number: 2008936777

ISBN: 978-0-9821374-0-6 (paperback)
ISBN: 978-0-9821374-1-3 (hardcover)

Printed in the United States of America.

To order additional copies of this book, contact:
Ebner Properties
3455 East Broad Street
Columbus, Ohio 43213
www.chosenforreasonsunknown.com

This book is dedicated in loving memory to my wonderful parents, Hershel and Feigel Ebner, and to my dearest brothers Abraham, Zishe, and Nuta. May their memory be an inspiration to all who survived and their legacy be a beacon of strength for future generations. They should know that all that I have overcome and achieved in my life has been a tribute to their stewardship from the heavens and in my heart.

Contents

Acknowledgments

Gene Church — It is with tremendous gratitude that we give special thanks to Gene Church. Gene was the impetus that started the writing of the book. He saw a story about me in the *Columbus Dispatch* and thought that the story would be most worthy of publishing a book. He called and introduced himself. He was very eloquent in making the argument to me as to why a book on my life was indeed so necessary. In spite of Gene's urging, I continued to be reluctant to the idea until he mentioned to me that there is nothing more permanent than the written word; after considering those words, I realized that the time had come for me to pen my story for future generations. Gene flew several times from where he was living at the time in California to interview me, gather information for the book, and write the initial manuscript. His questions were deep, pointed, thoughtful, and creative. He asked them in a most interested and caring way. It was due to his easy manner that I was able to recall so many of my thoughts and senses that I thought had long slipped away. I am most thankful to my dear friend Gene Church.

Pat LoBrutto — Pat has been the sculptor who has taken a fairly molded object and chiseled it in a most masterful way. His talent to find just the right proportion and clarity to every nuance can be seen throughout the book. His dedication to thoroughly articulate the picture he paints goes unmatched. It is with privilege that we had Pat as a part of our team.

Acknowledgments

There were so many people with a vested interest in this project — their efforts and loyalty have been appreciated more than words can say. Just to name a few:

Kelley Evans — It is with a heart full of affection that I give special thanks to Kelley Evans. Her expertise in good readership has added a critical flair that otherwise might have been overlooked. It was her goal to assure the readers clarity and visualization; she left no stone unturned. Flow and accuracy were paramount to her. Most of all, I cannot thank her enough for her nearly single-handedly administering all facets of editing through publishing and distribution. The care and concern she displayed were immeasurable. All her efforts were most appreciated.

Sam Nahem and his entire team — For numerous interviews and film footage shot to create "A Survivor's Journey," which was a very important research tool for this book.

Lapiz Design — For the graphic work used on the cover of the book.

Milton Kahn — For his opinions and advice given to promote the book so that this very important story could be shared with as many people as possible.

To the entire Ebner family — For their love and support from the very beginning.

To all of the friends, new and old, who have been there for the Ebner family through the years.

PROLOGUE

MONIEK EBNER CAME BACK to the little Polish town where he lived for the first thirteen years of his life in 2000. He was Murray Ebner now. He had been away for sixty years; the happy place of his memories had become a catastrophe. The Nazis had seen to that.

He flew into Krakow with his wife, Sylvia, son, Mark, daughter-in-law, Nicole, and daughters, Cindy and Lisa. They left almost immediately for Nowy Wisnicz. Murray had been gone so long he could barely speak Polish any longer; they had to bring a translator. Murray had told his family about his town and home for a long time. Everyone wondered whether his memories were accurate, whether he would be disappointed because the house was gone, or because nothing was recognizable.

His son, Mark, asked him, "Do you think you can find the house?"

"What are you talking about?" Murray said. "Of course I can find my own house." They were to find out that Murray's memory would be entirely accurate time after time, in the minutest details.

Why have I returned?, Murray thought. His family, his mother and father and brothers, were not there when he returned from the camps in 1945. They were not there now. He had not heard a word from them or about them in all these years. Still, he wondered. Often, he would say, "That man looks just like my brother Abraham"; "That fellow over there looks like Nuta all grown up"; or "That woman looks like my mother."

Other survivors had miraculous reunions with loved ones lost during the war. Other families found each other after years of separation. *Why not me?* A part of his soul and heart always expected to find them — maybe his brothers were alive in Argentina or Israel, *maybe Mama and Tata will be waiting for me at the house*. A part of his mind and heart knew, however, that he would never see them again. He swore he would never return…but Murray always worried that he hadn't done enough to find them, that they were alive somewhere…. So here he was, driving past the farms with his family, looking, as always, for his family. It was as if he had two families; the family that was lost, that existed in his mind alone because there was no one else to remember them; and then there was his American family, his wife and children, the loving family of the new life he had built from the ashes of the old.

He thought of all this as he sat in the car that drove up the street to the home where he grew up and took him back to the time when the world was his mother and father and brothers, and the little town of Nowy Wisnicz.

One

An enormous crash of thunder shattered the stillness of the night sky. Ten-year-old Moniek Ebner snapped straight up in bed, wide awake, covered in cold sweat. The flash of lightning that followed illuminated the entire room. He trembled with a fear unlike any he had ever experienced.

Nuta, his younger brother, slept beside him in the double bed and didn't respond to the noise, or the light.

Another boom of thunder caused Moniek to shudder and sent chills down his spine. He reached forward. "Nuta," he whispered, and shook his younger brother's leg. But the youngster didn't respond. A second flash of lightning showed him that Nuta's eyes were wide open, staring into nothingness.

He jumped from the bed and stared down in shock. Nuta was dead.

Moniek slowly backed out of the room and into the hallway. What was happening? How could this be? The youngster trembled as he made his way to the bedroom next door where his older brothers Abraham and Zishe slept.

More thunder, more lightning, and his worst fears came to fruition. His older brothers each had the same open-eyed, blank stare and were laying perfectly still, just like Nuta. He shook both of them. There was no reaction and they were cold. He bit his fist to stop himself from crying out.

His parents would know what to do; they always did. His three brothers were gone and life as he knew it would be irreversibly altered.

He eased himself out of the room and made his way across the hall. As always, the door to his parents' bedroom was open.

More thunder rolled through the night sky. Another flash of lightning illuminated everything. Neither his mother nor father moved. Like three of their sons, they lay silent, their eyes were wide open and lifeless. Moniek's life was over. He tried desperately to speak, to call out to his parents, but no sound would come.

There was another flash of lightning that lit up the room. Moniek was momentarily blinded, he stood motionless, his feet glued to the highly polished wooden floor…

Feigel stirred. Through sleep-filled eyes, she quietly asked, "Moniek, is that you? Are you all right?"

With great wonderment, he softly answered, "Yes, Mama. Are *you*?"

"Am I what?"

"Are you all right?"

She sat up in bed. "You look terrified."

"I'm fine," he replied.

"Did you have a bad dream?"

"No, Mama."

Hershel stirred as well and with a raspy, sleep-filled voice asked, "Moniek, is that you?"

"Yes, Tata," he whispered. "It's me."

His father rolled over and as he did gently said, "Get under the covers and sleep with us tonight."

When both parents were soundly asleep Moniek eased his way out of the bed and went back down to check on his brothers. All three of them were fine. The entire experience had been a horrible nightmare.

Sadly, it was a premonition of tragic events to come.

Prior to breakfast the following morning Hershel offered the usual, daily prayers and Feigel, a thin, attractive woman with straight dark hair, fixed lunches for all four of the boys. Moniek, normally the talkative one in the family, was abnormally quiet. His unusual silence was teased by the rest of the group seated around the table. He was ashamed of his gruesome nighttime thoughts and as a result never mentioned them to anyone. Ever.

"What's that on your finger?" Feigel asked, pointing to his hand. Moniek looked down. The marks on his knuckle left by his teeth from the night before were still clearly visible. He shook his head, unable to answer. Perhaps his nightmare was more real than he initially thought.

A few moments later the four Ebner brothers and three of their friends walked toward the school in the main square of their small town. The mid-November sun provided a degree of warmth to the chilling wind which cut through their heavy winter coats. For all practical purposes the public school they attended was more a Catholic school, on the town square surrounded by the court house, police station, small shops, and local businesses.

Each morning the brothers would walk, joined by several of their friends, to the public school where they studied mathematics, geography, and Polish history. The hundred and fifty students learned very little world history, and public events were seldom if ever discussed. Perhaps this was because their neighbors to the east were going through a time of enormous turmoil following their humiliating defeat in World War I. The majority of the children in their school were never really aware of what was going on in the country right beside them or, for that matter, in the world around them.

The brothers had an hour break in an empty classroom to enjoy Feigel's delicious lunch. Following that they all walked two blocks down the street where with fifteen other students they spent the balance of the afternoon in Hebrew school, learning the vast expanse of Jewish history, Jewish Law, and studying the Torah, the first five books of the Bible. Moniek had been incessantly teased throughout the day for being so reserved and quiet, totally out of character for the normally vocal youngster.

On the way home from school that afternoon one of their friends, a Catholic boy named Jacob, without really understanding what he was saying, called Moniek a dirty Jew. Jacob was much larger and two grades ahead of him but Moniek held his own in the resulting scuffle, while the others watched and cheered. By the end of the fight (which was actually more of a pushing match and produced no appreciable damage because of the heavy clothing they both wore), their friendship remained intact. All was well and all was forgotten. A neighbor told Hershel about the scuffle he had witnessed earlier and that brief and harmless exchange ended up being the main topic of conversation during dinner. While the understanding father didn't admonish the youngster for his actions, he clearly made the point that fighting was not the answer to anything. In truth, and as he confided to Feigel, he was proud that his son had both stood up for himself and defended himself admirably against the larger adversary.

Following dinner and homework, the neighborhood kids all congregated in the street in front of Moniek's house for a rousing game of soccer. Animosity no longer existed. That fight was history and now few would even remember it.

That was the way it was in Nowy Wisnicz, a small town about thirty-five miles southwest of Krakow, Poland. It was a peaceful place where the Catholics and the Jews got along exceptionally well. There was seldom any trouble between the population of about four thousand who lived in and around the town. Nowy Wisnicz was an agricultural community serving to support several local businesses located on the town square, two schools, and a few places of worship.

That starless night there was no booming thunder and no flashes of lightning. But still Moniek snapped awake in another cold sweat. Like before, Nuta was dead. So were his two older brothers. So were his parents. And, like the previous night, Feigel woke from a deep sleep and invited the frightened youngster to join them once again in their bed.

"Please tell me what's wrong," she whispered with motherly patience.

"It's nothing Mama. It was just a bad dream."

"What was it about?"

"I don't remember," he quietly replied. But he did remember. Down to the very last detail. And he never revealed his nighttime visions to anyone, though this incredibly painful nightmare would continue on a regular basis for nearly a year. He was too embarrassed and filled with overwhelming guilt to ever discuss it.

The second nightmare occurred on November 10, 1938. That night as well as the previous night, a tragic event had taken place throughout Germany and the adjoining country of Austria. Like so many other events which would follow, the actions of those two evenings would alter the course of history and that of an entire culture of people. Moniek was not conscious of the event, never heard about its occurrence, and would not even become aware it had happened at all for several years to come.

At the direction of Joseph Goebbels, the German Minister of Propaganda, but never actually authorized over Hitler's signature, it was decreed that the Nazis, the true followers, should have implied approval to attack and destroy Jewish synagogues, businesses, cemeteries, schools, and houses. Thousands of structures throughout Germany and Austria were burned to the ground because local fire departments were instructed not to assist in any way. Jews were openly attacked in the street and in their homes.

At least ninety-six Jewish people were killed and hundreds more injured. More than one thousand synagogues were burned to the ground. Nearly seven thousand five hundred Jewish businesses were completely destroyed. Cemeteries and schools were mindlessly vandalized. By the end of the ordeal, more than thirty thousand Jews were arrested and sent to concentration camps which Hitler had established throughout Germany.

Because of the immense damage done to literally countless windows in businesses, synagogues, schools, and houses, the two evenings became universally known and referred to throughout the world as *Kristallnacht,* "The Night of the Broken Glass." The tragic event occurred on the nights of November 9th and 10th of 1938.

The very same nights Moniek had his first two frightening nightmares.

Two

Moniek Ebner was born on September 20th, 1928, to loving parents Hershel and Feigel. He was their third son and Nuta, his younger brother, would follow two years later. A midwife assisted with Moniek's birth at their home since there was no hospital in the small town of Nowy Wisnicz.

Like his older brothers Abraham, who was now three, and Zishe, who was one, he was a pampered child, a treasured addition to the family. Life and time moved slowly in their little town, a peaceful farming community. His adolescence was as pure as the snow which covered their home during the long and bone-chilling Polish winter months. Neighbors would periodically visit, bringing food and small gifts for each of the youngsters.

Hershel was enormously proud of all his sons and treated them with great respect and quite naturally he expected the same in return. Based on the life-lessons he offered the children, his reward was returned in kind. He was a doting and protective father over all of the boys but not any more so than Feigel. Their collective lives in this quiet and uneventful community were ideal in relative terms to the times and their location. It was a wonderful place for the children to grow up and be nurtured.

Hershel Ebner was a tall man, six feet two, with a well-trimmed goatee, and was always impeccably dressed in a finely tailored suit each morning before he set off for his long day's work. Hershel was one of seven sons, each brother living within the farming community surrounding the town. Every morning, as he patted his sons on the head and offered them a kiss, he would leave Feigel some money for the family *Pushke,* a special box which held several coins for her to give to poor people who lived in town or were just passing through and needed assistance. He was a very generous man and considerate of other's hardships. As was the tradition, he religiously gave ten percent of his total income to charity, all of which was carefully distributed by the synagogue throughout the local Jewish community.

Early each morning, on foot or on his bicycle, Hershel would traverse into the local countryside and deal with the farmers surrounding the town. He was in the wholesale farm products business and as such would purchase animals, including cattle and sheep, or merchandise such as various fruits or hay, wheat, and corn. It was common for him to hire someone else to transfer the purchased items to the nearby town of Bochnia, about five miles due north up the dirt road, where Hershel would attend the local, bustling market square later in the afternoons and sell whatever merchandise he had acquired.

Bicycles, horses, and wagons were the primary modes of transportation. There was only a tiny smattering of automobiles throughout the town. They were actually rare and seldom seen. When they were, it was such an event that people would leave their houses and stand on the sides of the street watching in awe as they passed.

Hershel was a well-respected businessman, always fair with his customers, and successful in his endeavors. Over time and as a result of his business acumen he had acquired two fair-sized forests (which provided wood for people in town and on their farms to use for heating or cooking purposes) as well as a nearby rock quarry (which produced building materials for dwellings of various sizes). On occasion he would barter or trade his heating or building resources for other things he could use at home or sell in the market.

As a result of his prudent business practices, the family was able to purchase a lovely home on the north side of town at the corner of Bochenska and Ficher streets. The area was generally considered to be the Gentile side of town. The Jewish population lived on the south side, surrounding the Jewish cemetery. The Ebner house was situated near the town square and within clear eyesight of the police station where Hershel was close friends with the chief and most of the members of the small local force.

By comparative standards for the town the house was quite large, nearly four thousand square feet and one and a half stories high. The top floor was primarily used for storage purposes and the main floor provided a comfortable living space for the family. A full basement stayed cool during the summer months and provided adequate storage for various fruits and vegetables. In addition to the ornately decorated living room which displayed several paintings, a dining room, and kitchen, complete with a stove fueled by coal, it had four bedrooms. One was used by Hershel and Feigel and the boys slept two to a room. A fourth bedroom was always kept available for visitors.

On occasion during the summer months they would rent the spare bedroom to families or individuals who were on holiday or vacation. Moniek always enjoyed these times because it provided him the limited opportunity to learn just a little about life and the world outside their small community. There was a well-substantiated rumor that the house was once owned by a Polish prince.

The yard surrounding the house was unusually large for the area and covered a full city block. It was pleasantly filled with lush trees including pear, peach, and apple which provided a healthy food supply, well-trimmed shrubs, and a garden which produced additional fruits and vegetables for the family throughout the spring, summer, and fall. It was not uncommon for people passing through the neighborhood at night to help themselves. This was rather odd in that if they had merely asked Hershel or Feigel they would have given them whatever they desired or needed without pause or question.

Running out of patience from the regularity of the thefts, Hershel placed a six-foot tall, four by four piece of lumber into the ground at one end of the garden. No one knew what he was doing and he kept his secret to himself. The following day he placed another post into the ground on the opposite side of the garden. Then, without explanation, he strung a strong piece of metal wire between the two posts and secured it. Still no explanation. The family was dumbfounded.

The next day when Hershel returned home from work he had with him a large, mangy looking dog on a long yet very secure leash. The entire family watched in wonderment as he attached the leash to the metal wire, allowing the dog to roam freely through the garden. Whenever anyone approached, the dog would bark viciously, stopping any intruder dead in their tracks. From that moment forward the Ebners never experienced another case of thievery.

The house where Moniek grew up was always warm, heated by ornate, enamel-covered wood-burning stoves in each room. Their home was always filled with music. They had a small radio which played a constant variety of classical music and when that wasn't on Feigel nearly always seemed to be singing softly or humming to herself. Even with this overwhelming influence none of the boys were ever musically inclined. They were much too preoccupied with schoolwork and their studies.

From the time Moniek reached the age of six his father paid for special education with the local rabbi from their synagogue. The boys attended additional schooling three nights a week where they were instructed in more in-depth knowledge of the Jewish religion and, equally important, how to read and write in both the Yiddish and Hebrew languages. This meant they went to the public school each morning, Hebrew school in the afternoon, and special instructions from the rabbi three evenings a week. There was very little time for extracurricular activities. Still, their childhood in this peaceful community was filled with a sense of idealism as far as they were all concerned.

They still enjoyed an occasional game of soccer or dodge ball in front of their house. On warm, summer evenings a game of hide 'n seek was the order of the day. During the winter months several of the children would make their way to the nearby mountain with makeshift sleds for a full day of pleasure. On the weekends it was common to visit the large castle across town, the Castle Wisnicz which was constructed in the 15th century. It was an immense place filled with antiques, gold-plated furniture, rare paintings, and surrounded by a gently rippling moat. The castle was the major, actually the only, tourist attraction in the town and Moniek always enjoyed eavesdropping on strangers' conversations concerning faraway places they came from and other exciting places they'd seen and experienced. However, even with this fascination provided by others' encounters in the world, he never had any interest in leaving his family, their home, or their peaceful community. As far as he was concerned he was born at home and this was where he would spend the balance of his life.

Sadly, his frightening nightmares continued on a regular basis, at least once a week. And still, he never mentioned them to anyone.

Even Hershel, who tried as best he could to stay informed of international events, was not really aware of the enormous turmoil occurring in the country adjoining theirs. Poland, for all practical purposes, seemed as if it were light-years away from Germany, their neighbor. He tried his best to stay informed by reading the Polish newspapers *The Daily News, The National Tribune,* and whenever available *The Jewish Gazette.* However, there was little if any news concerning Hitler or what was actually going on. It was as if there was a news blackout on international news. Hershel was understandably interested in current events but not politically active in any organizations.

As a result young Moniek, during his formative years, had no idea of what was happening on the near horizon which would change all of their lives. He was blissfully ignorant of the coming tragedy Hitler would perpetrate on their secure and very comfortable family, their small town, their country, and the entire world.

He grew up in a peaceful environment, surrounded by loving parents, caring brothers, compassionate relatives, and friendly neighbors. For the time in history and the place he lived, it was an ideal existence. But soon, it would all come to a crashing and tragic conclusion.

THREE

EACH PASSOVER HERSHEL WOULD have the local tailor from the town visit their house and measure all of the boys for a brand new suit of clothing. Following their delivery and appropriate alterations the boys would each receive a new pair of shoes. The new clothing was worn to synagogue services and family gatherings throughout the following year.

They attended services regularly but not nearly as often as Hershel. Feigel normally only attended synagogue on the High Holy Days. It was a regular occurrence and, in fact, Hershel made a custom of inviting people to their home for the Friday evening meal. Many times these visitors would be total strangers, travelers moving down the road on foot or by wagon who were in need of a healthy meal and a place to rest weary bones if only for a few hours. Often the visitors would volunteer to offer a small payment for the Ebners' generosity, but Hershel refused, pleased that they were able to assist others less fortunate than themselves. The lesson was not lost on the four sons.

It was also common on Saturday evenings for Hershel to have a few friends over to their house for a friendly yet rousing game of cards. Ira Loman was the first to speak. "So Hershel, how's business?" Ira asked, smugly as usual.

"Could always be better," Hershel replied, studying his cards.

Ira flashed a smile through teeth which had never been adequately cared for. He was the local butcher, a portly man as a result of his chosen occupation, and as such enjoyed the others at the table as loyal and regular customers. "You say that every week. I talk to your customers and suppliers most every day. I know you're doing well." The others nodded in agreement.

Isaac Weisman, who owned the fruit stand in the town, rearranged the cards in his own hand and queried, "Did you listen to the radio today?"

The other four men, all dressed in the traditional black suits which were always worn to the synagogue, shook their heads "no." Even with limited access to information in general and especially any specific form in newspapers, Isaac prided himself on being the local expert in world events.

"Heard about this man named Hitler over in Germany?"

Again the others shook their heads. Isaac, pleased with being the undisputed information expert, continued. "He's taken over the country with a thing called the Nazi Party. He's become both Chancellor and President with total control over everything. And it sure sounds to me like he has it in for the Jews."

Joseph Weinstein raised a bushy eyebrow and asked in a raspy voice, "And just what's that supposed to mean?"

"Well," Isaac continued as he played the opening card of the hand, "He's claiming the Jews have corrupted their precious German culture with our foreign and mongrel influence."

"That's preposterous," Meyer Appel offered with a look of complete disdain on his face, ruddy and weathered from long days in the fields of his nearby farm.

"And ridiculous," Hershel said. "No one would possibly pay any serious attention to anyone who makes such outrageous claims."

"That's not what I hear," Isaac replied. "Supposedly he has a huge following that's growing every single day. He's also telling people that we're all evil and cowardly and the Germans are hardworking, courageous, and honest. It sounds pretty much to me like Hitler wants to rid the country of all Jews."

"Preposterous," Meyer said again.

"I tell you gentlemen, it really doesn't look like good times are ahead."

For the first time Josef Gutman, the reserved local banker, leaned back in his comfortable chair and gave what appeared to be a well-thought-out observation. "It doesn't matter to me what this Hitler person does. As long as he does it in Germany it won't affect us at all. The Polish government would never allow anything like that to happen here."

The card game continued as the others nodded in silent agreement. They had no sense of concern for the days in their collective future. Their lives would go on as they had in the past. With peace and tranquility being the order of the day. Business would go on, trouble would come, and it would be dealt with, just as before. Life would go on. Unfortunately, these intelligent men, like other intelligent people throughout the world didn't look closely enough, hadn't examined the facts. Everything was about to change.

The Ebner boys were all well-behaved, seldom getting into trouble and never anything of a serious nature. They were also better than average students and followed their parents' example of being thoughtful of and helpful toward others.

One warm summer day Moniek and his two older brothers were playing in a nearby field, chasing a small herd of dairy cattle. It was a harmless and childlike prank. But this day was different. On this day the cows strangely decided not to run away but rather to run menacingly toward the boys. They looked at each other in complete disbelief but only for the flash of a second because the cattle, their heads shaking wildly from side to side, horns flashing, were rapidly closing in on the three terrified youngsters.

At full speed the boys reached the fence surrounding the field and made their way over as rapidly as possible. Being the youngest of the group, Moniek was the last to make his way over the top of the barbed wire fence. And he didn't quite make it. His pants sustained a large tear on the right leg. After determining they were safely out of reach of the animals standing on the other side of the fence, Moniek showed his pants to his brothers.

Both Abraham and Zishe, in the way of older brothers all over the world, literally fell on the ground, rolling around, holding their sides, consumed in uncontrollable laughter. "Mama is going to be so mad at you," Abraham finally sputtered.

"Please don't tell Mama," Moniek pleaded.

"She'll know," Zishe said. "You can't keep that from her."

"I'll fix them," Moniek replied with complete seriousness.

"Not a chance," Abraham said as the laughter continued and the boys made their way toward home.

Later that afternoon Moniek quietly retrieved his mother's sewing basket from the top shelf of the hall closet and examined the various instruments within. He'd never taken any interest in his mother's sewing prowess and as a result had no idea how to deal with any of the things he held in his small hands. But in time, after considerable trial and error, he threaded the needle with the correct color thread and after two or three false starts actually began to mend the torn pants. By the end of the afternoon, while his brothers played soccer in the street in front of their house, he experienced the success he'd promised.

During the evening meal the brothers were giggling uncontrollably and making oblique comments toward Moniek's ill-fated attempt to cross the fence to escape the rampaging cows. They made no particular or specific reference, just snide comments meant to embarrass their younger brother and get him into trouble. Finally, Hershel had taken all that he could of their incessant teasing and continual innuendos. He looked at Abraham and Zishe and firmly announced, "If you can't say what you really want to say, you'll have to leave the table."

Before either of them could speak or even apologize Moniek announced, "We were all playing in one of the fields today and as I was climbing over the fence I ripped my pants." His brothers snickered, knowing Moniek would soon be reprimanded for both being clumsy and destroying clothing.

"Can they be fixed?" Hershel asked sternly. He was a prudent man and valued all things which had been purchased for the family. Moniek excused himself from the table, walked into his bedroom and returned with the trousers. As he handed them to his mother, the rest of the table watched in silence. Feigel carefully examined them.

"I can see where they were torn," she said. And then she smiled, "but they've been perfectly mended. I couldn't have done it better myself."

Moniek was enormously pleased and his older brothers were in total shock. After a second's hesitation Hershel announced, "Perhaps someday you'll become a fine and well-respected tailor. Sit," he decreed, with an ever so slight smile on his own face. "Now we'll all finish the dinner your mother has prepared."

Paul Joseph Goebbels studied history and literature at the University of Heidelberg. It was here during classic and intense debate sessions that he began to develop his remarkable abilities in the art of persuasion and altering others' thoughts and opinions. He had a crippled foot, the result of contracting polio when he was a child. The lasting influence of his relatively small stature and infirmity tormented him for the balance of his life

He joined the Nazi Party and was rapidly promoted to the position of business manager of the National Socialist German Workers Party (NSDAP) in the Ruhr district, the north German wing of the Party. Within a relatively brief period of time, driven by heightened political aspirations, he succeeded at taking control of the small, unorganized group. To further his growing quest for power he designed posters for himself which were widely distributed, published his own propaganda, staged impressive parades, and organized his personal bodyguards to participate in street battles, beer hall brawls, and public executions of his political opponents to further his own well-served ambitions. His skillful manipulation and open acts of terror transformed the small group he led into a major force within the Party.

Hitler quickly recognized Goebbels' remarkably effective achievements. His deep-rooted contempt for humanity, his urge to create confusion and spread hatred, and his unmitigated lust for power were all mixed carefully with his mastery of the techniques of mass persuasion.

On March 13th, 1933, Goebbels was appointed to the position of Reich Minister for Public Enlightenment and Propaganda. This reward, a direct result of his expertise in the ability to alter and reshape people's thinking patterns and beliefs, gave him total control of the entire communications media throughout the country. He was now completely in charge of all radio stations, the press, all publishing outlets, the cinema, and all other forms of the arts. His first exercise in total power was to eliminate all Jews and political opponents from any positions of influence in all forms of the media and the arts. Less than two months after his appointment he organized and staged the great ritual "burning of the books" in Berlin where all published works of Jewish, Marxist, and other "subversive" authors such as Albert Einstein, Sigmund Freud, Franz Kafka, Helen Keller, Thomas Mann, Karl Marx, Upton Sinclair, and H.G. Wells, were publicly burned in huge, raging bonfires.

Students carrying banners toured the streets, rifling libraries, synagogues, and private homes, confiscating all forms of what were mysteriously considered to be "radical" books. The general population joined in the frenzy with wild enthusiasm. Following the burning of the books people forced their way into Jewish publishing houses and completely destroyed their printing presses. The abject hatred of the Jews, once held closely and tightly to the vest, was now exploited openly in the public eye. They could now see without question that with well-orchestrated encouragement, the masses held the same and equally perverse contempt for all Jews.

Goebbels magnified the fueling of the growing fire of frenzy by continuing to demonize the Jew as the principal and eternal enemy of the Third Reich. He began to attack what he referred to as the "Jewish penetration of the professions," including law, medicine, property ownership, the theater, and several other areas. Within a short period of time, Jews were no longer permitted to practice these professions. Property was confiscated by the Party and once-successful people were left to fend for themselves as best they could.

Public schools were closed to Jewish children, they were excluded from all public events, and it became unsafe to walk the streets at night. The Jews were methodically and systematically being isolated from the German society.

The success which was achieved in feeding popular resentment, mobilizing the masses, and creating this common enemy in the form of the Jews was all a detailed component of a well-crafted master plan to rid Germany of all Jews. Hitler, Goebbels, and the others in their innermost circle of influence initially believed that if conditions became intolerable for the Jews they would leave the country on their own and resettle elsewhere.

Such was not to be the case. After experiencing thousands of years of persecution from country to country to country the Jews were a hearty people and had a tendency over their vast and storied history to adapt to adversity in any form and content, no matter how extreme. Families moved in with one another and total strangers were taken in as boarders. Living space was at a premium but a diminished form of life continued.

Food became a treasured commodity and in time diminished in volume, quantity, and quality. Tables once laden with feasts now became filled with virtual scraps, barely enough to go around. The Nazis forced nearly all Jewish businesses to close and shortened even further supplies which were necessary for a family to survive. But to the Nazis' anger, the Jewish people did just that, continued to stay put, refusing to leave their homes and what they considered to be their country. Times and circumstances for the German Jews were becoming more and more difficult by the day.

Many attempted to flee and thousands succeeded by immigrating to countries such as Belgium, Czechoslovakia, England, France, and Holland. Those with the means and foresight left the country, escaping to other places where their lives would be safer and hopefully more secure.

There was no such conflict in the peaceful town of Nowy Wisnicz. The businesses composing the town square, consisting of a bakery, a butcher shop, a livery stable, a florist, a tailor, a fruit vendor, a shoemaker, and the local bank, existed without disruption. Business at the small and only restaurant on the square, or the entire area for that matter, went on normally. The majority of the merchants were Jewish, proudly serving the mostly Gentile population. Life continued for the residents the same as it had for all their lives. They experienced no shortages and no restrictions of any sort. Their tranquility continued even with tragic news occasionally drifting to them from their neighbor to the east.

The Saturday evening card games became more vocal concerning this stranger named Hitler and what Germany appeared to be doing to the Jews, but the news was nearly always met with utter and complete disbelief. Such a thing like this could never happen. It was impossible to believe and dismissed without any noticeable concern. Nothing of this sort or magnitude had ever occurred and could certainly not be happening now.

One evening that week Feigel prepared potato soup as their main dish. Being Orthodox in their religion, their home was completely kosher and only served food which had been blessed by the local rabbi. The family would enjoy dinners consisting of chicken, chicken soup, veal liver, pumpernickel and rye breads, bagels, baked pears, assorted beans, potatoes, blueberry and apple pies, various fruits and vegetables, and Moniek's favorite thing of all as dessert, sugar cookies. On occasion, Moniek would take his small weekly allowance into the square and purchase either ice cream or a crystal candy which was hard and clear and composed primarily of sugar, his favorite.

But this night he turned up his nose as the bowl was placed in front of him. Moniek absolutely hated potato soup. It was common for Hershel to pay the youngster a few pennies to entice him to eat. His brothers, all following his lead and not wishing to miss out on anything, would pull the same stunt so they would be paid as well. Hershel found this to be amusing and always went along with the game.

"What's wrong, Moniek," Hershel asked knowingly.

"I don't like potato soup, Tata. You know that."

"That's right," Hershel replied, looking away from the table and barely suppressing a smile. "Guess I forgot."

"I'll just eat some bread and beans," Moniek quietly uttered, an exaggerated frown covering his young face. Then with sad resolve, "That'll be plenty."

"Yes, I suppose it will," Hershel said, never changing his expression. It was crystal clear that an offer of money was not going to be forthcoming. As a result Moniek and his brothers were all disappointed. They had been foiled. Their bluff had been called.

"I wish you'd eat more, Moniek," Feigel said with compassion. "You need your strength. I even made your favorite, sugar cookies, for dessert. But you can't have any unless you eat." It was very clear that she wasn't kidding.

"I just can't, Mama. I'm sorry." By this point it was unclear if even the few pennies would have made any difference.

"You're off from school tomorrow, aren't you?" Hershel asked, knowing with certainty that he was.

"Yes, Tata," he replied, already missing the delicious taste of the sugar cookies waiting in the kitchen.

"Eat some of your soup and I'll take you to work with me."

Moniek's eyes lit up brightly. "You will Tata?" Hershel nodded. The deal had been struck. Moniek forced down as many spoonfuls of the potato soup as he could stomach and later was treated to several sugar cookies. But the best treat of all was yet to come. He loved going into the country with his father. They would rent a wagon and he'd have him to himself all day long. They were special times which were close to his heart and he treasured them dearly.

The other brothers were jealous but they each enjoyed their own special time alone with their father. Moniek would dream about the day to follow and the words of wisdom that his father always shared during their outings. Those were the very last thoughts on his young, impressionable mind as he finally, in a state of impending excitement, drifted off to sleep.

And that night he snapped awake in a cold sweat to find his entire family dead. The dreaded nightmare had returned.

FOUR

THE FOLLOWING MORNING FEIGEL took special care to fix a hearty lunch for Hershel and Moniek as they prepared their trip into the countryside. Moniek was far too excited over the joy of the impending day to reflect on his unpleasant and sleepless evening.

"Is Marta coming today?" Hershel asked.

Feigel tapped her right foot softly on the floor, placed her hands on her hips, and glared. "You know she is," she replied. "Why do you always have to ask? I think sometimes you do that just to get my goat." It was a verbal exchange they shared on a regular basis, more of a game than anything else. Hershel and Feigel were a happy couple, a fact which was envied by a few others in the town.

Marta, an attractive young woman in her early twenties who lived on the outskirts of town, was their maid and visited the house three times a week to assist with cleaning and washing clothes. Feigel, being a perfectionist, would never allow Marta to clean any of her pots and pans. Feigel insisted on taking care of them all herself. Her collection was special to her and no one else in the house was ever permitted to touch them.

Hershel had already picked up the horse-drawn wagon from the livery stable earlier that morning while it was still dark and the rest of the family was sleeping. It waited in the backyard, the horse covered with a blanket, while they bundled themselves in layers of clothing in the protection and the warmth of the kitchen. The cruel December wind was cutting and as they climbed into the wagon, Moniek carefully protecting their lunch, they also covered themselves with a thick, warm blanket.

Feigel leaned out the door with a smile on her face. "What time will you be home?"

"We'll be back when we get back," he replied, suppressing his own smile.

"If you're not home by dinner, we'll eat without you."

"You wouldn't dare." And with that he made an ever so slight noise out of the side of his mouth and the well-trained horse moved out of the yard toward the nearby road.

Feigel waved and called out, "Have a wonderful day, both of you." Hershel returned the wave, blew his wife a kiss, and father and son were on their way to a day of wondrous adventure.

A pure white, glistening snow covered the ground as far as the eye could see and there was a thin and crisp layer of ice on the dirt road which continued to make crunching sounds under the wheels of the wagon. Moniek pulled the blanket closer around his neck, feeling the chill but still too excited to be in any real discomfort.

"Are you warm enough?" Hershel asked. "We have another blanket if you'd like to use it."

"No, Tata, I'm fine. Really."

They rode in silence for awhile, the horse seeming to know the way by heart. "Have you and your brothers been helping the nuns at the convent by your school?"

"Oh yes. We were there yesterday afternoon shoveling snow in front of where they live and also the church."

"Did they show you their appreciation?"

"They wanted to give us a little something but we refused."

"That's a good thing. I know from speaking with others in the town that the nuns appreciate all the help the four of you provide."

Moniek frowned. "Nuta doesn't offer much help."

Hershel smiled knowingly. "Nuta is young. Just as you once were. But now you're growing into a fine young man." Moniek was speechless. "I'm very pleased with your schoolwork and how well you're doing. What's your favorite subject this year?"

"Geography."

"Really? Why's that?"

"It's just amazing that the world can be so big and we live in so little of it."

"Yes," he softly replied, "but some of that big world out there can be remarkably cruel. Does it bother you that we live in such a small place?"

"Oh no," Moniek earnestly replied. "I love where we live. I never want to go anywhere else." Hershel smiled to himself, pleased.

After another few moments in silence, only the sound of the crunching ice beneath the wagon wheels, Hershel cautiously broke the stillness, "You had that bad dream again last night, didn't you?"

"Yes, Tata," Moniek virtually whispered, "but I promise it's not going to take away from all the fun you and I are going to have today."

Hershel nodded, choosing wisely to not pursue the subject.

Avi Cohen slowly sipped a near-boiling cup of coffee in his kitchen when he heard the crunching ice outside in his barnyard. He was pleased that as usual, no matter the weather or the circumstance, Hershel Ebner kept his appointments with all of his customers and suppliers. If he said he was going to be somewhere he always showed up on time or before. Avi slipped on his thick glasses with wire rims, wrapped his thin-framed body in a warm wool coat, and walked outside into the freezing temperatures.

As always, greetings and handshakes were the first order of the morning. Hershel and Avi had known each other since they went to school together years and years ago. They attended the same synagogue and had countless friends between them. While Avi didn't come into the town all that often they saw each other on a regular basis and their lifelong friendship was solid.

With a slight expression of confusion Avi looked down at Moniek and asked with serious curiosity, "And just who's this?"

"This is Moniek, my third son," Hershel replied with pride.

"Moniek," Avi repeated. "Goodness. Look at you. You're growing into a fine young man and now your father's introducing you to the business already. Goodness, child. I haven't seen you in ages."

They shook hands as well and it was time to take care of business. But not before coffee was offered. It was tradition. The three of them entered the kitchen and Avi poured a cup, handing it to Hershel. As he blew on the steaming concoction he suggested, "Moniek would like some coffee as well." Avi smiled as he poured the cup, not seeing Hershel as he winked at the surprised youngster. Moniek just didn't know what to say. It was the first cup of coffee he'd ever had in his entire life. It didn't taste all that good but he was with the adults doing adult things and he liked that.

Once in the barn, surrounded by pens holding various animals, Avi showed Hershel the dairy cow he had for sale. Dairy cows were more valuable than beef cattle because they could provide milk and also butter which could be used by families for a considerably longer period of time than just assorted portions of meat.

Hershel walked into the pen, completely familiar with all sorts of animals and not afraid of any of them. Truth be told he had an affinity with virtually all animals and them in turn with him. The cow stood perfectly still as he lifted its upper lip and looked inside, examining its teeth and looking closely at the inner linings of its jaws. "Moniek," he finally said, "come over here." Moniek was not quite as sure of himself as his father but followed his direction. "See here?" he whispered, out of Avi's earshot, "The teeth are all in place and the gums and walls of the jaws are clear. This is important."

"Yes, Tata," the youngster quietly replied, hanging on to his every word. Hershel rubbed his hands slowly and with a degree of expertise across both front legs of the cow as professionally as any veterinarian could ever do. After all, this was his business. This was one of the principal reasons he was so highly respected throughout the entire community.

Moniek listened quietly and attentively as his father and Avi discussed the sale. They bartered reasonably and went back and forth for a short time until a deal was eventually struck. Both men appeared to be pleased with the arrangement. Hershel reached into his pocket, removed a large roll of folding money, paid for the cow, and told his old friend that early the following morning an associate would arrive to pick up the animal and take it to the market. There were more handshakes all around and the Ebners were on their way toward their next destination.

As they moved down the road, wrapping themselves in their warm blankets, Hershel asked, "Did you learn anything back there?"

"Mr. Cohen's a very nice man."

"That's not what I asked."

"I learned that you're a very smart person."

"I appreciate that, son, honestly I do, but that really wasn't my question."

Moniek thought long and hard, and then finally replied, "I learned that you have to be an expert in what you do if you're going to be a success in business."

"And life," Hershel quietly said. "You learned a good lesson today. One I hope that'll last you for a lifetime."

Moniek beamed with pride. This would be a special day, one he would only share with his mother. Then Hershel added, "You know what, son? I made a very good deal with Mr. Cohen this morning. And I think a large portion of it has to do with the fact that I consider you to be my very own and very special lucky charm." Now the buttons on Moniek's clothing were about to burst. He lowered his blanket. All of the sudden it wasn't quite as cold as it had been previously.

Hershel handed Moniek the reins for the horse and in a manner only a proud father could express said, "I guess it's time you learned to drive."

In total shock Moniek took the reins and stared at his father as mist began to form in his eyes. Hershel noticed the tears of appreciation, returned his stare straight ahead, and calmly suggested, "Watch the road. You're in charge now."

In 1933, when Moniek was five years old, Hitler was appointed Chancellor of Germany; the first concentration camp, Dachau, was constructed and opened; a daylong boycott of all Jewish businesses was proclaimed in Germany; the feared and lethal Gestapo was formed; books were burned in massive bonfires throughout the country; and the Nazis outlawed all other political parties, giving themselves complete and total control over everyone and everything.

Moniek, completely oblivious to all these world-shattering events, enthusiastically rolled a barrel stay down the middle of the street in front of their house, guiding it as best he could with a long, thin stick. He wasn't as proficient as his older brothers or some of the other kids in the neighborhood but he was the youngest among them and in time would improve and eventually emerge as the best of them all.

Hershel, while a generous man, was also extremely frugal. He never bought toys for any of the boys. As a result they improvised, creating their own clay creatures molded from mud, and capturing assorted bugs such as spiders and horseflies of various sizes. Holding their legs or wings gently they would tie a string around the small insects and pretend they were training them or much to Feigel's consternation hold mock races in the backyard.

Another favorite toy the Ebner boys enjoyed consisted of a single rubber band and a small piece of folded-over wet paper. It was called shooting spitballs. With extensive practice one could become reasonably proficient, but not always.

"Ouch!" Abraham screeched, grabbing the side of his face with both hands.

"I'm sorry," Moniek yelled back. "I wasn't aiming at you. I swear I wasn't."

Everyone rushed to Abraham's side as he writhed in pain, kneeling in the grass. "I know you didn't do it on purpose," he said softly, which didn't make Moniek feel any less guilty or less responsible for his act.

At dinner that night Hershel asked the normal questions concerning the boys' day in school and what they had learned. Abraham was particularly quiet, turning away from the table as much as possible. It was Feigel who first noticed it. "What's that on your cheek?" she asked, reaching to touch the still red mark on his face.

"It's nothing, Mama," he quietly replied.

"I did it," Moniek softly confessed.

"And just what was it you did?" Hershel asked, leaning back in his chair and folding his arms across his chest.

Moniek was close to tears. "We were shooting spitballs outside. It was an accident. I promise. I'd never do anything to hurt any of my brothers."

Hershel was firm. "If your 'accident' had been one inch higher it could have put out your brother's eye."

Now Moniek's tears of shame began to fall. Feigel took his hand in hers and squeezed it, nearly shedding tears of her own.

"It was an accident," Abraham confirmed. "It wasn't on purpose and I'm going to be fine."

Hershel took a very deep breath and slowly exhaled before he spoke. "You boys are all aware we have no weapons in this house. That's because they're dangerous and all too often people get hurt just because they're around. The farmers outside the town are different. They have to have guns to protect their livestock. But weapons come in different forms. They can be rifles, or shotguns, or pistols...or even spitballs."

Moniek hung his head, still holding onto his mother's hand. Hershel cut a piece of veal, put it carefully on his fork and before he placed it in his mouth asked, "Has the lesson been learned?" He stared at each of his sons, especially Moniek.

"Yes, Tata," they replied in unison.

FIVE

TWO YEARS LATER, AND as was the custom, Hershel invited two strangers to join their family for the traditional Friday evening dinner. They were a young couple, recently married, and on their way to Bochnia where they both hoped to find work. The conversation that evening centered around Zabzez, the small town they recently left, their families, and their hopes and dreams. That's when it happened.

The front window exploded with a tremendous crash sending shards of glass flying in all directions. Everyone seated at the table ducked for cover, protecting their faces as the curtains blew in the wind and a projectile landed on the living room floor. It was a good sized rock, hurled under the cover of darkness.

From outside came shouts,"Get out, dirty Jews! Get out of town!" Then there was silence. After a moment, the people who had been enjoying a peaceful dinner straightened back up and just stared at one another, their faces consumed with sadness.

Hershel turned to the two older boys and without being asked they left the table. He then went into the living room and with Feigel's assistance as well as that of their two visitors picked up as much glass from the floor as they could.

The young male visitor was the first to break the silence. "I thought this only happened in our little town. That's one of the reasons we left."

"It seems to be happening everywhere," Hershel replied.

"Very often?"

"Unfortunately, more and more."

Abraham and Zishe returned to the living room carrying a large piece of plywood which they placed against the wall, covering the broken window. They were familiar with the procedure and had done it several times in the past.

In a fatherly manner Hershel placed his hand on the young visitor's shoulder and said, "It may be dangerous on the street tonight. You and your new wife will stay here with us this evening and you can leave in the morning after breakfast."

"I appreciate that."

"Feigel, would you please show our guests their room so they can get a good night's sleep?" Feigel, pleased with the suggestion, nodded. The young couple picked up their meager belongings and followed her down the hallway.

Moniek approached his father, pointed at the window, and quietly asked, "Tata, why do those people do that?"

"They drink too much alcohol which makes them think they're now brave men. Then they hide in the dark behind bushes, throw rocks at windows, and call people names. Doesn't seem very brave, does it?"

"But why do they hate us so much? What have we done to them?"

"We haven't done anything to them. We never have. It's just the alcohol which makes them do things they would never do normally. The people who did this terrible thing are probably neighbors and tomorrow, when they sober up and return to normal, everything will be fine again. You'll see. Don't worry about it."

But Moniek did worry about it. His worries were understandably confined to the protection and safety of his own family. As a result of the information blackout, just like the majority of the population of Poland, he was not aware that later that year "No Jews" signs began to appear throughout all of Germany. Jews were no longer permitted to do business with Germans.

Nor was he aware that on September 15th the German Parliament passed the Nuremberg Laws which severely restricted the rights of all Jews. This included having the ability to travel freely, own land, or even own businesses. The vice-like grip of the Third Reich was tightening on the entire country and few in the entire world were aware of it or cared one way or another. Another seemingly obvious fact which didn't seem to bother anyone was that all armament production in Germany was eclipsing heretofore record levels. Their military/industrial complex swung into full gear, manufacturing pistols, rifles, machine guns, land mines, incendiary devices, hand grenades, heavy armaments of assorted sizes, tanks, troop carriers, airplanes, and ammunition to such an extent that no one had ever seen or imagined. This was all in direct violation of the Treaty of Versailles which they had agreed to at the conclusion of World War I. However, no one in any position of responsibility ever questioned what was going on. No one ever asked. The size of the military ballooned exponentially, and all manner and description of weapons of destruction were being mass-produced at an alarming pace.

Moniek burst through the back door into the kitchen, as always a huge smile covering his face. "Hi, Mama. What's for dinner?"

"Not one single thing until I get a kiss." It was a daily exchange but one he always enjoyed. After reciprocal pecks on the cheek, Feigel added, "You remember Mrs. Levy, don't you?"

"Yes, ma'am." How could he not remember her? Mrs. Levy regularly visited Feigel at least once every two weeks and would normally spend the better part of an entire afternoon talking but not necessarily having a conversation. Mrs. Levy just liked to hear herself talk and had few friends who would sacrifice the time to listen for hours on end to her ramblings.

"Nice to see you, Mrs. Levy," Moniek said. He was a well-mannered child and always treated others with respect, especially adults.

"Nice to see you too, Moniek," she replied. "How are you doing in school?"

"Pretty well, ma'am." He was also a little shy when it came to bragging about himself or any of his accomplishments. It was normal that

Mrs. Levy would ask about his schoolwork in that she was a teacher herself. She was also one of the few serious town gossips and more than willing to whisper the latest tidbit of information to anyone who'd listen to the rumors she was always more than eager to share.

Feigel was an unwilling audience and completely uninterested in what anyone else in the town was doing. On the other hand, unlike so many other women in the neighborhood, she was always the consummate hostess and forced herself to politely pretend she was paying attention.

"Mama," Moniek announced. "I have some homework I need to finish so I'm going to go to my room." While Moniek was an extremely tolerant child, Mrs. Levy drove the youngster nearly out of his mind with her nonstop talking. It was as if she never even paused between words long enough to breathe. At the first possibility and being cautious not appear impolite he would escape the room as soon as was humanly possible.

"I have a much better idea," Feigel said. Then punctuated it with a tone of firmness, "Why don't you do your homework here at the kitchen table."

"Yes, Mama," he replied, a deep frown replacing the smile which carried him into the room barely moments earlier. He sat down, opened his workbook from school, and tried desperately not to hear as Mrs. Levy continued to drone on. He stared at his mother with pleading eyes, and when Mrs. Levy looked away for a second, Feigel winked. It was a signal they'd used successfully in the past and Moniek was thrilled — he was free.

"Mama," he said. "I'm going to finish some of my chores before dinner."

"That'll be fine," she whispered, a smile covering her face. "You're a good boy." Mrs. Levy smiled warmly, agreeing with the comment.

Moniek went to a small closet at the far end of the kitchen and removed a broom. He began to sweep the kitchen floor as Mrs. Levy continued to go on and on. Soon, as a direct result of his rather violent sweeping, small puffs of dust began to rise from the floor. Mrs. Levy let out a giant sneeze and apologized. Moniek swept faster, actually working up a sweat. Now Mrs. Levy began to cough to the point where for a pleasant change she was unable to speak.

While Moniek worked faster and harder Mrs. Levy finally excused herself and left their home. Once the door was securely closed behind her Feigel and Moniek shared a secret smile of satisfaction. "Like I said, you're a good boy. Thanks for rescuing your mama." Moniek beamed as he returned to his homework and Feigel began to prepare the dinner meal.

"Go ahead, Moniek," Abraham whispered. "You can do it."

"This is really not a good idea," he whispered back, concern in his voice.

"Of course it is. Tata has taken a wagon today and won't be home until dinnertime. What's the matter, anyway? Are you afraid?"

"I'm not afraid." His tone was nowhere nearly as confident as the words which came from his mouth. "But I don't know how to do it. I'm only afraid that I'll break it."

"You won't break it. It's easy. Anyone can do it. A lot of the other kids younger than you can do it."

Moniek had clearly been challenged by his older brother and could find no plausible way out of the dilemma in which he most unfortunately found himself. With great trepidation and extreme caution he pulled Hershel's bicycle away from the wall where it was leaning and slowly pushed it past the two small animal pens and toward the back door of their garage. He looked toward Abraham with eyes that almost seemed as if they were pleading. "This is not a good idea," he repeated.

"No one will ever know," he said. "Nothing will go wrong. It's easy. I've done it before."

Abraham opened the garage door, looking both ways to make sure no one was watching. Moniek slowly pushed the valuable bicycle through the door into the alley behind their house. He shook his head, angry with himself that he had accepted the challenge. He knew without question that if he did anything to damage his father's primary mode of transportation he would be in enormous trouble. But now it was too late for him to back out. He hoped beyond hope that his brother was right, that it would be as easy as he described.

He swung his right leg over the crossbar but his legs were too short for him to sit in the saddle. If he were to ride at all it would have to be while standing up. By this time Zishe and Nuta appeared around the side of the garage. In addition to everything else, he now had an unwanted audience. He glared at Abraham, "Why didn't you just invite the whole neighborhood?" he hissed sarcastically.

"This is just family," he replied.

"You can do it, Moniek," Zishe said. "I've done it before."

"I'm not going to do it," he announced firmly as he got off the bike. "One of you will tell and I'll be in trouble with Tata."

"We won't tell, Moniek. None of us," Abraham calmly expressed.

Moniek pointed at Nuta, his younger brother, "He will."

"No I won't," Nuta said, shaking his head from side to side. "I promise."

Moniek took a deep breath, let out a slow, long exhale, and swung his leg back over the bicycle. Abraham moved in to steady him and offer a degree of balance. Then, without warning, Abraham, with all the strength he could muster, gave Moniek a mighty push and the youngster careened down the alley.

The bicycle went first one way, and then the other, weaving wildly from side to side, completely out of control. Moniek was terrified, hanging on for dear life. Having no instruction whatsoever in operational skills, he was completely unaware of how to operate the brakes. He barely missed running into a garage on the other side of the alley and then came an incredibly close call with a large tree, missing it by mere inches. Thankfully his forward, and mostly sideways, progress was diminishing as his brothers watched in near shock. They were now aware of the consequences they would all suffer if anything happened to their father's bicycle as a result of what they initially considered to be an innocent stunt.

The bicycle eventually ground to a halt and fell over on its side, throwing its young rider across the alley. The brothers all rushed to him, concern on their faces. Moniek was scratched up a little bit, nothing life threatening or serious, and the first words to come from his mouth were, "Is the bicycle all right?"

Fortunately it was. Nothing was broken or bent, a fact which brought great relief to them all. The boys returned it to its proper place in the garage and made a sincere pact that not a word was ever to be spoken of the experience again. To anyone.

Six

Yitzechak Ebner was Moniek's grandfather. He owned a farm in the surrounding area and in contrast to most of the farms around the town his was one of the largest and most productive. His crops included carrots, hay, turnips, potatoes, beets, beans, onions, and wheat. These were all seasonal crops but via rotation, other than during the bitter winter months, he was always occupied, spending the majority of his days in the fields.

Moniek's other grandfather, Yanison, on Feigel's side of the family, also owned a farm but it was considerably smaller and as a result he could not produce anywhere near the same volume of crops as his good friend Yitzechak. The entire family got along well and on rare occasions would get together for a celebration of some sort. Whenever this happened it was common for the extended family to spend the night at whichever place they were visiting.

While only a few miles outside of the town it was still a full day's buggy ride to get to either farm and by evening's end it was too dark and on occasion too dangerous to travel through the countryside at night. Moniek dearly loved these infrequent gatherings. He had seven uncles, six aunts, and more cousins than he could even count, and they all spent the night together, sleeping as well as was possible in every nook and cranny of the entire house.

Since his cousins lived in the country on various farms, most of them adjoining in one form or another, they all attended different schools in the surrounding area and these rare gatherings provided the only opportunity for him to actually get to see the majority of his relatives.

One treasured weekend each summer Hershel would rent a "fancy" buckboard from the livery stable in the town and the family would pile in for a three-day excursion to visit grandpa Yitzechak. It always proved to be an exciting trip. Feigel would prepare great amounts of food and everyone would take along an extra change of clothing, for the boys were all well aware they would be assigned work duties in the fields, an experience they all looked forward to with great enthusiasm.

After two days of hard but satisfying work in the fields, enjoying great mounds of delicious food, and the opportunity of listening to adult conversation, it was as if life just couldn't get any better. And just then it did.

"Moniek," Hershel announced with authority, "tomorrow you and I are going to take a ride together." Moniek was pleasantly shocked because he knew well what that pronouncement indicated.

"Yes, Tata," he replied, a smile as big as all outdoors covering his face. His brothers could not express any degree of jealousy because they'd already had their turn with their father. Now it was Moniek's time. Sleep came with much difficulty in that he was so excited about the day ahead. But sleep always and eventually comes to a ten-year-old child. However, it was not the blissful sleep he had envisioned. The nightmare returned with all its gruesome details. In the nightmare he was not at his grandfather's farm. He was in his own home, going room to room, witnessing the open eyes of his entire family and their blank lifeless stares into a void filled with nothingness.

In the morning, Hershel could tell that the youngster had experienced yet another sleepless night. The glow of excitement from his eyes, which was so bright and beaming just the night before, was gone. The father felt enormous empathy for his son but knew from experience there was nothing he could do or say to ease whatever it was the boy was going through.

"We're going to have a fine day, son," Hershel said as the buggy rolled away from the barn where the horse had been tied.

"I know, Tata," he replied without enthusiasm. Hershel felt helpless. He'd asked about the bad dream on countless occasions and each time Moniek continued to tell him that he couldn't remember any of it. Moniek turned around, noticed the wicker baskets and poles in the rear of the buggy, and knew with a certainty what their destination was going to be. It brightened him slightly but he was still disturbed.

"I guess you know where we're going," Hershel said enthusiastically.

"Yes, Tata," was the flat two-word response offered as the youngster stared straight ahead.

The buggy was drawn to a halt by the side of a river which drifted peacefully through the center of Yitzechak's farm. Hershel had fished in this very spot since he himself was a youngster growing up here. He wanted desperately to help Moniek but knew in the bottom of his heart that there was nothing he could do.

"Tell you what," Hershel said, "I think it's time you started to help out a little bit rather than just sitting on the bank watching me do all the work."

"Really, Tata?" Moniek asked, beaming at the suggestion.

""Sure," Hershel said, "I was your age when I began fishing in this old river. We'll do well today. After all, you're my lucky charm."

Moniek always loved hearing his father say that and it always brightened his spirits. As they removed the gear from the buckboard thoughts of bad dreams and nightmares began to diminish.

This was somewhat unconventional fishing by all normal standards. They attached the lines from the poles to the wicker baskets, lowered them into the water, and waited patiently for a fish or two to swim into the basket and become momentarily trapped. Feeling the additional weight on the baskets they would haul them up, drop them on the ground nearby, and dip the empty basket right back into the river.

Moniek had an exceptional morning for a first-timer and actually out-fished his father. In the various excitements of the moment he did not see the fish Hershel caught and released, wanting his son to achieve a sense of accomplishment and perhaps relieve him, at least momentarily, from his painful recurring dream.

Their morning excursion developed into a tremendous success. Tonight's dinner would be a feast for all and Moniek would be the hero of the day. After counting their catch and complimenting each other on their fishing prowess, they sat down on the bank of the river for a moment in silence, quietly watching the gentle water as it rolled slowly across the rock-filled river bed.

Hershel quietly breached the silence, "Moniek, do you remember when I took you with me and we visited Mr. Cohen where I bought the dairy cow?" Moniek nodded, having no idea where his father was going with the conversation.

"I was just teasing you about becoming a tailor."

"Oh?" Moniek replied, still a bit confused.

"I was thinking," Hershel said. "I realize you're still young but I was thinking that when you get a little bit older perhaps you'd like to become a part of the family business."

"Seriously, Tata? And work with you?"

"Why not. You're a bright young man, follow directions well, and you're a quick learner."

"But I thought Abraham was going to join you in the family business. I thought that was always the plan." Moniek was flabbergasted. He was also deeply touched.

"Our business is big enough for all of us. I can't handle it all anymore. Besides, there's no reason we can't expand a little." Moniek was stunned and didn't know what to say. As was usually the case Hershel took the lead. "Why don't we get these fish back into the wagon, take 'em back to the farmhouse, and have ourselves one fabulous dinner."

As they were placing the fish in the wicker baskets in the back of the buckboard Hershel softly asked, "Did you have a good ride on my bicycle a little while back? I heard it didn't work out all that well."

Moniek was stupefied. "Who told? Which one of my brothers?" he asked.

"None of your brothers. It was a neighbor who watches our house for me when I'm gone." Moniek didn't know what to say. "I'm glad you didn't get hurt. One of these days I'll give you some lessons so you won't fall off anymore. How's that sound?"

"That sounds wonderful, Tata," he responded enthusiastically. "Really wonderful."

"Good," he said with a smile of satisfaction. "Now let's get all these fish back to the house."

Spring of 1939 brought a welcome relief from the bitter winter months. Flowers in the yards began to bloom and healthy green leaves returned to the abundance of trees in the immediate and surrounding area. Farmers' fields began to come alive and experience their annual revitalization. It was a pleasant and delightful time of rebirth and renewal. Via the wondrous miracle of nature, the small town of Nowy Wisnicz magically transformed itself from the cold, gray, snow-covered streets into a burst of color exhibited in every yard and on every street corner. Peoples' moods began to brighten as they greeted each other on the street. No longer was it necessary to move rapidly from one warm and comfortable place to the next. Now conversations would pick up where they left off the previous fall and neighborly friendships would be rekindled.

Moniek dearly loved the spring months. It meant he could begin to wear a thinner jacket to school. It also meant he could eat his lunch outside the schoolhouse on the playground with his brothers and some of their friends. In their geography class they never learned that all Jews were completely banned from working with Germans or that Jews in that country were now required to apply for identification cards from the police and further required to show them on demand to any police officer or German official. Failure to apply for the ID card or inability to provide it when requested usually resulted in unpleasant repercussions.

Springtime provided a sense of bliss for the happy and energetic youngster. He was immersed in school, with his studies, and all forms of regular boyhood pastimes enjoyed by most ten-year-olds. His life, based on all standards of which he was aware, was completely normal.

However, two events which occurred earlier that year would have a profound effect on the balance of his innocent existence.

While German Jews were flooding into Poland for the most part they ended up virtually homeless in the larger cities such as Lodz, Krakow, and Warszawa. Few if any made their way to smaller towns such as Nowy Wisnicz. As a result there was still little if any exchange of information concerning what was actually going on in Germany. On occasion, when Hershel went to the market in Bochnia, he would hear these wild yet unconfirmed rumors from traveling strangers but paid little attention, choosing instead to both mind and take care of his own business.

During the Saturday evening card games he would casually mention things he'd heard at the market but most of his friends dismissed them. Isaac Weisman, who owned the local fruit stand and listened to the radio as often as was possible, had also heard ripples of information from people traveling through the town. Even Josef Gutman, the banker, had heard the same things from occasional customers.

However, as it had always been in the past, no one honestly believed what was happening even though they heard it clearly from actual victims of the Nazi persecution. They chose to close their own ears to the truth, believing that if there were indeed severe or massive problems they would all certainly stay within the boundaries of Germany. Like they'd discussed so many times before, the Polish government would surely never allow anything like that to happen here. Not in their country and certainly not in their small, peaceful town. It was literally unthinkable. They couldn't even believe their own ears after hearing Hitler on May 24, 1939, vow to attack Poland at the earliest opportunity.

Moniek experienced a delightful summer filled with mornings off from the public school, more time to spend playing in the street and visiting the castle with his friends, the wonderful three-day vacation to his grandfather's farm, and the fishing excursion with his father. It just couldn't have been better.

Except for the recurring nightmare.

One afternoon that fall, as the leaves were turning and a slight chill began to fill the evening air, Moniek and his brothers returned home following Hebrew school to find their parents covering all of their windows with thick paper. The boys were all confused and asked, nearly in unison, "What on earth is going on?"

Hershel was as serious as any of them had ever seen him. "Get a roll of paper and cover some of the windows," he instructed. They did as they were told without further questions. Nor were there any questions asked during a very quiet dinner that evening. For a change Hershel didn't instigate the traditional exchange concerning what each of them had learned at school that day. It was clear he was deeply troubled over something but never said a word to explain what it was that was bothering him.

When the boys all retired for the evening several men from the synagogue visited their house but this night it was not for the purpose of playing cards. Their whispered conversation in the dining room became louder and increasingly animated as the discussion continued. Moniek listened closely and while he couldn't really discern the words spoken he could tell clearly from the tone of his father's voice that he was very concerned about something.

And once again Moniek was plagued by the all-too-familiar nightmare.

The following morning he was greeted at the breakfast table with an out-of-character and eerie silence from both of his parents. "This is my birthday month," he announced, trying to break the silence. But to no avail. "Only nineteen more days." Still nothing.

"We'll do what we can, Moniek," Hershel sadly said, looking down at the table rather than making eye contact. "But it probably won't be like before."

"That's all right, Tata," Moniek brightly replied. "Just being with my family is the best birthday present anyone could ever ask for." Feigel pushed her chair back, silently left the table, and moved to the sink, pretending to wash dishes, her eyes filled with tears noticed only by her husband.

The discussion the previous evening had not been positive. This very day, September 1st, 1939, the Germans were clearly expected to invade Poland with a massive force. Hershel stared blankly into the distance, deeply concerned about what would become of his family. Then he walked to the sink and put a comforting arm around his wife's shoulders as she wiped away tears.

Later that afternoon Moniek ran all the way home from school. Even as both the sun and the temperature were falling he was covered with perspiration. In a state of utter excitement he burst through the kitchen door of the house without the traditional, "Hi, Mama, what's for dinner?" He was taken aback to find his father there. Hershel wisely chose to stay at home this day rather than travel into the countryside and conduct business.

"Tata! Tata!" he exclaimed, "Is it true!? Are we really at war with Germany? That's what everyone at school's talking about. Is it true?" There was a sense of desperation in his young voice.

"I'm afraid so," Hershel reluctantly replied.

"But what will we do? Where will we go?"

His father tried to be as reassuring as possible. "I expect our army will stop them at the border. If not," he hesitated and took a deep breath, "we'll do whatever they say and probably stay right here." Even Hershel didn't believe his own words but he continued, doing his best to calm his young son. "Everyone is well aware that the Germans have the most industrialized, advanced, and civilized society in all of Europe. They just want to occupy the land so they can call it their own, not really to harm anyone unnecessarily. Certainly not civilians. We're all going to be just fine."

This was not what Hershel had heard in the countryside and from several others while taking care of business at the market. He'd heard unbelievable stories concerning the viciousness and the atrocities the Germans were perpetrating on the Jews in their own country and while trying desperately to remain consoling he was worried to the very depth of his soul for the future of his family.

Talk of any sort was at a minimum at the dinner table that evening. There was very little which could actually be discussed because no one really knew anything. It all came down to a matter of a deadly waiting game, hoping for the best and desperate for news from the front. From anxiety-filled discussions at school Moniek's brothers were also familiar with the news of the day and equally disturbed. Hershel made the decision that tomorrow the boys would stay at home rather than be on the streets of the town.

The following morning Moniek was awakened by an unfamiliar sound outside his bedroom window. Nuta was already awake, staring wide-eyed at the sight outside. "What is it?" Nuta asked, concern on his face.

Moniek rushed to the window and witnessed an amazing sight. Their backyard was filled with uniformed soldiers, many of them climbing down from horses and securely tying them to everything in sight. They were all carrying rifles, an arsenal unlike anything he had ever seen. "What is it?" Nuta repeated, his voice now consumed with fear.

Moniek dressed as quickly as possible. "I don't know," he finally replied. "Tata will know." He finished dressing and rushed down the hallway into the kitchen. Abraham and Zishe were already there with their parents, watching the soldiers and horses filling their backyard.

"Tata, what..."

"It's all right, son," he quietly replied. "These are our soldiers. They just wanted to stop and rest for awhile and give their horses some water. I told you we were going to be fine." And once again, he still didn't believe his own words. There was a knock at the door and Hershel opened it to find a disheveled officer, his barely teenaged face covered with sweat and dirt stains.

"Excuse me, sir," the officer said with respect. "We found water for our horses but I was wondering if I could get some for my men. We've had a long ride and a pretty difficult night."

Feigel immediately began to fill pans with water and collect glasses for the soldiers. The officer was polite and appreciative as he passed the much needed refreshment to the men standing around him on the back porch. Hershel asked, "Would you like to come in for awhile and rest?" The officer was somewhat taken aback with the offer.

"I'd very much appreciate that, sir," he said.

"You're more than welcome to bring some of your men as well."

Several soldiers entered the house, but not before removing their boots. They tipped their hats, nodded thanks to Feigel, referring to her as "ma'am," and relaxed in chairs in the kitchen, dining room, and living room. They were all very quiet and appeared to be exceptionally tired. Moniek and his brothers stood against a far wall in the kitchen, cautiously examining their strange visitors. A cursory look from Hershel indicated that they were to remain silent. And they did.

Hershel carefully asked the officer, "How's it going?"

The officer nodded, as if to himself, and quietly replied, "Our unit was at the front. The fighting is pretty heavy and severe, but we seem to be holding our own."

"That's good," Hershel said. "Many casualties?"

The officer looked up into Hershel's eyes with a sense of near disbelief covering his face. "We're in a war," he said with intense seriousness. "A shooting war. People are getting wounded and people are dying." He hesitated before softly explaining, "We have to go back." His words trailed off as he stared out the kitchen window. Hershel felt badly that he had asked.

There was another knock at the door and Feigel opened it. Standing there, nearly bursting with excitement, was Jacob. "Is Moniek home?" he asked.

"Yes," Feigel replied. "would you like to come in?"

"No thank you, ma'am. Could Moniek come out?" Moniek looked at his father, seeking permission.

"Don't go too far," was all Hershel said.

Jacob was a friend and classmate. As the two of them left the yard Jacob, obviously impressed by the soldiers, whispered, "Wow, this must be the whole Polish army."

"I sure hope not," Moniek replied. "Where are we going, anyway?"

"Have you seen it? Have you heard about it?"

"Heard about what?"

"You'll see. It's just down the street." They quickly rounded the corner and Moniek stopped dead in his tracks. Whatever it was, it was the largest thing that he had ever seen in his life.

"What is it?" he asked his friend.

"It's a tank," Jacob said. "Don't you know anything?"

"Of course I do." As they cautiously approached the huge thing parked silently in the middle of the street Moniek continued his questioning. "What's that big long thing in the front?"

Jacob shook his head. "You really don't know anything do you. It's a gun."

"Wow," Moniek exclaimed. "Must be one heck of a gun. What's it doing here?"

"Somebody said it just broke down and they're trying to get it fixed." Both youngsters stared in wonderment at the giant machine until some soldiers politely shooed them away, explaining that it wasn't safe for them to be there.

At dinner that evening when Moniek related the story of his adventure Hershel was not at all pleased that he had drifted so far away from their house. But with all that was going on he didn't feel that any form of punishment was in order. However, he did tell all the boys he wanted them to stay near the house if they were to venture outside at all.

After the boys and Feigel were safely asleep Hershel sat at the kitchen table, alone, in the dark, staring out the window. Outside the Polish soldiers covered the backyard, sleeping side to side with their horses still tied everywhere. The officer Hershel had spoken with began to move among them, waking them up, and instructing them to be as quiet as possible. Wiping sleep from their tired eyes and moving slowly they saddled their horses and mounted.

With a hand signal the officer directed them all to follow him and they left the yard, heading down the dirt-covered alley. Hershel was very confused and walked out onto the back porch, watching with interest as they disappeared into the distance. That's odd, he thought to himself. They're headed due north, toward Bochnia. But the front and the German's are in the south. It didn't make any sense. None at all. He'd been with the soldiers all day long and no one had delivered any new orders. Why on earth were they heading north?

Then it suddenly occurred to him as if it were a bolt out of the black night sky. They weren't going back to the front. They weren't going back into more horrific, bloody battles complete with death and destruction. They weren't going back to the war effort to protect their own country. They were deserting.

Hershel stood in silence on the back porch of their fine home, his head hung in despair, wondering how many other Polish troops were also retreating and deserting on this dark and quiet night. Mostly he continued to wonder what would happen to his family when the Germans finally arrived, as they most certainly would. Staring blankly into the starless sky there were no answers to the questions weighing heavily on his mind. Moniek slept barely a few yards away, tragically experiencing the same vicious nightmare he'd been having on a semi-regular basis for nearly a full year.

Seven

Moniek stared out the kitchen window, confusion covering his face. "Where did all the soldiers go?" he asked.

Hershel continued to sip his steaming coffee, looking blankly into the distance, and quietly said, "They left in the middle of the night."

"I guess they must be going back to the war."

"I suppose they are." Hershel had never lied to Moniek or any of his sons. He felt his answer was fair and reasonable because what he had assumed when the soldiers left was just that, an assumption.

"Do you think any of them will be hurt?" Moniek, as fate would have it, was unfamiliar with the concept of death. Both of his grandmothers had died before he was old enough to understand or begin to comprehend what it actually meant.

"War is a terrible thing, son. But yes, to answer your question, some of them will probably be hurt." Hershel took another sip of coffee. This was a conversation he'd hoped to avoid, at least at this point of his son's young age. "Some of them will not be coming home when the war is over."

"Why, Tata?" It was a sincere question born of the simple fact that he had lived a protected life in a very small community where nearly everyone looked out for and took care of each other.

"In wars there are guns, some of them very large..."

"You mean like that tank I saw in the street yesterday?"

"Yes, like the tank. They also have other guns, lots of other guns. And when they shoot those guns sometimes people die. Do you know what that means?"

"Sort of — I remember when Jacob's father died last year he was real sad. And he cried. I didn't understand why."

"Because that meant his father was never coming home again."

"Ever?"

"Never, but Jacob's father was a good man and he lived a good life. He's gone to a much better place."

"If some of those soldiers die will they go to a much better place?"

This was a difficult question for Hershel because he believed in the bottom of his heart that the soldier's had all deserted and failed to protect their own country. "I don't know," he said with extreme caution. "That's not up to us."

"Who decides?"

Hershel smiled, "I think that's enough conversation for now. This is something you'll learn when you're just a little bit older. Okay?"

"Sure, Tata."

"Why don't you and Nuta clean your room this morning? Since you're going to be home it'll give you something to do."

Moniek smiled as he left the room and moved briskly down the hallway. He still had no real concept of death. This would change dramatically in the near future.

He was in his room when he first heard it. It was a giant rumbling on the street, right in front of their house. Moniek ran into the living room, opened the front door, and was astonished at the sight before his eyes. There were soldiers wearing different uniforms than the ones he had seen only yesterday. Countless soldiers in what seemed like an endless column. There were several tanks like the one he had recently seen only larger. There were huge trucks and open cars carrying even more soldiers. It was exciting. It was exhilarating. It was overwhelming.

"Mama! Mama!" he shouted. "Come quick! Come and see this!"

Feigel moved to the front door, took a quick look outside, and instantly shut it quietly but with authority. She was noticeably flushed and took a deep breath to compose herself.

"Mama, it's..."

"I know who it is. Listen carefully to me. I don't want you to open the door anymore. And you're not allowed to leave the house without permission. Is that absolutely clear?"

Moniek nodded, not really understanding. Feigel had never before been so forceful with him and he found it confusing. His brothers entered the room consumed with equal excitement and peeked through the bottom of the papers which were draped over their windows. Hershel walked in slowly and joined the rest of the family, his face understandably deeply troubled.

Feigel could only whisper, "They're here."

"I know," he replied, also quietly. "I've been watching from the window in our bedroom."

"What will we do?" There was a minor yet desperate tremor in her voice.

"We'll stay inside and wait. We have no other options."

However, there had been other options. Hershel had spoken with customers of his in the countryside, several of whom were more than concerned about the impending Nazi occupation. A couple of them, more concerned than most, were planning on leaving their farms, taking their families, and heading north, away from the direction that the German army would most likely enter their country. At the time Hershel felt that this was extreme and tried to talk the people out of such a drastic and unrealistic decision.

Now, standing silently in his own living room while what seemed to be the entirety of the German army marched down the street in front of their house, he questioned if the decisions a few of them had made had not been correct.

Later that evening he cautiously visited some nearby neighbors and learned that the occupying force was the 14th Army of the Wehrmacht, the HQ of the First Operational Group of the Security Police and Security Service under the direct command of SS-Brigadeferer

Bruno Streckenbach. The town wisely offered no resistance whatsoever, the residents choosing to stay within what they hoped desperately would prove to be the safety of their own homes. As the day wore on and more and more soldiers marched through the town, the Polish army was nowhere to be seen. The people of Nowy Wisnicz and the surrounding area had just become the newest residents of German occupied territory. Tragically not one single person had the faintest idea concerning what was going to happen to them now that their lives had been completely uprooted and forever altered.

The Nazis, as Hitler had promised, had invaded Poland, a country with a Jewish population of more than three and a half million people, by far the largest in all of Europe. The massive war machine, ignored by the rest of the civilized world, had finally begun its callous and vicious march toward their vision of world domination and the expulsion or extermination of all those considered to be "subhuman."

By sundown the army had made its way through the town, on its way heading north, toward Bochnia. They left behind only about a dozen men wearing finely tailored black uniforms and a comparable number of other soldiers who carried rifles at the ready, prepared to shoot anyone for any reason. Because no violence occurred, some of the residents were actually optimistic that perhaps the "occupation" wasn't going to be that bad after all.

At dinner that night Hershel explained as best he could what was going on. No one was to leave the house for any reason. It was too dangerous to be outside. This was the first time Moniek had heard the name Adolf Hitler or any reference whatsoever to the Third Reich. Being a ten-year-old the severity of the information didn't register with him at all. Hershel also sadly reported that earlier on this very day France, Britain, India, Australia, and New Zealand had declared war on Germany. If the war didn't officially begin when Germany invaded Poland, it most certainly would be formalized by these declarations.

Moniek tossed and turned in his bed, unable to find the benefit of sleep. He was afraid to sleep, afraid of the nightmare. As often as he'd experienced the terrible dream, he felt that what had occurred this day would most certainly cause its painful return. When he woke up the following morning he was enormously relieved that the feared nightmare had in fact not returned. Actually, since the very day the Nazis marched through and occupied their small town, he had not had the nightmare. The nightmare had become a frightening reality.

Things in the town changed rapidly. The Germans closed the Jewish school and both synagogues. Religious services or gatherings of any sort for Jews were strictly forbidden and repercussions were promised if the rule was broken. That night a small group of men met in the dimly lit Ebner kitchen, but not for the traditional card game. Their conversation evolved into a whispered political discussion concerning what they could possibly do now that they were under control of the SS and the Gestapo. And of course, there was absolutely nothing they could do.

The feared Gestapo commandeered the police station, forced all the officers to leave, and established that building, virtually next door to the Ebner household, as their headquarters for the entire area. They let the police chief stay in the office to assist them. Hershel and the chief, who was not Jewish, had been close friends for years.

Tension mounted throughout the town. Those brave enough to venture out onto the street for necessary chores or shopping were always polite to the Germans and in kind were always met with blank, hateful stares which they could not comprehend. They had done nothing to these people. Why were they filled with such hate and vengeance? Who could have possibly created such feelings of animosity toward total strangers who were trying their best to be courteous and friendly?

Many of the local merchants were ordered to close their businesses, especially the ones owned by Jews. Hershel was notified in writing that he was no longer to conduct his own business. In one single day the SS and the Gestapo seemed to know virtually everything about the small town and its inhabitants. While Hershel kept this information to himself, the edict was a blow of enormous proportion to his entire family. How would they eat? How would they possibly survive?

Fortunately, for them, unlike many others in the town, they had a fair-sized stockpile of food, especially in the well-chilled basement. They'd probably be all right for awhile but no one knew how long this was going to last.

On September 4th the Germans surrounded and cut off Warsaw, one of the largest cities in the country. Two days later they occupied Krakow, another major city west of, but reasonably close to, where Moniek lived. In all probability the army which marched through their small town took part in that action. Unlike Nowy Wisnicz there was minor resistance followed by much bloodshed in the streets. It was as if David was once again fighting Goliath.

Two days later the Gestapo ordered that all Jewish businesses exhibit a Star of David in their windows. Failure to comply would call for their immediate closure. This was an odd and nonsensical order in that everyone in the town knew who the Jewish business owners were. However, as they were sadly to learn over time, much of what the Nazis did was nonsensical.

"Tata." Moniek asked as he watched his father put on a heavy winter coat, "What are you doing?"

"I just need to go see some people," he replied. "I'll be fine."

"I thought none of us were supposed to go out at night," he said with a degree of innocence only a child can provide.

"I'll be very careful. And I'll be fine." After patting his son on the head he quietly opened the door and slipped into the darkness, careful to look in all directions for armed soldiers who by now were patrolling the streets on a regular basis. Unknown to virtually everyone in the town or the Ebner circle of friends and associates, on September 17th the Soviet Union invaded Poland from the east. The entire country was under siege, cut off, completely surrounded.

Hershel silently rode his bicycle into the countryside to a nearby farm to visit one of his regular customers. When he arrived all the lights were off. The small, frame house was completely dark. But Hershel knew the habits of his customers well. He knew with a certainty someone was still awake. He parked his bicycle and knocked softly on the back door. After three tries a raspy voice harshly whispered, "Who is it? What do you want?"

"Soloman, it's me, Hershel. Let me in." The door opened slowly and Soloman Weiss waved Hershel into the small kitchen of the farmhouse. Soloman was a large, burly man with bulging muscles, a result of working a lifetime in his fields. Normally he was gruff and quick with an insult. But recent events had changed all that. He was resigned, nearly what Hershel would consider to be frightened. This was an entirely different demeanor in that Soloman had never been afraid of anything in his entire life. He quickly closed the door and locked it, something which before yesterday was never done.

"What are you doing here?" he asked, continuing to whisper. "We're not supposed to be outside after dark."

"I need a special favor. You remember the favors I've done for you over the years."

"I remember. You're a good and honest man who's always been more than fair with me. What favor are you asking?"

"Our food supply is growing short..."

"Everyone's food supply is growing short," he said, cutting him off.

"My family needs some food. That's why I came to see you. I can pay."

Soloman looked away, clearly pained by the ultimate intrusion in their lives. It almost appeared as if the large hunk of a man was going to cry. "I'll do whatever I can. And you can pay later. You don't have to pay me now."

Hershel thanked him and then cautiously made his way back home with two chickens in the bicycle basket. He felt bad for Soloman. He felt bad for everyone in their town. But mostly he felt bad for his own family and the fact that he couldn't do more to protect and provide for them.

The dining room was lit by only a few flickering candles. Feigel entered from the kitchen carrying a small cake with one single candle on its top. "I'm sorry it's not more, Moniek," she said, trying to sound as upbeat as possible.

"Mama, it's perfect. It couldn't be better." They were celebrating his eleventh birthday, a mere nineteen days after the Germans occupied their country and their world was literally turned upside down. The cake was the perfect dessert to the delicious chicken she had prepared. Unlike the normal dinners, this one small chicken was shared by the entire family. The portions were considerably less than normal, but then nothing was normal anymore.

"I'm sorry we don't have a gift for you," Hershel said, deeply embarrassed.

"That's all right, Tata. I've heard that nearly all the stores and shops in the town are closed."

Abraham chimed in, "Those that aren't will be soon."

Hershel nodded, "Sad but very true. The Germans aren't allowing any of the merchants to replenish any of their merchandise. Soon it'll be nearly impossible to get anything."

Feigel cut the cake, passed equal slices around the table to Hershel and their sons, and returned to the kitchen. "But what will we do, Tata?" Zishe asked with concern.

"I've made arrangements with some of my customers. We're going to be fine."

"But that means you'll have to go out. And we're not supposed to go out," Abraham countered.

"It means we'll survive," was the flat response.

Feigel returned from the kitchen carrying a small wrapped package. "We do have a little something for you, Moniek. It's not very much but I hope you'll like it."

Moniek was taken aback as he carefully unwrapped the package. Inside he discovered his very favorite thing: four good-sized sugar cookies. He was speechless, looking up at his mother with tears in his eyes. "I hope you enjoy them," she said, tearing up as well.

"Thank you," he whispered. Then, he gave each of his brothers one of the cookies and kept the last one for himself. As the four of them enjoyed an enormous treat, magically transforming them away from their dilemma for only a fleeting moment, Hershel and Feigel smiled warmly at each other.

The warmth and pleasantries shared during the birthday celebration were short-lived. The Nazi newspaper, *Der Sturmer* ("The Attacker"), circulated five hundred thousand copies weekly to loyal and passionate readers. The paper was published by Julius Streicher and regularly printed quotes announcing that, "The Jewish people ought to be exterminated root and branch. Then the plague of pests would have disappeared in Poland at one stroke."

The day following Moniek's birthday Reinhard Heydrich hosted a conference in which he stressed the absolute necessity of keeping the Jews in "as few concentration centers as possible as a prerequisite for the ultimate aim." He issued instructions to the SS Einsatzgruppen, which came to be an integral part of the Gestapo known as the Task Force, that all Jews were to be gathered in ghettos near railroad tracks for transportation and the conclusion of the future "final goal." It was their specific function to round up all the Jews and other "undesirables" living within Germany's newly occupied territories and send them to the recently ordered ghettos or simply put them to death.

The ghettos were unbelievably overcrowded, remarkably unsanitary, and within a short period of time less and less food was available for the inhabitants. Heydrich also ordered a census of all Jews in the country and the establishment of Jewish administrative councils within each of the ghettos to implement a host of outrageous and demeaning Nazi policies and decrees.

These councils were referred to as *Judenrats* and were composed of Jewish elders and leaders within their various communities. If a town had a population of less than ten thousand Jews the *Judenrat* had twelve members. If the population exceeded ten thousand, the council had twenty-four members. They were elected by the residents of the individual ghettos and once the elections were completed they themselves would elect a chairman and a deputy from their members.

They were under the direct control of the SS and forced to comply explicitly with their every order, no matter how simplistic or extreme. If the SS wanted fifty men for a particular work patrol, it was the responsibility of the local *Judenrat* to make sure that the appropriate number of men appeared at a specific spot at the appointed hour.

Failure to comply with any order usually resulted in steep fines levied toward the Jewish ghetto. The Jews were being systematically bled of everything they owned because the fines had to be paid or severe penalties would be meted out to several within the boundaries of the respective ghettos.

Nowy Wisnicz had a relatively small Jewish population and no proximity to any railroad tracks. As a result, a ghetto was never formed there. However, the majority of people who lived on the Jewish side of the town, shortly after the Nazi occupation, simply disappeared, as if they just vanished. And no one had any idea where they went. It was rumored that they were taken to the newly formed ghetto in Bochnia but it was never confirmed.

There was a knock at the front door. Hershel motioned for Feigel and the boys to move down the hallway before he answered. There were three uniformed German soldiers with scowls on their faces and rifles in their hands. "Do you have a radio? And if you tell me you don't we'll search your house and you won't be happy with what we leave."

Hershel nodded and the soldiers followed him into the living room. Without hesitation he handed them the small radio which rested on a table. "Is this the only one?" Hershel nodded again. The soldier gave him a blank stare. Then, without another word he turned and the three of them left the house.

The confiscation meant that they were now completely without any contact with the outside world. They were alone.

Eight

Seven days after Moniek's birthday Warsaw surrendered to the mighty German war machine. Two days later the Nazis and Soviets divided up Poland. Over two million Jews now resided in Nazi controlled areas, leaving 1.3 million Jews living in the Soviet area.

Even though the Jewish population in Nowy Wisnicz was very small the Gestapo still formed a Jewish Polish Police Force. They acted as an adjunct to the SS and patrolled the streets issuing orders and organizing work patrols. At first the restricted number of recruits were hesitant to comply but within a short period of time began to rather enjoy their somewhat limited position of power. In addition to their alleged authority they also took pleasure in having the advantage of access to more food than was available to the other remaining Jews.

Many Jewish people who lived in the nicer homes in the town, including Josef Gutman, the local banker, were forced to vacate their houses which were then occupied by SS and Gestapo men. There were no resettlement or relocation plans offered. The people were left to their own devices to find new housing or live on the street as beggars. Because of the closeness of the community all those forced out of their own homes found lodging elsewhere, either with family members or friends. In nearly all cases the living conditions were crowded and worst of all, the food supply was evaporating at an increasing pace. Those who moved to farms in the country were most fortunate because of their access to food.

Hershel was somewhat bewildered in that the Nazis had not taken over their home because of its proximity to the Gestapo headquarters and the simple fact that it was one of the larger and nicer houses in the entire town. He guessed to himself that it was a result of being close friends with the police chief but never expressed his feelings vocally. Instead he chose to not "rock the boat." A lesson they were all learning rapidly.

Because of the complete blackout on all news or any information at all from the outside world none of them were aware that on October 6th the country of Poland officially surrendered to the German army. The Nazi noose was rapidly tightening.

"Do you think the German soldiers celebrate Rosh Hashanah, Tata?" Moniek asked.

"I don't think so, son."

"Why not?"

Hershel looked his inquisitive son square in the eye, "As you've seen, they think and act differently than we do. We believe in peace and getting along. They believe in war, and power, and controlling other people."

"But why?"

Hershel looked into the distance, his eyes nearly glazed over. "A very, very bad man tells them what to believe. And they do whatever he says."

"Are we going to celebrate this year?"

"Of course we will."

"But how can we when we can't go to the synagogue? The soldiers closed it."

"I know they did. We'll celebrate at home."

"I've been a good boy this past year, haven't I, Tata?"

"Yes, Moniek, you've been a very good boy."

"I'm going to be even better next year," he said.

Hershel smiled. But it was a smile laced with sadness. "I know you will, son. We're all going to be better."

Rosh Hashanah is one of the holiest days of the Jewish year. It literally means "head of the year" or "first of the year," commonly referred to as the Jewish New Year. It is a time for introspection, looking back at mistakes made over the past twelve months, and vowing to correct them. It's also a time for planning positive changes in the coming new year.

The name "Rosh Hashanah" does not appear in the Bible but is referred to as Yom Ha-Zikkaron, the day of remembrance, or Yom Teruah, the day of the sounding of the shofar. This was one of the last lessons Moniek received before the Nazis closed the Hebrew school.

The shofar is a large, hollowed out ram's horn which is blown somewhat like a trumpet. People throughout the town would hear the sounding of the shofar coming from the synagogue, a total of one hundred notes sounded each day during each of the High Holy Days, ending with Yom Kippur, a day of fasting, probably the most important holiday of the Jewish year. The name "Yom Kippur" literally means "Day of Atonement," a day set aside to "afflict the soul," to atone for past sins.

While there is no specific reason for this practice it has been suggested that the sound of the shofar is a call to repentance. But this year there would be no sound of the shofar. This year the synagogue would remain silent, just as it had since the first day of the Nazi occupation. The previous year would be the last time young Moniek would hear the shofar.

After dinner that evening, both Feigel and Hershel disappeared into the kitchen. This was highly unusual in that Hershel normally sat at the table, speaking with the children. The boys looked at one another, wondering what was going on. After a few moments they reappeared, both carrying plates of apples which had been quartered and small bowls of honey. The boys were delighted because they certainly hadn't expected this delicacy.

"Tata," Abraham asked, "where on earth did you..."

"A customer of mine had some extras and gave them to us for the celebration."

A popular observance of the holiday was eating apples dipped in the honey, a symbol of their wish for a sweet new year. The treat was delicious as it always was and certainly much appreciated. This year, because of their circumstances and the fact that both German soldiers and the Polish police were patrolling the streets, they would not practice the Tashlikh, the casting off. In all previous years, following the Rosh Hashanah dinner, the family would go to a nearby stream and toss whatever leftovers they had into the flowing water. This tradition was carried out to symbolically cast off their sins and cleanse them for the beginning of the new year.

"Do you think my name was written in the good book, Tata?" Moniek asked as they finished the last of the delicious apples and honey.

"May you be inscribed and sealed for a good year. I'm sure it will, son." Moniek beamed.

"Me too, Tata?" Nuta parroted.

This brought a slight smile to his face. "Yes, Nuta. You too."

"Do you think the German soldiers' names will be in the good book?" Abraham asked.

The smile instantly dissipated and Hershel became completely serious. "No. They will not."

"Will they have a bad year and a bad life?" Zishe queried.

The father lowered his sad eyes toward the table, "I certainly hope so, son. I certainly hope so." Being Orthodox Hershel studied and followed the widely accepted teachings of the thirteen principles of faith which many believe are the minimum requirements of Jewish belief. Among them the eleventh belief states that, "God will reward the good and punish the wicked." He closed his eyes, hoping beyond hope that this would indeed be the case.

The ten days beginning with Rosh Hashanah and ending with Yom Kippur are generally known as the Days of Awe or the Days of Repentance, a time for serious introspection, a time to consider the sins of the previous year and repent for those sins before the arrival of Yom Kippur.

One of the ongoing themes of the Days of Awe is the concept that God has "books" in which He records peoples' names. He writes down who will live and who will die as well as those who will have a good life or who will have a bad life for the coming year. These books are initially inscribed on Rosh Hashanah and are then sealed on Yom Kippur.

It is generally believed that those who have not atoned for their sins of the previous year before the arrival of Yom Kippur will not find their names in the book of people who will have a good life and a good year.

After what had been done to them and their small town so far, it was impossible for Hershel to even begin to believe that the Germans, any of them, could possibly atone for the sins they had perpetrated over the last twelve months within the finite time frame of the next ten days. His perspective was completely localized and understandably very personal. He was not aware that, in the middle of that month, Hitler announced to his general staff his plans to conquer the west.

Another event which would affect their lives was the appointment of Hans Frank as the governor-general of the country, becoming the supreme chief of occupied Poland's civil administration.

Frank, an enthusiastic proponent of Nazi racist ideology, ordered the general confiscation of Polish property and increased the number of residents forced to move into various ghettos that were being established throughout the country. He was also responsible for transporting countless Polish workers, all non-Jews, to Germany for the purpose of slave labor. By the end of October he issued a forced labor decree for all Jews aged fourteen to sixty.

Moniek could feel the pain shooting through his small fingers. His prowess with a needle and thread was being utilized but in a terribly unpleasant way. He sat at the dining room table beside Feigel and together they sewed the six pointed, blue, Jewish Stars of David on white armbands. They worked in silence as the others watched. The newly appointed Governor Frank had ordered that all Jews over the age of twelve must wear the armbands whenever they were outside. Moniek and Nuta were not affected by the decree but that mattered little.

The armbands were designed and used for the purpose of identification so that all Jews could be easily recognized by the Germans whenever they left their homes. It was demeaning and humiliating to say the very least but they had no other choice. If you were stopped on the street while not wearing the armband and questioned by a German soldier, or even worse, someone from the Gestapo, a severe punishment would normally follow.

It was widely rumored that the basement of the police station, now the Gestapo headquarters, was being utilized primarily as a torture chamber designed to "teach these subhumans to follow the rules we establish or pay dearly for their insubordination." Those who had firsthand knowledge of the basement, probably out of fear of further reprisals, would never corroborate its existence or the things which occurred there. On the other hand, there were never any denials as to the cruelty they more than likely experienced.

This was but a minor point in the Nazi master plan and policy which was now in full force. The Nazis were determined to transform Poland into a massive reservoir of slave labor to be used by the German war industry. To accomplish this end they established several points prior to their occupation:

1. To exterminate the Polish elite consisting of professors, lawyers, doctors, scientists, and anyone who could offer any degree of influence to others and be detrimental to the Reich.
2. To exterminate any and all potential opponents.
3. To close all places of education, all schools, colleges, and universities.
4. To forbid any cultural or political activities with death being the ultimate penalty.
5. To create an exclusive German Zone by confiscating all private property.

During the winter of 1939, the Polish elite and anyone who had any role in the cultural or scientific life in Poland mysteriously disappeared and were eventually exterminated. The Nazi's justification for this incredibly vicious act of cruelty was, "the slaves don't need culture."

There was a fair sized, two-story prison high on a hill on the far side of Nowy Wisnicz. Within days of their arrival the Gestapo, without any justification, arrested the mayor, several city council members, and the priests from the Catholic church. They were incarcerated, completely cut off from the general population of the town, and as such could provide no leadership, advice, or sympathy to their followers for the plight they were being forced to endure.

On a regular basis Moniek would peek through their front window and see the group being marched through the street, under heavy armed guard, to various work patrols where they were forced to perform back-breaking labor for hours on end until they were physically spent and could barely make the trek back up the hill to the prison.

Seeing the town leaders and elders marched through the street on a regular basis was, as it was intended, completely intimidating to the rest of the population. Moniek turned to his father who sat silently in a nearby chair, wondering, worrying. "Tata," he asked, confusion on his young face, "is this the end?"

Hershel rubbed his chin thoughtfully and stared at his favorite painting on the far wall. After a long moment of hesitation he finally answered, "No, son. This is not the end. This is only the beginning."

While these initial tragedies were occurring the entire populations of countless towns in western Poland were deported to various ghettos without receiving any compensation for their property. This was done in order to make a place for what the Nazis referred to as the German "colonists." The new German population settled on the expropriated farms and houses and several regions became exclusively German.

Nowy Wisnicz, again, because of its relatively small size and location, was initially not one of the main regions to be occupied by the "colonists." A few Germans moved into the town and took over the nicer houses and some of the farms in the surrounding area. Still confusing to Hershel was the simple fact that no one ever bothered them or forced them to move. He still felt quite strongly that it had to be a result of his relationship with the chief of police. For the time being they still had their house and for the time being, in that several others did not, it was considered to be a blessing. A small blessing, but a blessing to be sure.

The dining room was dark. Hershel struck a match and lit the shamus, the servant candle which was necessary for the religious observance of the evening, and handed it to Nuta, the youngest member of the household. Then he offered three blessings. The first was a general prayer over the candles. The second was a prayer thanking God for all their ancestors. And the third was a general prayer thanking God for allowing them to reach this time of the year.

Nuta moved to the front of the menorah, an ornate candelabra holding nine candles, and lit the one on the far right. Hershel then placed the shamus in its proper place in the center position of the menorah and they all observed a moment of silence.

The story of Chanukkah, the Jewish festival of rededication also known as the Festival of Lights, an eight-day festival, actually began with the reign of Alexander the Great who conquered Syria, Egypt, and Palestine but allowed the Jews to continue to practice their own religion and was relatively benevolent in that he was not particularly oppressive.

More than a century later, Antiochus IV was the ruler of the region and began to oppress the Jews on a massive scale. He placed his own priest in the Jewish Temple, massacred Jews, prohibited the practice of the Jewish religion, and desecrated the altar of the Temple by requiring the sacrifice and slaughter of pigs, non-kosher animals, to be conducted there.

Two groups joined forces and conducted a successful revolution opposing him. Following their victory the Temple was rededicated. However, at the time of the rededication there was very little oil left that had not been desecrated by the Greeks. The Temple menorah needed oil that was supposed to burn throughout the night, every night for eight nights in a row. Sadly there was only enough oil to burn for one evening.

Miraculously, it burned for the entire eight days offering the precious time needed to prepare a fresh supply of oil for the menorah. Soon after this incredible event occurred the Jewish people declared an eight-day festival to commemorate the miracle.

So that the story would never be forgotten and following family tradition, each night the boys would rotate, all having the opportunity and the privilege of lighting the candles and hearing the story retold.

As the family eased into their chairs around the dinner table Her-shel pondered the third blessing offered each night prior to the candle lighting: the general prayer thanking God for allowing them to reach this time of the year. His concern was focused on this time next year and wondering whether or not another Chanukkah would be celebrated by the entire family.

NINE

GERMAN AUTHORITIES ORDERED THE seizure of all Jewish property in Poland. The first step in this detailed plan was initiated in the form of confiscating all military and civilian institutions. They were then utilized as temporary German barracks for the continuous flow of soldiers passing through the country and warehouses to store the massive amounts of supplies which were to be used in the growing war effort. Shortly thereafter all accounts and safes in all banks were frozen and emptied, their contents sent back to the Third Reich headquarters in Berlin to assist in financing Hitler's sweeping plan of world supremacy. If anyone had any money or anything of value in a bank it was now just gone and there wasn't one thing in the world which could be done about it.

Next came the looting of personal and private property. Soldiers, usually in groups of three or more, would go to an individual's home and demand entrance. Once inside they conducted extensive searches, looking for any objects made of gold or silver. They also confiscated money and various artifacts.

This made living conditions even more difficult and harsh because most of the people who were robbed blind had been using many of those artifacts and objects to clandestinely trade for food, a practice that the Nazis frowned upon. Conversely, by now virtually all of the merchants in the town were completely out of merchandise and had no prospects of ever getting any more.

Hershel continued to make occasional nighttime trips into the countryside to visit nearby farms. He was usually able to obtain some sort of food to bring back home but each of his excursions was dangerous and fraught with peril. Still, food was a necessity and the risks had to be taken if they were to eat.

One evening, well after the sun had gone down, Hershel silently made his way to visit his old friend Avi Cohen at his farm. He clearly expected the house to be dark but as he approached he could see that all the lights were on. Loud voices filled with boisterous laughter emanated from within. He carefully eased his way closer until he could clearly see that the voices and the laughter belonged to German soldiers, seated around the kitchen table, enjoying a huge meal and having a wonderful time. It occurred to Hershel that it had been a long time since he had heard the sound of laughter.

Filled with sadness and as silently and cautiously as possible he made his way back to his own home. It was obvious that Avi had lost his farm, the most important thing in his life. Actually, the only thing in his life. Accepting this as a probability Hershel also felt it was more than likely that Avi had by now been taken elsewhere by the Germans. It was anyone's guess when he would be able to see his old friend again.

The Germans seemed to be confiscating more and more farms and homes, displacing the residents, creating organized discomfort. The food supply was diminishing at a rapid pace, especially with the loss of farms where food could be obtained. On his way back home that night, unfortunately empty handed, Hershel vowed that his family would never starve. They may not have all to eat that they were used to but they would never starve. He committed to himself that he would do whatever was necessary and take whatever risks were appropriate to obtain enough food to keep them all alive.

Hershel was aware of the forced searches being conducted throughout the area and as such had taken appropriate measures. When the three soldiers came to their front door he let them in without hesitation. "Do you have any gold or silver or money in the house?" the soldier asked curtly.

"No I don't," Hershel earnestly replied. "Everything we had was in the bank in the town, locked up in the safe." No further explanation was necessary. The German knew clearly what that indicated. But still the three of them conducted a thorough search, rifling through drawers, cupboards, and closets, breaking things, leaving a complete mess. They checked the basement especially closely and were somewhat surprised at the food stuffs they discovered. There were separate bins, mostly holding dwindling sized piles of potatoes, carrots, and turnips.

"You have a lot of food here," the soldier said, raising an eyebrow. "Did you steal it or have you been trading illegally with the local farmers?"

"Neither," Hershel replied. "I follow the rules you've given us and do exactly what I'm supposed to do. As you can tell, it's very cold down here during the winter months. It takes a long time for the food to spoil. We've had this stored since the end of last summer."

"Perhaps we should take this food with us," the soldier announced, a slight smile of sadistic satisfaction on his face. Hershel looked down at the ground.

Another soldier spoke up. "Look, Sergeant, we've done a thorough search. He doesn't have anything. We have plenty of food ourselves. I'm not interested in carrying fifty pounds of potatoes back to the barracks when there's already more there than we'll ever eat."

"That's right," the lead soldier said as they turned and started back up the stairs. Then he stopped, turned around, and stared Hershel straight in the eye. "Besides, we can always come back whenever we want." And with that they climbed to the top of the stairs, walked through the living room, and out the front door, which they left open. Hershel found it interesting that power and authority had somehow erased the very concept of decent manners.

Hershel let out an extended exhale of relief. Had the soldiers rummaged through the potatoes in all likelihood they would have discovered the menorah, some other elaborate candlesticks, several gold and silver items, and a shoebox filled with jewelry and money. This time the family had been enormously fortunate but he promised himself as he looked at the potatoes in the bin that he would find a much better and more secure hiding place for their valuables.

When he reached the top of the stairs and entered the living room Feigel and the boys were already busy cleaning up the mess the German's had made and putting things back in their proper places. The entire family ceased their activity and looked at him with wide eyes. He offered a slight smile toward each of them and offered, "This time we were fortunate, very fortunate."

There was a knock at the front door and as now became the custom, if Hershel was at home, he was the only one who would open it. Jacob Kreiger stood there, wearing the ill-fitting blue jacket and blue cap supplied to the Jewish Police Force by the local SS. Hershel did not invite him into the house but left him standing on the porch in the chilling cold. The two men stared at each other. "Hershel Ebner," Jacob said without emotion, "you have to come with me."

Hershel knew he had no choice and it would be futile to argue the point or refuse the order. The Jewish Polish Force had a certain degree of authority and failure to follow their instructions to the letter usually resulted in severe punishment. Hershel nodded and moved to the closet where he put on a warm coat. Walking through the front door Jacob tapped him on the shoulder. Then he tapped him on his arm.

"If you come outside without your armband I'll have to arrest you."

Hershel turned around and Feigel helped him attach it to his sleeve. Feigel whispered, "Be careful."

"I will. And I'll see you soon." And with that the two men walked off the front porch and made their way down the street.

They walked in silence for a few blocks until Jacob finally asked, "Why don't you ever talk to me when I see you on the street?"

"I don't like what you're doing," he flatly replied.

"I'm doing this for my family."

Hershel and Jacob had known each other for the majority of their lives. At one time they were considered the closest of friends. Before the occupation they even attended the same synagogue and had served together on various committees.

"What you're doing is an embarrassment to your family, to yourself, and to every Jew in our town. By doing what you're doing you have become shameless, just like the Nazis."

"I should put you in jail for talk like that." But his voice was shaky when he muttered the words.

"But you won't because you know I'm right."

The silent walk continued. Several in the Jewish Police Force had indeed emulated the Germans persona and resorted to violence when dealing with people who not that long ago had been their neighbors and good friends. This violence nearly always occurred in the presence of soldiers, SS men, or the Gestapo who took great pleasure in watching the Jews being openly beaten in public.

When they reached their destination Hershel joined several other men wielding picks, shovels, and sledgehammers, working on the side of a road, digging, breaking rocks. Jacob handed Hershel a pickax and pointed toward a place where he was to work. The work patrol was breaking large rocks into smaller ones which would be used to reinforce the main road coming through the town so it could support the heavy German equipment as it continued to roll through.

There was no lunch break or any food provided. In fact, there was no rest at all during the entire day. Several times Hershel, while continuing to work, would look at Jacob. Each time the look was noticed he would quickly look away and move to another spot. Jacob knew what he was doing was an embarrassment.

After dark that night Hershel walked slowly up the steps of their front porch, his legs, arms, and back burning with pain. Once inside he collapsed into a chair while Feigel brought him a cup of coffee, his first food of the day. The boys all volunteered to do anything they could to help but in reality there was nothing any of them could do.

"Tomorrow I'll take some food with me," he quietly and sadly announced. "I have to go back."

In 1920 Karl Binding, a widely respected judge, and Alfred Hoche, a renowned psychiatrist, both members of the German Eugenics Society, wrote and published a book titled, *The Permission to Destroy Life*

Unworthy of Life. The book would eventually become one of the cornerstones of the Nazi philosophy and practice.

In their book they stated without equivocation that the elimination of "worthless people" should be legal. It clearly suggests "the elimination of those who cannot be saved...whose death is an urgent need...and those who are below the beast with neither the will to live nor to die." The book also makes reference to those who are mentally dead and who form a foreign body to the human society. Their words, while admonished when first published, were a precursor to what was to become a tragic reality barely two decades following its initial printing.

Hitler, Goebbels, Himmler, Bormann, Eichmann, Heydrich, and others believing in the supremacy of the Third Reich justified their actions and later their crimes by claiming that their victims were *Untermenschen*, "underlings," "subhumans," who were viewed as both biologically inferior and, in the case of Jews, a potential and probable challenge to the superiority of all pure Aryans.

The Nazi leaders felt that by eliminating all those designated and deemed to be unfit, they would be creating a better race for the entire world. In this regard Himmler once told a group of senior SS men and party leaders, "What about the women and children? I decided to find an absolute solution here too. I regard myself as having no right to exterminate the men. In other words, to kill them or have them killed, and to let the avengers in the form of children grow up for our sons and grandsons to deal with. The difficult decision had to be taken to make those people disappear from the earth."

Himmler also decreed in a screaming tirade that, "The Jews are our misfortune," and "We are the race that must rule the world. The rest will be our slaves."

Heydrich echoed the sentiments when he proclaimed, "The Jews are unbearable to my very soul."

The Nazi agenda of hate was preached continuously, night and day. It focused on the master race protecting itself by eliminating all subhumans. It constantly reinforced the theory of racial purity and Aryan supremacy. While many felt it was understandable that extreme anti-Semites in nearly all positions of leadership within the Third Reich would harbor these feelings and attitudes, it was the master of propaganda who in a brief period of time turned an entire country around to accept and passionately believe in their radical theories.

Once Josef Goebbels, the ultimate controlling and authoritative speechwriter, creative designer of posters, creator of brilliant and powerful documentaries, and accomplished public speaker, gained complete control of the radio waves, newspapers, films, and loud speakers, 80 million people were totally deprived of independent thought. Because of this constant barrage of propaganda it was thereby possible to subject them all to the will and beliefs of one man.

The fate of the European Jews and all others considered to be undesirable, according to the Reich, was clearly sealed and carried with it the approval of the vast majority of the German population. Without the collective assistance and protection of the world community it seemed tragically that their time on this earth was destined to be either short or pain-filled and remarkably oppressive. Only time would tell.

TEN

THE WINTER WAS EXCEPTIONALLY harsh. More and more of the Jewish residents of Nowy Wisnicz disappeared mysteriously, without explanation. The Ebner family was spared for the time being but never felt any sense of security because they knew without question that at any given moment they could be the next ones who, for reasons unknown, just didn't live there anymore. As had been the case since the Nazi occupation last September, no one knew anything.

While the majority of the synagogues in Poland had been tragically burned to the ground the two in Nowy Wisnicz were left untouched. After completely desecrating the places of worship and savagely destroying the Torahs and sacred altars, the Germans used the buildings as storage areas for war materials which were allegedly on their way to the front. When Hershel had rare conversations with friends they wondered where the front actually was. The occupation of Poland had been a swift and outstanding success. The country had unconditionally surrendered. Why were the Germans still there? And where were all their Jewish neighbors disappearing to?

"Faster, Ebner, or I'll give you the stick." Jacob Kreiger had assimilated all too well into his position on the Jewish Police Force. He relished the temporary circumstances of power he had achieved and wielded those powers with authority over former friends, neighbors, and even people he once worshiped with. He held the stick high in the air in a raised position, ready to strike. But when Hershel turned and looked at him with sad, tired eyes, Kreiger lowered the stick to his side and silently walked away to physically intimidate another worker on his patrol.

Hershel and Kreiger no longer spoke to one another. No words could possibly bridge the chasm created by the extreme difference in their positions. Hershel, for all practical purposes, was now little more than an insignificant Jew while Kreiger willingly played the part of a significant ploy for the Nazis in their grand scheme of things. Hershel felt that he and virtually all of his fellow Jews had been betrayed. Kreiger had violated all laws of civility, all the teachings of the Torah, and all basis of reasonable understanding and friendship.

Breaking rocks and road construction was halted as a result of the freezing weather and heavy snowfall. Now Hershel and the others, including older sons Abraham and Zishe, spent long days shoveling snow, clearing the roads for the military equipment to pass through the town. The war, wherever it was, was going on and would not be stopped for any reason.

Hershel and the boys literally dragged their exhausted souls across the back porch, barely able to walk, a result of a day of backbreaking labor, and entered through the kitchen door. Once inside they collapsed into chairs, slowly and painfully removing their heavy winter clothing. Feigel produced steaming cups of broth for each of them and hung their jackets on nearby hooks on the wall. Conversation was understandably sparse.

"Did you see Kreiger?" she quietly asked.

Hershel nodded and could barely speak. "He remains the same, only worse."

"How can he be that way?"

Hershel shook his head from side to side, a look of confusion on his face. "How can any of them be that way," he replied.

"I've fixed a chicken soup for dinner," she quietly said. "But I'm afraid it's the last of the chicken. Somehow we'll make do."

Their food supply was running dangerously short. Their stockpile in the basement now consisted solely of potatoes and even they were rapidly disappearing. Potatoes became the staple of their diet. Feigel fixed them in every imaginable way. Mostly it was potato pancakes. Moniek balked at first but after realizing that on several occasions that was all they had to eat he capitulated and joined the family in the meager meal without complaint.

With the Germans taking over more and more farms in the area it became increasingly difficult for Hershel to find any of his previous customers who would deal with him and provide food for the family, no matter how little it might be. He usually made at least one trip a week into the nearby farmlands to try and negotiate but the supply was growing alarmingly slim. On many of his excursions which proved fruitless he would drift into empty fields and pick raw vegetables with his bare hands so the family would have something to eat. Each day became progressively harder and harder. The weather certainly didn't help. Nor did Jacob Kreiger.

Moniek knelt at his father's knee and helped take off his ice-caked boots. "Tata," he pleaded, "please let me come with you and Abraham and Zishe tomorrow. I can help. I can make it easier for you."

Hershel smiled at the youngster, "You're doing what needs to be done right here. You're helping your mother and while I'm gone you're the man of the house."

"But I can shovel snow. I can work."

"There's plenty of snow right here that needs to be shoveled. Are you and Nuta still helping out the nuns at the church?"

"Yes, Tata, we were over there today."

"That's good. I'm proud of you. How are they doing?"

"Not very well — like everyone else they're running out of food."

"I wish we could help them." And his words drifted off sadly into a pained silence.

Hershel had heard rumors from others on his work patrol about the ghetto which had recently been established in Bochnia, the town up the road where only months ago he used to take his products and animals to the market. The free market, with free people. Now the town had been reconfigured, turned alarmingly upside down. The Jews were all segregated into a relatively small enclosed area where conditions were deplorable, virtually unlivable. He felt that from a comparative standpoint his own family was still doing well. They still had each other and while not quite their normal bill of fare they still had enough to eat. At least enough to keep them alive and keep them going, for awhile.

On January 25th of 1940 the Nazi high command held a top-level conference and unanimously chose the town of Oswiecim, also known as Auschwitz, located in Poland near Krakow, as a site for a new concentration camp. Like several others before, it was selected because of its relative isolation in the countryside and the simple fact that railroad lines from nearly all of the country could connect easily with the site. The two and a half story, brick buildings were initially constructed and used as barracks and a training facility for Polish soldiers, now either surrendered or long gone. Within days construction began on a tall, double barbed wire fence surrounding the entire facility. Once completed the wires were all electrified, deadly to the touch, and guard towers were built around the facility and equipped with high caliber machine guns. From its conception the camp was designed to hold political opponents of the Reich and any other dissidents found to be potentially dangerous to the Nazi master plan.

Barely days later, *Der Sturmer*, the official Nazi newspaper, quoted that, "The time is near when a machine will go into motion which is going to prepare a grave for the world's criminal — Judah — from which there will be no resurrection." In this simple comment, authorized and endorsed by the Third Reich, the fate of the Jews had been once and for all sealed. It was now crystal-clear to the entire world that Hitler and his minions felt that the elimination of the Jews was necessary for the national salvation of all Germans. And while this news permeated the world stage, few did anything at all to quell its growth or the path of its demonic destruction.

Declaring war is an unbelievably massive undertaking. Virtually unthinkable to most rational and or logical people. Creating a World War and having grand delusions of ruling the planet greatly magnifies the equation. None of what the Third Reich was in the process of doing occurred by accident. It was remarkably well thought out, brilliantly well planned, and exceptionally well executed. The war was going well for them with their invasions of Denmark, Norway, France, Holland, and Luxembourg. All of these countries swiftly surrendered to the Reich. As the Germans methodically devastated Europe it seemed as if the world was theirs to take. And the United States remained silent.

It was late in the evening. Long after the sun had gone down. Moniek shook his head from side to side, standing in their garage with his father and brothers and actually couldn't believe his own eyes. Hershel had returned from his weekly late night visit into the countryside and one of his regular customers who was going to be evicted the following day gave him two calves rather than relinquish them to the Nazis. The calves were both in the same pen, fortunately weaned and being very quiet, thankfully unknowing of their fate.

Hershel cautiously eased his way through the well-patrolled streets of the town until he was able to locate Mordechi Reuben, the local sochet, the only man left in town that could properly slaughter the animals according to Jewish laws and tradition and declare them to be kosher and therefore edible.

"Yes," Mordechi quietly answered in the relative safeness of the shadows surrounding them. "I can perform the butchering for you for the price of a small piece of meat, but we have a slight problem."

"And what would that be?" Hershel asked.

"I can't take the risk of carrying my knives in public. If they should catch me they'll be determined to be weapons. If they catch me… well…I don't even want to think of what they'll do to me and my family."

"What if I have someone else carry your knives to my house?" Hershel asked. "Would that be acceptable?"

Mordechi nodded with a degree of reluctance and softly replied, "We can do it tonight."

Upon his return home Hershel related his conversation to a family filled with stunned silence. They had food waiting in the garage, which would be discovered by either the Germans or the Jewish Police in short time and without a relatively quick solution there was nothing they could do about it.

Moniek finally broke the silence. "I can bring the knives back here." It was a bold statement. Feigel totally disapproved.

"I can do it, Mama. No one's going to bother a kid on the street this late at night. If I'm stopped I'll just say I'm lost and pretend that I'm crying." He looked at his father with passionate and pleading eyes. "I can do it, Tata."

Hershel looked at Feigel and softly replied, "He can do it."

Moniek eased his way through the few back streets to Mordechi's house and silently entered the back door.

"Your father sent you?" Mordechi asked with a degree of amazement.

"I came for the knives," he curtly but respectfully responded. "Not for conversation."

Mordechi nodded and handed the youngster two, very long, and very sharp butcher knives. Moniek carefully placed them inside his pants, one on the side of each leg, and returned to the dark streets of the town. His short trip, while fraught with peril, was fortunately uneventful. Feigel, understandably, was enormously relieved when he came through the back door and most proudly produced the knives.

"I was so worried about you," she said.

"Mama," he replied, standing as tall as possible. "Tata tells me that when he's not here I'm the man of the house." Then he offered a huge smile. His mother responded with a long hug. Perhaps her young man wasn't all that young any more.

Less than an hour later Mordechi appeared at the back door, prepared to do duties which have been passed down from countless generations. He carefully examined the knives which Moniek had transported home and washed them repeatedly with a sense of reverence. Each washing deserved a prayer. The Ebner family observed each prayer in silence.

Then it was time for the ritual. "Hershel," Mordechi quietly said, "It'd be better if the children weren't in the garage. It can be kind of…messy."

Hershel nodded acknowledgment and, although the boys didn't agree, they went along with the wishes of the adults without questioning. For them and their family this was a matter of food and they all knew better than to do anything which might disturb the process.

The sharpened knife was quick, slicing the throat and causing instant death as the other calf looked on without any awareness that he was next in line. It was very quiet. No one made any sound for fear of discovery. Within half an hour the ritualistic butchering was completed. Mordechi took a piece of what amounted to the size of a small roast, placed it underneath his coat, and quietly disappeared into the night. Hershel summoned the boys and together they carried the balance of the beef into the house where it would be stored in the basement and provide sustenance for at least two months — possibly longer, with smaller portions than they were once used to.

Judaism focuses considerably more on actions than beliefs. When beggars appeared at their door or what few neighbors who were left asked assistance, Feigel would always share whatever they could spare. Because of her generosity the two month supply of beef lasted the family barely a month. Hershel, whose religion by no means faded or waned in the least, never said a word concerning her sharing with others who had less than they did.

The streets during the daytime were reasonably quiet, reasonably safe. And they had been for several months, even as the Nazi war machine continued to rumble through their town. Because of the apparent safety permeating the air and following much pleading Feigel finally allowed Moniek to visit his friend Jacob who lived nearby. He was thrilled with the opportunity because it seemed to the youngster like ages had passed since he'd been allowed out of their own yard.

Moniek heard it up ahead, in the distance, growing closer with each step taken. It was music coming from somewhere down the street. Since the Germans confiscated their radio it seemed almost as if all forms of music had become a thing of the past. Even his mother, who was always singing or humming a Polish tune of some sort or another, now remained eerily silent.

But he heard the music and was attracted toward it. While cautious and keeping a safe distance he crouched down behind a leafless bush and could see a finely appointed house, one which had been occupied by the Germans. The living room was filled with soldiers, laughing, drinking, and singing along boisterously with the music. Moniek was totally intrigued with the sight and watched for several minutes.

Here were all these normal looking people laughing and singing and having a good time. Moniek was confused because the picture before his eyes certainly didn't fit with all he'd been told about the Germans. From all outward appearances they seemed to be all right. Most of them were young looking, actually not that much older than Abraham. These certainly couldn't be the vile and vicious people described by the few others he'd spoken with.

Perhaps the others were wrong, he thought. The people inside the house enjoying themselves couldn't possibly be as cruel as everyone seemed to think they were. He promised himself that later that night, when his father and brothers returned from their work patrol, he'd tell him of his excursion and ask why everyone seemed to be so upset with the Germans. After all, they couldn't possibly be as bad as everyone says. Could they?

Hershel and his two older brothers returning home each evening from their work patrol was always the highlight of his day. Moniek, as had become the tradition, sat at the kitchen table, watching out the window so he could catch the first glimpse of his father as he entered the backyard. But something was wrong. Something was very wrong.

"Mama!" he shouted. "Come quick!"

Feigel rushed to the window and without putting on a jacket or scarf quickly ran outside. Abraham and Zishe were helping to support Hershel as they slowly eased their way across the yard.

The face she loved so much had been transformed. It was now bruised and bloody, with welts under both eyes. "What happened?" she quickly asked with true panic in her voice.

"Inside," Hershel whispered, barely able to force the word through his swollen lips.

Once inside the kitchen Feigel and the boys all helped remove his jacket and boots. It was all Hershel could do to lift his arms. His eyes were filled with sadness, expressing much more than the pain he was obviously experiencing.

"I was on the patrol," he softly began. "An officer came up and told me I was to go to the forest and cut down some trees on the property we own. They needed them to heat some of the homes they took over. They provided a wagon and some saws. Two armed guards came along as escorts. They told me I'd be paid."

Feigel listened attentively as she prepared a cup of broth. The boys were captivated, hanging on each spoken word. "After awhile," he continued, "we filled the wagon with the lumber and delivered it, as I was ordered, to the Gestapo headquarters."

"The one right down the street?" she questioned.

Hershel nodded. "They took me inside, down into the basement. They tied my hands behind my back and a man in a black uniform told me I didn't bring enough lumber. He began to beat me with a stick, and then another man joined in. Other soldiers stood in the background laughing. I think I must have passed out before they threw me outside into the yard and the boys found me. I'm fortunate to be alive."

Feigel prepared a warm cloth and began to wipe the blood from his face. Each time she touched him, ever so gently, it still caused a great degree of pain. He grimaced but went along with the procedure because he knew it had to be done. He closed his eyes, also knowing that tomorrow he'd be back on the work patrol, wondering and worrying when the next time would come when he'd be ordered into the forest, and even worse, the basement of the Gestapo headquarters.

Moniek held his father's hand, watching with great compassion, fighting back tears. Any questions he might have harbored earlier in the day concerning the Germans and the Nazis had now been answered.

Winter slowly dissolved into spring but certainly not like the one last year or all the others preceding it. The streets were still patrolled and it was still dangerous to be outside at night. Hershel, Abraham, and Zishe still put in laborious efforts on their work patrol. But now, with the snow receding they were back at the task of breaking rocks to shore up the main road through the town. And the heavy military equipment and army kept rolling through their small and once peaceful town toward parts unknown. Why were the Germans still there? There was no logical reason. The remaining residents of Nowy Wisnicz certainly provided no resistance or challenge to the mighty Nazi war machine.

Whenever there was a knock at the door the family held its collective breath. The boys retreated to a bedroom down the hall. Feigel stood silently against a far wall, her arms folded, always expecting the worst. As Hershel opened the door that warm August afternoon there were three soldiers, armed with submachine guns. One handed Hershel a folded piece of paper. In a flat tone and without emotion or expression the soldier announced, "You will join the others on the road. You have one and a half hours to collect whatever you can carry. You're going to Bochnia." And with that the three of them turned and walked away.

Hershel looked across the room at Feigel and sighed. That was all he could do. Like so many others their lives had now been completely changed, totally altered. And, just like the German occupation of their once peaceful country, there wasn't anything they could do about it.

"Have the boys pack some warm clothes and blankets," he whispered. "I have no idea how long it'll be before we can come back home." Feigel nodded sadly and moved down the hallway. Hershel stood alone for a brief moment, looking at the home that they'd shared for so long, wondering when and if they'd ever see it again. He moved into the kitchen and collected some food they could carry for their trip. A tear eased out of his right eye, slowly creeping its way down his cheek and he quickly wiped it away. No one in the family had ever seen him shed a tear before. He vowed to himself that today would certainly be no different. His own worst nightmare had just become reality.

ELEVEN

THE BOYS FOLLOWED THEIR mother's wishes without questions or conversation. They could clearly determine from the seriousness in her voice that there was no time for that. Talk would come later. They didn't understand why they were taking heavy clothing with them, in that it was the middle of August, but they weren't about to challenge any instructions from their father.

Hershel made his way down the stairs into the basement and carefully removed two planks of wood from the wall behind the bin holding the few remaining potatoes. It was a safe and secure place he had established for their valuables. He took out four boxes and rubbed them gently as if they were treasures. And indeed they were. One held the cherished family menorah, another was filled with silver and crystal candlesticks, various other family memorabilia, and heirlooms. The third held silverware which had been in his family for generations. And the last was a miscellaneous assortment of gold items, including an antique pocket watch, all of Feigel's rings, some of which were inherited from her mother and grandmother, a smattering of diamonds, objects made with pure silver, and money, some of which was actually American currency.

In the market in Bochnia after conducting business, it was not uncommon for Hershel to trade Polish money for American because it was worth more on the open market. This money was normally placed away as an investment for the future. But their future was now. He carefully folded a stack of bills and placed them into one pocket, placed the rings into the other, picked up the four boxes, and returned to the kitchen.

The boys were all there, each carrying winter jackets and a blanket, each registering confusion and disbelief. "We're going to be fine," Hershel said. "This is temporary and we'll be back home before you know it." Then he turned to Feigel, "Prepare some food we can each carry. Make it as light as you can." She nodded and began to make an assortment of sandwiches.

Hershel went into the backyard carrying the boxes he had retrieved from the basement, the boys watching intensely from the kitchen window. He disappeared momentarily into the garage and then reappeared carrying a shovel. After checking carefully to make sure he was alone and no one was watching he dug four shallow holes, close to his favorite fruit-bearing trees in the yard, and carefully buried the boxes, covering them up and tapping the sod so no one would discover the hiding places. He stood and momentarily looked at the house and the garage and the trees and the garden. Everything he owned. Everything he loved. Their entire future was now buried in four, small wooden boxes.

As he reentered the kitchen he was greeted with looks of desperation which unfortunately caused him even more anguish and pain than he was already experiencing. The entire family had small cases or canvas bags beside them, filled with items which would be beneficial during their trek. He studied the faces of his wife and children for a moment and then finally offered, "I told you, we're going to be fine, this is only temporary. We'll be back home soon."

"Yes, Tata," the boys meekly responded. But Nuta began to cry and rushed to his mother's side, hugging her desperately. "I don't want to leave," he cried.

"Your father has always taken care of us and he will today as well." Feigel looked at her husband and held back her own tears. "I made several sandwiches and we have a few loaves of bread. We'll be fine."

People were walking down the street in front of their house, heading north, the same direction the mounted Polish soldiers had gone about nine months earlier. But that passage of time now seemed like an eternity. The travelers were carrying blankets and bedrolls and suitcases for their excursion into the unknown. Hershel stared through their front window, wondering himself about what eventuality lay ahead at the end of the road.

Bochnia was only about five miles away but the blistering summer temperature, the additional burden each of them was carrying, and thick, boot-grabbing mud on the road from a heavy rain the previous night, made each step more and more difficult. The boys grew tired but kept up as best as they could. Hershel whispered to Feigel, out of the earshot of the others. She nodded agreement to whatever it was he said.

The slow moving and unguarded column was made up of families and individuals (from Jurkow, Zakilcyn, and as far away as Limanowa, small, insignificant towns in Poland) who had absolutely nothing at all against the Germans. They walked down the road following instructions passed down by the Third Reich hierarchy because they were well aware of the repercussions should they dare to refuse them. For the most part there was silence in the entire group as they made their way toward Bochnia. What little conversation that transpired between them was carried out in hushed whispers, exactly like Hershel to Feigel.

Hershel nodded toward Feigel, and then subtly pointed toward each of the four boys, silently instructing them to follow him. The children shrugged, having no idea what was going on, and followed without question. As the column continued to move slowly forward and the sun began to set, Hershel and the rest of his family casually left the column, disappearing into the trees on the side of the road. They were in the forest, alone, protected by heavy foliage, but relatively safe for the time being. Hershel felt that living in the country and off the land would be better than the stories he had heard about the Bochnia ghetto. He also hoped with all his heart that their ordeal would soon be over and they'd be able to return to their home.

Their first night in the forest was relatively calm. Because of the comfortable temperature there was no need for a fire for warmth and Hershel wouldn't have allowed one anyway for fear of giving away their position. The boys mostly felt as if they were on a camping expedition, an exciting adventure. But Hershel knew far better and kept all family conversation to a very quiet level. Nuta, not truly understanding the seriousness of their situation, occasionally raised his voice expressing excitement over this, that, or the other, and was quietly corrected.

The sandwiches, while reasonably rationed, lasted only a few days and the bread a few days longer than that. Most evenings after the sun went down Hershel would travel into nearby fields and pick potatoes, carrots, or turnips for the family to eat. Once back at their always-moving campsite they would rub the vegetables on the moist grass and eat them raw. It wasn't much but it was certainly better than nothing. No one complained. Hershel managed to find a small bucket in a barnyard and used it to bring drinking water from nearby streams close to where they were spending the night. With what was left over they washed their hands. That was the total extent of their hygiene.

August drifted into September and the temperature began to fall. And with that the boys became well aware of why their father had instructed them to bring along jackets and blankets. Their days were spent mostly in silence, grouped together, trying to avoid detection. Occasionally they would hear other rumblings in the forest surrounding them but couldn't tell if it was others avoiding the ghetto like themselves or a German patrol searching for people.

Most evenings after the sun had retreated the family cautiously moved to a new location. By working here virtually all of his life, Hershel was intimately familiar with the countryside, the forests, and all of the farms in the area. After careful observation to determine the safety of such a venture he would visit an occasional farmhouse which had not yet been taken over by the Nazis. He normally returned to his family in the forest with little more than scraps of food because the Germans had confiscated as much as they could to feed their own traveling army.

That night they had a few bites of cold beef and some raw carrots and turnips as their supper. And still, no one complained in the least. Moniek found it somewhat strange and could not understand that no prayers were ever offered over the food. This had been his experience for as long as he could remember but apparently it was no longer to be. He never questioned his father's decision. They ate in restrained silence, grateful for what they had.

As darkness became total, thousands of stars filled the sky, and the temperature continued to fall. They each put on their coats and made themselves as comfortable as they could under their blankets on the ground. What began as an adventure for the boys was rapidly turning into a truly unpleasant experience for each of them. Feigel kept up as best as possible but crossing streams and climbing hillsides in the dark eventually began to take its toll. The boys were all young and could put up with the hardship. Feigel was becoming remarkably fragile, both physically and emotionally, from the nightly moving and the shortage of food. Hershel was well aware of her situation and was determined to do whatever he could to make things easier for her.

It began as a mere drizzle, chilly but almost refreshing. After their meager evening meal it was time to move on to a different hiding place for the evening. The drizzle evolved into a steady rain and then intensified dramatically. What was initially chilly became cold, to the point of near freezing. But the family moved on, now looking for a safe place as well as protection under trees which for the most part were now leafless.

Hershel spotted a stand of pine trees across a stream and knew from experience that their branches would provide the protection from the relentless deluge they were now experiencing. The sloping banks on both sides of the stream were mud-covered as a result of the driving rain and they were extremely cautious in crossing the narrow waterway. The boys held hands with each other and Hershel firmly had a hold of Feigel's arm.

Going down the first bank was successful and the water on their feet was icy cold but fortunately very shallow. The boys made it up the other side of the stream without incidence but as Hershel and Feigel climbed up the far bank she slipped and began to slide back into the water. Hershel lost his grip for a second but grabbed her hand just before she slipped into the stream. The boys all ran back to assist and fortunately pulled her to safety. After breathing a collective sigh of relief they all made their way up the bank and off toward their new hiding place.

There were pine needles underneath some tall trees which had been protected from the rain and were still dry. They provided a bit of a much appreciated mattress but no real additional warmth. Sleep, like so many nights before, was difficult, now even more so as a result of their feet being drenched.

"Feigel," Hershel whispered. "Are you all right?"

"I'm fine," she softly replied. But he knew she wasn't. She wasn't fine at all.

None of them had a calendar so they were completely unaware of when September became October. All they knew was that the temperature continued to fall drastically and when they woke the following morning a light dusting of snow covered the ground. Nuta was the first to wake, well before daylight.

"Tata," he whispered, "can't we build a fire?"

"No, son, I'm sorry. We can't. Try to get some more sleep."

Nuta shivered and turned back over, pulling the blanket closer around his neck. "Nuta," Hershel quietly offered, "Come over here closer to me." The youngest of the boys moved beside his father and was comforted by his warmth. Hershel didn't move the rest of the night. Nor did he sleep.

Within the next two weeks the temperature dropped even further. Now at nighttime the entire family slept side by side, as close as they possibly could, each trying to capture the warmth of the other, trying to forget the accumulation of the snowfall and the difficulties that additional element provided.

Sometimes during the night they'd hear strange, moving sounds in the distance, causing everyone to snap to attention. They didn't know if it was a German patrol on the prowl or a wild animal looking for food. It was most unnerving. Feigel, showing enormous bravery through the entire ordeal, was clearly coming to the end of her rope. She and her children had all been pushed beyond their limits.

A week later the temperature continued to plummet and more snow accumulated on the ground. The family huddled together as closely as possible, trying their best to avoid both the freezing elements and the Nazis in the forest.

"Ouch!" Feigel exclaimed, loud enough to wake the others. She smacked her right leg over and over, rubbing it furiously.

"What is it?" Hershel asked quietly but with grave concern. "What's the matter?"

"I've been bitten," she replied, this time without the benefit of a whisper. "I've been bitten by something nearly every night we've been in the forest but I've just never said anything. This is different."

"Are you all right?" Hershel asked. "Is there anything I can do?"

Feigel reached underneath her blanket and also her skirt, producing a large, black bug. Its origin was unknown. All she knew for certain was that when it bit her leg it was very painful. She threw the carcass into the darkness of the night.

"You're doing all you can." And with that she turned back over and pretended she was sleeping. Hershel edged closer to his wife and did the same. This became yet another sleepless night, shared in the forest.

The following day, for the first time since they began their excursion, Hershel left the family alone and ventured off by himself. But not before instructing, "Stay right here. Stay as warm as you can. I'll be back in no time." And with that he disappeared into the forest. The family huddled together, sharing and nibbling on a carrot left over from the previous night.

"Where's Tata gone?" Nuta asked quietly.

"I don't know," Feigel replied. "But I'm sure it's important."

Hershel eased his way through the woods, ever mindful and careful of the sounds emanating around him. The snow continued to fall, growing increasingly deeper by the day, and the temperature fell as well, becoming considerably colder. He knew with a certainty he had to get his family to some sort of shelter as soon as possible or their days would literally be numbered. His sons, while understandably uncomfortable and experiencing increasing hunger as each day passed, were resilient. Feigel, on the other hand, needed desperately to be protected from the elements.

It was near sundown when he returned to the family, bringing with him some raw potatoes which would constitute their meal for the evening. They were gratefully accepted and everyone waited patiently for an explanation of the disappearance.

"After we eat, and when the sun goes down, we're moving." This was not unusual in that they did that most every night. It was unnecessary to issue instructions for the boys to collect their belongings. They'd done this on countless occasions and knew exactly what to do.

"Feigel," he softly said. "I've found us a place to stay. It's not very much but at least you'll be inside."

She nodded and smiled as only she could. "We'll all be inside."

After dark, in single file and as silent as possible, the family moved through the forest. None of them had any idea where they were going. They just hoped that somehow they'd finally be out of the freezing weather and not wake up in the morning covered with snow.

Hershel had managed to make contact with an old customer of his. Actually it was the wife of an old customer. The man, Mr. Kline, had mysteriously disappeared one night and had not been seen for several months. His wife, Miriam, was a very considerate and compassionate person and offered to help the Ebners in whatever way she could. It was a dangerous proposition for her and Hershel did not in any way want to take advantage of her hospitality. Harboring Jews on the run or hiding from the Germans would carry a serious penalty.

The family quietly made their way across the barnyard. There were no lights visible so they negotiated the short trip in the darkness. Hershel cautiously opened the barn door and the family entered behind him. The darkness was even more severe than outside. But they weren't outside any longer. While certainly not warm by any stretch of the imagination they were in a shelter, protected finally from the cruel elements.

Feigel reached out in the darkness, took Hershel by the hand, gently squeezed it and whispered, "Thank you. This'll be just perfect." Compared to what they'd experienced for nearly four months in the forest, their new accommodations would easily qualify as the most exquisite five-star hotel.

A sound of shuffling on the ground coming from nearby startled them all. Abject fear permeated the entire area. Hershel huddled Feigel and his sons close to his side and held them tightly. As their eyes adjusted to the darkness they could see that they were sharing quarters with two dairy cows and a calf. This was actually quite fine in that the animals body warmth provided a much needed modicum of heat to the drafty barn.

They all smiled at each other, something which hadn't occurred for a very long time. But they were finally inside, finally underneath a roof, and their lives would, at least for the time being, be considerably better.

TWELVE

THERE WAS A DECENT sized mound of hay in an empty stall, leaning against the far wall. The rest of the family followed Hershel toward the area, wrapped themselves as warmly as possible in the blankets they were carrying, and did their best to tunnel their way underneath the pile. The extra layer of protection provided additional and much needed insulation. It was the first time they'd slept in relative warmth in nearly two months.

It was still dark when Hershel heard the barn door as it slowly creaked open. He froze, fear gripping his very being, concerned about their discovery. As the others stirred at the intrusion he touched each of them gently and whispered, "Stay very still. Don't move."

Less than thirty seconds later they heard the barn door open and then close again. The family had been undetected but still lay motionless, still in mortal terror. Another sixty seconds passed and Hershel silently eased his way out of the pile of hay, carefully examining the inside of their new dwelling. They were alone. "Feigel," he whispered. "Whoever it was is gone."

The rest of the family eased their way to the center of the barn as their eyes slowly adjusted to the darkness. Nothing seemed unusual or out of place. Without speaking they all wondered not only who had entered the barn but equally important, why. Hershel moved to the front door, looked through a crack, and could see lights on in the kitchen of the farm house.

"Tata," Moniek quietly said. "There's something here on the top of this barrel." The rest of the family moved cautiously to the far wall where he was standing and looked down at the unbelievable sight before their eyes. They looked at one another, thinking their eyes were deceiving them.

Reposing on the lid of the barrel were two small loaves of freshly baked bread, still warm, and a bucket half filled with cold water. Compared to what they'd been eating since they walked away from the column marching toward Bochnia this vision appeared to be a veritable feast. Hershel picked up one of the loaves with reverence. They had not tasted such a morsel since the bread they brought with them on their journey ran out after only four days in the forest.

He tore off a chunk of the sweet smelling bread and handed it to Feigel. She held it in her dirt-stained hands, not honestly believing they had real food, warm food. She raised it to her face and inhaled deeply, savoring the aroma. Then, dutiful mother as she had always been, handed the morsel to Nuta, her youngest son. Nuta held it in his own little hands, examining it, studying it as if it were a foreign object. He raised it toward his lips and then suddenly stopped. Without being told he handed it back to his mother. "No, Mama," he said. "The first piece is for you."

Hershel nodded with fatherly pride as Feigel gingerly took the piece. "It's pumpernickel," she said, a smile easing its way across her face. Then she savored the first precious bite while the others watched, smiling at their good fortune. Hershel patted his youngest son on the head and then tore off more chunks, distributing them to all four boys, saving himself for last. "We'll save the other loaf for later," he softly offered. "You never know if or when another angel is going to appear with more delicious food."

It had been four months since any of them had enjoyed even the smallest bite of warm food. The one they were now enjoying, based on their current circumstances, could easily be compared to the finest meal any of them had ever experienced. The best part was that they had another loaf leftover for later that evening. Following that it was altogether possible they'd be back to eating raw vegetables. But right now, as the sun began to slowly rise, that mattered little. They had a bite of food, cooked and warm food. They also had a roof above their heads.

After the feast was quickly devoured the family followed the same routine they had grown used to in the forest. For the most part they just sat in silence, pondering their remarkable good fortune and appreciating the warmth provided by the shelter of the barn. On occasion the boys, being boys, would tease or poke each other and a quick cat-and-mouse-like chase around the barn would ensue. No one objected as long as the game was kept quiet and there was no yelling. The parents actually enjoyed seeing their children at play for it had been such a long time since that had occurred.

Hershel had each of the boys take turns watching diligently through the slats of the door, staring with vigilance into the barnyard, acting as lookouts for any unwelcome or potentially dangerous intruders.

"Tata," Moniek whispered excitedly. "Someone's coming toward the barn." Everyone looked toward Hershel, awaiting instructions as to what they should do.

"Everyone," he said without panic or emotion in his voice. "Over here." The family followed him into an empty stall on the far side of the cows, near the end of the barn. They all hunched down and stayed perfectly silent. Each of the parents held two of the children close to their sides. The only sound heard in the enclosure was the rhythmic, peaceful breathing of the cows.

A young girl, perhaps fourteen or fifteen, entered the barn carrying a pail. She moved to the side of one of the cows. She was wearing a thick winter coat and her cheeks were rosy, attractively complimenting her dark eyes and hair. A small, three-legged stool was at the edge of the stall and she placed it beside the cow. After removing her gloves she rapidly rubbed her hands together, warming them. Once the pail was placed in its proper location she sat down and professionally began to milk the cow.

The only sound Hershel and the others could hear now was the milk as it was rhythmically streaming into the pail. The boys stared at their parents, wondering what on earth was going on. But both parents could only offer a shrug for they had absolutely no idea.

The young girl finally broke the silence with, "Mr. Ebner, are you still here?" It was a soft and kind voice. Hershel rose slowly and walked around the end of the stall. He looked down at her as she continued the milking.

Hershel was taken aback and speechless for a second. Then he cautiously questioned, "Rachel? Is that you?" The young girl nodded and offered a smile. "My goodness, you've become quite a young lady. I guess I haven't seen you in close to two years."

"I've usually been in school when you came to visit my father." Hershel already knew that there hadn't been word from her father in nearly four months and wisely chose to not bring up that most painful subject.

"Feigel," he said. "Come out here and meet an old friend of mine. You too, boys." They all slowly came around the side of the stall, still wondering what was going on. When the boys saw the attractive young woman they hurriedly brushed themselves off and straightened their hair as best they could. The boys were suddenly conscious of the fact that they had not cut their hair in five months.

Hershel pointed to each family member as he made the introductions. "Mrs. Ebner, Abraham, Zishe, Moniek, and Nuta, I'd like you to meet our benefactor. This is Rachel Klein, Mr. and Mrs. Klein's daughter. They're the ones being so kind as to let us stay here."

"Thank you very much, Rachel," Feigel said with great sincerity. "We truly appreciate your hospitality."

"My father has always admired your husband for his honesty during all the times they've done business together. My father is a very wise man." Rachel seemed and sounded equally wise beyond her own years. "He always told me that loyalty and honesty should be rewarded."

"That's in the Torah," Moniek blurted out.

"Yes son, that's correct." But then Hershel offered a look indicating that this was not the proper time for him to be entering into the conversation. Rachel continued the milking without missing a stroke. She didn't have to watch what she was doing. Her actions were automatic.

"Did you find the bread I brought this morning?" she asked.

"Yes, and thank you for that as well. It's been quite a long time since any of us have enjoyed any warm food. And yours was absolutely delicious."

"I'll try my best to bring some each morning but please don't be angry if I should miss a day or two. I'm sorry we can't provide more. Our supplies are pretty depleted with the Germans stopping anytime they want and taking anything they see."

"Do the soldiers come here often?" Hershel asked, concern on his face.

She shook her head as she moved to the second cow and began to milk her. "No. And to tell you the truth my mother and I have been surprised that they haven't just taken over our farm like they have so many others in the area. I guess they think our place is so small it really wouldn't do them much good." The cow stood perfectly still, accustomed to the daily process. From trips to the countryside with their father the boys had all seen cows being milked but they watched with growing curiosity and a sense of respect because they had never seen a girl performing the task.

"My mother says she thinks it would better if you stayed inside, at least during the day." Hershel nodded agreement as the attractive young woman finished her milking chores. She picked up the pail, placed it on the barrel where she had left the bread earlier that morning, and took a pitchfork in her hands. With expertise born from experience, she forked a bunch of hay and placed it in front of one of the cows who began to chew with an attitude as if she didn't really care one way or the other.

When Rachel got the second forkful filled with hay, Hershel gently took it from her hands and placed the hay in front of the second cow. He smiled at her, "I know a little about animals."

She returned the smile. "That's what my father has told me since I was old enough to understand what he was talking about."

"From now on I'll feed the cows for you. I know it's not much but it's what little we can do to thank you and your mother for providing us shelter."

Rachel nodded, picked up the pail of milk, and moved toward the door. Before she exited she turned and said, "We have very little to offer, but is there anything I might be able to provide?"

Feigel hesitated for a second, and then quietly asked, "Do you have a pair of scissors in the house that I could use?"

She smiled again, exited the barn and moved toward the house. The family looked at each other in total wonderment. They had a loaf of bread to eat that evening and more coming in the morning. They truly felt as if they were blessed.

After the sun had safely disappeared and stars filled the sky, Hershel took the pail which earlier that morning had been filled with water and ventured into the darkness toward a field in a neighboring farm. The ground was virtually frozen and he had difficulty finding produce but as a result of his years in the fields working with farmers during all seasons of the year he knew carrots would still be in the ground. They wouldn't be as tasty or as large as the summer carrots but they'd be edible. Following considerable digging he found what he was after and produced the desired result. On his way back to the barn he stopped by a stream, washed the carrots, and filled the bucket with very cold water. The waterway was only partially frozen but he knew it would only be a short time before the stream would be covered by a sheet of ice, growing thicker by the day, making access to the water more and more difficult.

That evening the family shared and enjoyed the second loaf of bread, ate all the carrots, and washed it down with cool, clear water. Following dinner they all bundled up and crawled into the haystack for the warmth they appreciated so much.

Hershel heard the door creak open again in the morning and unlike the morning before, smiled to himself and returned to sleep which was nearly peaceful. When the family awoke later they were delighted to discover one loaf of bread, the pail half filled with water, and a pair of scissors.

Before sundown Hershel had fed the cows, Rachel had milked them, and the boys, including Hershel, were all sporting brand new haircuts. Rachel smiled warmly and nodded approval as she left the barn. The boys beamed with pride.

Their evening was the same as the previous one. The routine they followed was basically similar to what they had experienced in the forest except that for a delightful change they now had real food, sparse as it was, and a roof over their heads.

Mrs. Kline and Rachel only left the farm on the rarest of occasions and even then when it was an absolute necessity. As a result they were able to glean little or no information with reference to the war effort or what was happening anywhere. Their caution was based on the fact that the Germans, because of their omnipresence, could just show up at any time at any location for random searches or the purposes of confiscating whatever they wanted. It was common for patrols to roam the forest looking for people who were in hiding.

The absolute faith Hershel once held that this whole invasion and occupation thing would be over soon and everything would return to normal began to slowly dissipate. Late one night he made the long walk back into town, being exceptionally careful and cautious along the way. He froze in his tracks each time he heard a sound, gripped with fear of discovery. But this was a trip he felt he had to make.

Several hours later he returned to the barn. The boys were all soundly sleeping but Feigel stirred and joined her husband. She gently took his hand in hers and quietly asked, "Did you get anything to eat?"

He nodded. "I found some food on the road."

"You must be awfully tired. That's such a long way to walk." She was avoiding the real question on her mind which was, what had forced Hershel to make such a dangerous journey? He decided to answer it anyway.

"The town was mostly dark. There seemed to be more soldiers than when we left. No one was on any of the streets."

"It's too cold to be outside."

Then, his morose voice quietly announced, "Someone is living in our house."

Feigel looked sadly at the dirt floor and shook her head. "I guess we both knew that was going to happen. It was just a matter of time."

"We'll be back there again someday." But his words seemed hollow, as if he didn't believe them himself.

"We're doing fine right here, thanks to Mrs. Klein and Rachel. And we're all going to stay that way until the war's over," Feigel replied. But somehow her own words sounded as hollow as her husband's. "You must be exhausted. Let's go to bed so you can get some sleep."

Hershel nodded and they moved toward the mound of hay which provided some degree of warmth from the elements. After burrowing underneath the hay he closed his eyes but even being completely spent sleep would not come. Instead thoughts of their home filled his mind. Some were reflective, pleasant, wonderful thoughts about times they spent there, having children, and watching the four boys growing up. Other thoughts, the ones which concerned him and prevented much-needed sleep, were the new people living in their home and whether or not he himself, Feigel, or any of their sons would ever see it again.

A few days later, as they finished their evening bread and raw vegetables, Moniek commented, "Tata, isn't it about time for Chanukkah?"

"Yes, son," he sadly answered. "But this year we'll have to celebrate it in our hearts. There will be no menorah, no lighting of the candles, no wonderful meal, and no small gifts for each of you."

"We have you, and Mama, and each other, and food to eat, and a pretty warm place to stay. What greater gifts could there be?" Both his parents had to look away but the youngster continued, not seeing the expression on their faces in the near darkness. "We can still say the three prayers, can't we?"

Hershel began to speak but before a word came from his mouth and totally out of character Feigel cut him off and softly offered, "Of course we can, Moniek. Of course we'll say the three prayers."

The last of the three prayers was the one thanking God for allowing them to reach this time of the year.

THIRTEEN

THE EFFICIENTLY TRAINED GERMAN army was continuously indoctrinated with the concept of Aryan supremacy. As a result of their deep-seated feeling of superiority there was a clear sense of indifference toward anyone and everyone who felt and believed differently than they. Hitler asked, actually demanded, that his soldiers "give all that they have to give." And they were consciously willing to do just that. They carried out his will without thought or emotion.

Indifference and intolerance for nonbelievers of Aryan supremacy became the central focus of their lives. They had little or no regard for anyone not wearing the same uniform or sharing the same thought processes as themselves. The once highly civilized nation was transformed into small-hearted, cold-blooded assassins, willing to do anything asked of them by their Fuehrer. The tragic reality of it all was that a modern, civilized society was engaged in the most horrific of organized behavior.

Most other so-called civilized nations throughout the world found the stories emanating from Germany and Poland literally impossible for a rational person to believe. As such they just turned a blind eye and simply chose not to acknowledge them. Large German forces remained in Poland without rhyme or reason.

Summer arrived and Feigel cut the boys hair again, each of them laughing and pointing fingers at the other. With the exception of a few close calls, all of which proved to be uneventful intruders looking for food handouts, they had achieved a relative degree of safety for the better part of six months, having no idea what was going on in the world outside their humble yet comfortable dwelling.

Feigel made a special point of making each of them wash their hands and clean off their faces on a daily basis from water leftover in the pail. They had no soap and this was the total extent of their hygiene. While it wasn't much it was all they could do. They each still wore the same clothing they had when they left their house in what now seemed like ages ago. But they were together, alive, and still eating. Certainly not like they were before they were forced virtually at gunpoint to leave the comfort of their own home.

Rachel and Mrs. Klein continued to provide fresh baked bread on a regular basis and Hershel would make routine nighttime visits into adjoining fields for whatever he could find to add to their dinner. Now that the temperature was rising the boys found it more and more difficult to stay within the confines of the barn. They were boys and wanted to be outside, playing. Nevertheless, that was too dangerous. They never knew when German soldiers might be conducting a sweep through the countryside.

Because they had no access to newspapers or radio reports they had no idea that on March 1st of that year Heinrich Himmler had made his initial visit to Auschwitz and ordered Commandant Hess to begin massive expansion including a new compound to be built at a location called Birkenau that could eventually hold one hundred thousand prisoners. People living in the immediate area were evicted, houses were demolished, and the largest prison camp ever built was under construction.

The camp at Birkenau was to be known as Auschwitz II. It was completely isolated in the middle of what had now become a vast and open field, surrounded by a double electrified fence and guard towers every fifty yards. While only a few miles away from Auschwitz I it was out of sight and mind of all who lived there but were not involved with its construction. Like so many others it was greeted with a mere shrug and yet another turning of the eye. It wasn't as if the people were ignorant, they just ignored reality with the justification that "it's not my business or my problem."

A railroad running directly into the camp brought new prisoners on a regular basis who were worked until they dropped. For the most part they were the ones who built and constructed the huge compound. The very size of the place was difficult if not impossible to comprehend. Barrack by barrack by barrack was rapidly constructed. None of the prisoners working on the camp had any idea of what the place was to eventually become. No one could possibly conceive of it.

In *Der Sturmer*, the Nazi newspaper, it was quoted, "Now judgment has begun and will reach its conclusion only when knowledge of the Jews has been erased from the earth."

Hans Frank, the newly appointed governor of Poland stated publicly, "I ask nothing of the Jews except that they should disappear."

And the Ebner boys played in silence in the confines of the barn and under the watchful eyes of their parents. Wishing they could play outside like they imagined other regular children were. Wishing they could all be at least reasonably normal again. But "normal" was yet another word which would no longer exist in any dictionary.

Barely a year before, a man named Winston Churchill became the Prime Minister of Great Britain and was now responsible for the war effort against the Germans. He proved himself to be a remarkably competent leader and was highly respected by not only his own people but also heads of state throughout the entire free world.

On July 9th of 1941 the German *blitzkrieg* on London began, causing hundreds of thousands to flee for safety into bomb shelters beneath the streets of the city. The attack was relentless and continued on and on and on. The people taking refuge would shudder as they heard a high-pitched shrill, the warning sound of a buzz-bomb about to explode on the streets above. Explosions, flying debris, or collapsing buildings killed many of those not fortunate enough to have made it into the shelters. The Nazis murdered civilians callously by the thousands.

The nonstop attack was well planned by Hermann Goering, the Commander-in-Chief of the Luftwaffe, the German Air Force which he created, a position he held since March 1st of 1935 when he was appointed by Hitler. He was also responsible for organizing the remarkably rapid build-up of the expanding German aircraft industry, the total rearmament program, and the training of all pilots.

"Tata, can't we please play outside in the barnyard?" Nuta was literally pleading, begging to escape their confines. Hershel was firm yet polite.

"You know you can't. It's too dangerous to be outside, especially in the daytime."

"But we'll be quiet," the youngster replied, wide eyes filled with eternal hope. "I promise."

"I know you will, son, but the soldiers have been seen all around the countryside and we can't take any chances. You'll have plenty of time to play outside in just a short time." Hershel had to look away because he doubted his own words. Words which he hoped would provide some degree of reassurance to his youngest son. Feigel noticed the expression on her husband's face and gently suggested that the boys play a quiet game of tag inside the barn. While not the solution or the answer they were each looking for they proceeded half-heartedly with the game. But it wasn't the same. It certainly wasn't the same as the games they played after dinner on the street in Nowy Wisnicz. Nothing was the same anymore.

The entire world was changing and they had no concept at all of what was happening. The Nazis had occupied Bulgaria, Yugoslavia, and Greece, all of which fell to the German superior power in a short time. They had also defeated Denmark, Holland, and Norway. Hitler's incredible war machine was gobbling up all of Europe in large chunks and it didn't appear as if there was anyone or anything which could stop them. The "master plan" of world domination seemed to be successfully traveling on a well-designed track. Sadly, and most unfortunately, the plan for the elimination of all Jews and all things Jewish from the Reich-controlled territories also seemed to be the process of the day. No one was safe. No one.

Rachel slipped quietly into the barn, but not to milk the two cows. The entire family was there and they could clearly see the concern covering her face. She hushed them unnecessarily. They weren't about to speak until they heard what information the young girl had to offer.

"The soldiers are nearby. Very close. They're searching every farm. It's too dangerous for you to stay here. They'll find you for sure."

Hershel knew that the danger was double edged. If the Germans discovered his family at the farm, Mrs. Klein and Rachel would also be severely punished. After the generosity they'd both shown over the past several months, especially the brutal winter months, he wasn't about to do anything that might possibly place them in peril. Without hesitation he turned to the boys and quietly announced, "Collect your things. We're leaving."

Feigel, without asking a question, grabbed the few things she had and within minutes they were all ready to leave the domicile which for all had saved their lives during the freezing winter. There was a moment of silence. Rachel knew how grateful they all were but words at this moment were difficult and expressed with great emotion. Finally she spoke, "I have a loaf of bread in the oven. It'll be done in about fifteen minutes and you can take it with you."

Hershel, with a remarkable degree of calmness asked, "Do you think we have fifteen minutes?"

Rachel looked down at the dirt floor and silently shook her head. "They're very close," she whispered. "I think you should leave."

Hershel thanked her for their hospitality and everything she and her mother had done for them. The boys each nodded acknowledgment for the blessings they had received. As the family cautiously moved through the door of the barn, Feigel took the young girl in her arms and hugged her tightly. Words were unnecessary at this precious moment in time. As the two of them shared a soft yet sad smile, they each wiped the tears from the face of the other.

Feigel could barely whisper the word. "Shalom," she offered.

"Shalom to all of you," Rachel replied. And with that the family disappeared across the once relative safety of the barnyard and into the forest. As they walked in silence toward the green trees in the distance they each contemplated the exchange. "Shalom," used both as a greeting and a salutation literally meant "peace." Peace was something they hadn't known for what now seemed like forever. Collectively they wondered if they'd ever find it or have it again. The only sound was their footsteps.

The forest was the same as they had remembered from the previous year. Fortunately it wasn't nearly as cold as they last experienced. Other than that, the conditions were remarkably similar. Moving every night to a new hiding place. Sloshing through gentle streams. Eating raw vegetables stolen from farms in the area. Sleeping under trees which would hopefully provide some shelter and protection from the elements. They each missed the nearly daily warm loaf of bread but no one ever spoke about it. But they certainly thought about it every single day they were away from the farm.

With the onset of summer came more and more bugs and various insects, biting, digging into the skin during sleeping hours, causing moments of pain.

Nuta stirred, smacking the right leg of his now extremely filthy, tailor-made wool suit. He sat up, wide awake, considerably more than a little distressed. Hershel sat up beside him, wiping sleep from his own eyes. "Are you all right?" he whispered.

"I'm fine, Tata. It was just a bug." Then he lay back down, twisting slightly, and tried to resume sleep. Precious sleep was developing into a luxury which few of them experienced on a regular basis.

It seemed as if the warmer weather had created an infestation throughout the entire forest. Everyone was being eaten alive by the insatiable pests. In addition, it wasn't just the bugs. Now there were lice, disgusting little white things which would bore their way into your skin, sucking the blood from your body. There was no relief whatsoever. Hershel watched in anguish as Feigel rolled from side to side, trying to achieve any degree of comfort. Moniek stood up, attempting desperately to wipe the bugs off of his own tattered suit. Hershel stood up and joined him. They each examined the other's face and Hershel offered a look of controlled desperation. The father offered his hand to his son and quietly suggested, "Let's go for a walk."

The weather was fine but the bugs and the lice were slowly driving them all out of their minds. Moniek was the first to break the silence and innocently asked, "Tata, will we ever forget this?'

Hershel walked a few more steps, deeply contemplating the question. After a heavy sigh he finally replied, "Unfortunately, son, some things are unforgettable."

"We'll get through this somehow, Tata. I know we will." Moniek's voice expressed considerably more confidence than his father had felt in a very long time.

As they walked hand in hand Moniek reflected on happier times they'd shared in the past: visiting various farms and meeting customers, summer excursions to his grandfather's farm, fishing with his father, and learning. He couldn't remember ever spending time with his father without learning something. The lessons were kept deep within his heart. While he never expressed it vocally Hershel was more than just his mentor. He was his hero. And somehow, some way, he would see to it that they all made it through the very bad times they were experiencing.

They'd been in the forest and away from the comfort of the barn for several weeks. The infestation of bugs and lice continued to magnify on seemingly a daily basis. Everyone was covered with an assortment of bites, some of them quite painful. Feigel did everything possible to maintain some slight degree of hygiene. She made the boys wash their hands and faces and occasionally their hair as best as they could without the benefit of soap. She even went so far as to collect twigs which were used to clean their mud-caked fingernails on a semiregular schedule.

She was making a massive effort to keep everyone as clean as she could and unfortunately losing the battle. She was also losing her own battle. Hershel could tell that her health was failing. She had made a comeback when they were staying in the barn so delightfully provided by the Klein family but the forest and the bugs were taking a serious toll.

One afternoon when the boys were nearby collecting blueberries Hershel took Feigel's hand in his and softly announced, "This is too difficult. It's just too hard on you."

She nodded slowly, accepting the reality of the statement. "I'm afraid, Hershel, really afraid. I'm afraid we're all going to be caught out here and they're going to do something terrible..." She could not complete the sentence.

Hershel looked deeply into her eyes with an enormous degree of compassion, concern, and understanding. "We need to find some shelter," he offered. "A roof over our heads, and a place where you can get better. We need to get back to civilization." She shook her head, not understanding. "Tomorrow we will go to Bochnia. Whatever is there can't possibly be worse than this. We'll find a place to live and work and even food that doesn't have to be dug from the earth."

She slowly nodded, acknowledging the fact that he was the man of the family. He had always made the decisions and in virtually every circumstance had always been proven to be correct. Feigel knew in her heart of hearts that his primary concern was for her and their children.

That night after a dinner of raw potatoes and blueberries, Hershel told the boys that they were going to Bochnia. "Will we be able to go back to school?" Abraham asked.

"I don't know. We'll find out when we get there."

"Will our friends be there?" Zishe questioned.

"Again, I don't know. We'll find out tomorrow."

"Maybe we'll get some clean clothes," Nuta added, wiping a crawling bug off of his leg.

"I certainly hope so, sweetheart," Feigel replied maternally. "That'd be a very nice thing for all of us."

"I hope so as well," Hershel said. He thanked the boys for picking the blueberries and suggested they collect some more in the morning for their short trip. Like so many nights before, sleep was difficult, but this evening it wasn't a result of the crawling and biting bugs. This night was filled with concern about what they'd find tomorrow. He just wanted all of them to be all right and have enough to eat. It didn't seem like so very much to ask.

In the morning the boys collected enough blueberries to fill all their pockets and the family made its way toward Bochnia. They wisely avoided the road and stayed on the fringes of the forest, snacking on the berries and wondering about their future.

FOURTEEN

AS THEY LOOKED THROUGH the trees they could see a handful of other travelers, all headed north, the same direction as themselves. Most of the people were walking but a few rode in horse or ox drawn carts or wagons filled with all the earthly belongings they were capable of carrying. The procession on the road was eerily silent. There seemed to be no sound from anyone, certainly no conversations. Even the youngsters and infants made no appreciable noise. For the most part the faces of the adults all seemed to be tired, resigned. Like the Ebners, virtually all of them had been forced out of their homes, the majority from small farms in the countryside, and required to make their way to Bochnia. Only an anxious few of them had the vaguest concept of what they were facing. The majority of the travelers had absolutely no idea.

Hershel fell securely into the latter group. He was completely unaware of what they might experience over the course of the next few hours. But as he explained to the rest of the family the previous evening, whatever they found couldn't possibly be worse than what they had just gone through during the painful months spent hiding in the forest and at the Klein farm.

The family was remarkably fortunate that they had avoided detection by the roaming bands of soldiers throughout the countryside. Many other families and individuals did not experience the same degree of luck. Those caught in hiding, along with their benefactors, were taken away at gunpoint by the Germans. They mysteriously disappeared and were never seen or heard from again. Remaining family members and friends mourned and others accepted a resigned shrug, saying, "I'm glad it wasn't me."

Within a few short and very quiet hours they saw the city of Bochnia up ahead. Initially it didn't seem to look all that imposing. It had been quite awhile since Hershel visited the local market and the outskirts of the city had changed appreciably since his last trip. There were now two very large buildings just off to their right and a beehive of activity surrounding them both.

As the family joined the procession along with the others, they saw in the distance German soldiers standing on either side of the road, directing the way toward the gate where they would all finally enter the ghetto, the dreaded place they had successfully avoided for nearly a year. Hershel made a hand signal and quietly directed the family back into the shelter of the forest on the side of the road where they watched in silence for several minutes.

When the concept of forcing all the Jews to leave the Reich-controlled territories throughout Europe became a reality, the Nazis reestablished the century's old and once forgotten medieval ghetto to make the Jews conditions even worse. A specific section of large- and medium-sized cities was cordoned off and surrounded by walls or barbed wire fences. German guards patrolled the outside perimeter to keep the residents from leaving or entering. On occasion the gates were opened so more people could come into the area which was generally referred to as "The Jewish Quarter." The number of ghettos throughout Europe was expanding on a daily basis. Within a brief period of time the vast majority of them were characterized by overcrowding, shortages of food, and forced labor.

The entire family watched intently as the others tentatively walked into the ghetto through the gate on Kraszewska Street and entered what was referred to as ghetto "A". The new arrivals looked around with understandable apprehension as the gate was closed behind them and armed soldiers took their sentry posts. The enclosure appeared to be surrounded by a seven-foot-tall fence constructed of pieces of lumber eight inches wide with a three-quarter-inch space between each plank.

Hershel pointed at the gate and whispered to the others, "I don't like the looks of that. There has to be another way to get in without all the soldiers around." In single file the family quietly made their way around the side of the enclosure to an area which was very familiar to Hershel. It was the market where he had done the majority of his business in what now seemed like a lifetime ago. The market was directly adjacent to the fence and there were no soldiers patrolling the perimeter. As quietly as was possible Hershel moved to the fence and eased one of the boards back and forth until it came loose from the ones on either side. He motioned for the family to join him and one by one they slipped through the fence and into the ghetto. Once inside, Hershel replaced the board as well as he could.

There were very few people on the street and Hershel wondered silently where they all might be. Like the others they had seen earlier that day on the road, there was little conversation between the few they did see and absolutely no smiles. It was obvious that no one was happy or pleased to be here. The family slowly moved down the street, examining their new surroundings.

"You there!" a gruff looking Polish policeman bleated out. Hershel looked around, a little confused. What had he done wrong? "Yes, you!" the policeman shouted again. He carried a two-foot long rubber club and Hershel was not about to challenge him. While the SS did not trust the Polish police members with firearms it was still their responsibility to patrol the inside of the ghetto and keep order. Like Jacob Kreiger, many of them truly enjoyed their elevated position and the benefits which they accrued.

"Are you new here?" The portly man wore an ill-fitting blue jacket and cap which under normal circumstances would have looked funny.

Hershel avoided eye contact, choosing instead to look at the ground and quietly answered, "Yes, sir."

"You and your family are to report to the local Judenrat office. It's in the two-story building at the end of this street on the right side. Do you understand me?" Hershel nodded and the policeman scowled before he walked away to harass other new arrivals. They all breathed a collective sigh of relief at the fact that their entry into the ghetto had been undetected.

The family moved in silence past several one-story houses which lined both sides of the street, no doubt once well-kept but now deteriorating from lack of care. All Jews who owned houses in the "Aryan" section of Bochnia were forced to move into the ghetto and exchanged houses with Poles who were trying desperately to get out. All other Jewish families, especially the new arrivals, were completely dependent on the Judenrat for their living arrangements. A few families were fortunate enough to be assigned to single apartments while a house with two or three bedrooms and a kitchen normally accommodated at least three or more families. Typically all basements within the enclosed area were utilized for housing purposes and more than one family was usually the norm.

It was August and extremely warm. The family was dead-tired. They all carried their coats and blankets over their arms, sweating profusely. The older boys were doing their best to hold up but Nuta and especially Feigel had just about taken their last step. After a few blocks they began to walk through a small business district which contained numerous stores, now nearly all closed. One had a series of three steps leading up to the front door. Hershel indicated for all of them to sit down and rest for a moment. They willingly complied and appreciated the opportunity to catch their breath.

Hershel whispered to the family, "I don't like the sound of this Judenrat thing at all. I'm sure we can find something here on our own." Everyone nodded. They didn't have an opinion. They were all much too exhausted to engage in conversation. An elderly gentleman with a long gray beard and wearing a heavy black suit walked past them. He kept his half-closed eyes focused on the sidewalk, lost in his own personal world.

"Excuse me, sir," Hershel said.

The man stopped. "My name is Rabbi Siegal," he softly and flatly replied without emotion, still not making eye contact.

"I'm sorry, Rabbi. I didn't mean any disrespect. If I may ask you a question?"

"You can ask but that doesn't mean I'm going to give you an answer."

"I've heard that there were a lot of people here. Where are they all?"

"I guess you just arrived. Obviously a 'greenhorn,'" he said, again with absolutely no emotion. Hershel nodded. "You came in from the south?" Hershel nodded again. The Rabbi pointed toward the east, "Then you must have seen the two very large buildings over there."

The Rabbi went on to describe the two large buildings as massive workshops where about two thousand people from the ghetto engaged in long days and difficult labor to produce products for the German war efforts. Their existence became one of the countless cogs essentially vital for the continuation of Hitler's ever-growing machine of destruction. The largest department was designated for tailoring and produced uniforms for the German army. They also manufactured underwear, shoes, brushes, handkerchiefs, electrical appliances, and even toys. Other departments exploited the services of locksmiths, box-makers, and had an extended and very large carpentry facility. Their finished products were sent by truck to the front for distribution.

"Are the people who work in these places paid?" Hershel asked.

The Rabbi shook his head and it almost looked as if a slight smile came to his face. "Very little," he replied, nearly sarcastically.

Hershel chose not to pursue that line of questioning and instead asked, "Would you possibly know of any place my family could stay without having to go to the Judenrat office down at the end of the street?"

If there had been a slight smile it disappeared completely. "In time you will have to deal with the Judenrat. We all do." He hesitated for a moment, looking in both directions to make sure no Polish policemen happened to be traveling past them before he spoke. "Next door," he whispered. "It's open. Go up the stairs and be as quiet as you can. The attic is empty. You can stay there for awhile."

And with that the Rabbi shuffled on down the street without another word. Hershel looked at his family. "I told you we'd find a place to stay and be all right."

When they reached the top of the stairs and opened the door to the attic they found a completely empty room with no furniture. It was stark, bare, without any ventilation, not even a window. As a result it was sticky hot and incredibly uncomfortable. Following their father's lead the boys placed their blankets on the floor and sat down. Silence followed.

"We need to have some food," Hershel finally said. "Boys, I hate to have to ask you this, but there have to be some people here from our town. See if you can find anyone who can help us or tell us how to get some food."

"I'll go," Nuta said enthusiastically.

"No, son, you're a little too young to be on these streets by yourself. You stay here with your mother."

"But it's too hot," the youngster replied. "I can't breathe." Feigel was also having difficulty breathing but didn't complain. Hershel noticed and while feeling great empathy and concern couldn't do anything to relieve their discomfort.

"During the past year we have been very hot and we've also been very cold. We'll make do just fine here for awhile."

Even with all they'd been through the boys never actually felt they were in any serious degree of peril. They still held the thought that Poland was just going to be an extended part of Germany and in a short period of time their lives would return to normal and they'd be able to return to their home. Because of their youth, continued optimism, and belief in their father their fear factor was minimal. They looked at the quest for food and trying to locate old friends as an adventure. They also looked forward to getting out of the stifling attic.

Hershel studied Feigel's lovely face as sweat began to form at her temples and her cheeks started to turn bright red. He took a deep breath, which was difficult and painful because of the heat, and exhaled slowly. "I'll be back in just a little while. Stay here and stay as quiet as you can." And with that he made his way down the stairs.

When the three boys returned to the attic later that afternoon their faces clearly reflected the failure they had each experienced. They felt as if they had let their parents and their family down. They sat on the floor and sweltered in the blazing heat, saying little.

Hershel returned moments later. "Get your things together," he said. "I've found another place for us to stay." They were all thrilled with this news. Any place out of this blistering furnace would be a welcome relief. As they gathered their things the boys explained their failure in finding any food. The patient father responded with, "We've been without food several times before and one more night isn't going to make that much of a difference. We've always gotten through it before and we can certainly exist for one more night."

As they made their way down the stairs and into the relative coolness of the air outside the front door Hershel continued. "Tomorrow we'll meet some more people and find out what's necessary to obtain food. After all, everyone else in the ghetto must have something to eat. It's just a matter of us finding out what we have to do ourselves." He paused momentarily, "And we will."

The city of Bochnia had a long, storied, and violent history of anti-Semitism. In 1445 several Jews were burned at the stake, watched by a cheering crowd. In 1605 the town council decided to expel all Jews and several of them resettled in the nearby town of Nowy Wisnicz. The city was restricted to all Jews until 1867 when they regained citizen rights and were once again allowed to purchase land and build their own houses. Collectively they built a synagogue, a library, established charity organizations for the needy, operated a medical clinic with a physician on staff, and provided medical services. Some of the charity organizations provided money for the poor, others gave coal for heating during the brutal winter months, made clothing available whenever necessary, and established feeding programs at schools.

In August of 1939 the tensions in and around Bochnia mounted due to anticipation of the upcoming war. Many Jews deserted their homes and fled toward the east, hoping to avoid the atrocities and persecution they had experienced over the past several centuries. When Germany attacked Poland on September 1st they initiated the invasion with heavy bombing. While the city of Bochnia itself was spared, the train system and miles and miles of tracks were destroyed.

There were widespread rumors that the Germans were killing all the Jews as they advanced forward. This caused a panic among many of the Jews and they left the town. The refugees were forced to make their trek on foot toward what they hoped would be their escape route along with the retreating Polish army.

And then, on September 3rd, the German Wehrmacht, the same one which only hours before had passed through Nowy Wisnicz, captured Bochnia, taking over the entire city without opposition. Jewish families were immediately evicted from their homes, Jewish businesses were broken into and looted, and Jewish workers had to provide the Germans with services free of charge. It was not only the Germans; local Poles also took advantage of the situation and broke into stores and homes of the wealthy Jews. In March of 1941 the ghetto was established, the wooden wall was constructed, and people began to move out of the homes they had built and lived in for many years, some of them for their entire lives.

As the family moved down the sidewalk Hershel offered, "This place is on a first floor and there are windows so at least there's some ventilation."

"That'll be wonderful," Feigel said, her voice seeming to wither and grow fainter with each spoken word.

"There are two other couples in the small apartment but they've agreed to let us stay with them. It's going to be crowded."

"I'm sure it'll be fine," she replied. "Are they friends or old customers of yours?"

"No."

She was confused. "Then how did you arrange for us to stay with them?"

"Let's just say we made a business transaction," was all he said and that was the end of the conversation.

Their new dwelling was a small, one bedroom apartment directly beside a bakery, separated only by a thin wall. While the bakery had been closed for some time the aroma of the long-ago baking bread remained, which only added to their hunger. It brought back fond memories of Rachel and Mrs. Klein baking them a warm loaf of bread on so many occasions. However, their eternal hope was that tomorrow would be a better day and that they would stay together.

Two other couples arrived at the apartment and introductions were made. Hershel had been correct: it was certainly going to be crowded. But at least they could breathe. Windows were opened and a slight breeze made their most uncomfortable afternoon a thing of the past. Conversation was sparse. Both couples were all too tired from their day's work to be talkative. The entire family slept on the floor on top of their blankets and jackets while the two couples shared the bedroom. Arrangements like this were commonplace in the ghetto.

Just before they drifted off to sleep Feigel reached over and gently touched Hershel on his arm. At first he was alarmed. "Are you all right?" he questioned.

"I'm fine," she replied. Then with a trembling voice added, "I just wanted to say...thank you."

He was momentarily choked up but finally and softly said, "Sleep well."

The following day the boys set out to find old friends and once again the excursion proved ineffective. Hershel as well traversed the streets of the city looking for any source of food and collecting information concerning their new whereabouts. Two very kind women each gave him a quarter of a loaf of bread. While not much it was considerably more than they'd had to eat the previous evening. When he returned to the apartment they divided the bread between the six of them and they listened closely as he further explained why there were so few people in the ghetto during the day.

In addition to the two large manufacturing buildings to the east of the ghetto a place called Camp Klaj was recently opened. It was about six hundred meters from the ghetto and well-hidden in the woods among pine trees, many of which were twenty-five meters high. The camp was surrounded by an electrified barbed-wire fence and had observation towers with permanent guards. Its purpose was to manufacture ammunition which was vital to the German army and the war effort.

Its staff consisted of one hundred fifty Jewish men and ten Jewish women who looked after the kitchen and cleaned various living quarters. They served five hundred German soldiers and assorted ammunition technicians. The soldiers carefully searched every worker as they left the facility each evening, making sure nothing was smuggled out of the camp which could somehow be used against them.

In addition to the permanent staff there were more than five thousand Jewish workers who came from nearby towns and the ghetto. They would come early in the morning, leave late in the evening, and received a small monthly salary. This was a prized position, highly desired, one which was eagerly sought out on a regular basis.

Work in the two major workshops or the ammunition manufacturing facility generally resulted in a much better chance of survival in the ghetto due to the modest salary which was provided. However, there were far more people wanting to work than there were jobs available. To facilitate this on a minor scale the Germans also operated numerous other workshops as well but they were considerably smaller. Others in the ghetto joined work battalions maintaining city streets, pruning trees, doing gardening, and other assorted forms of manual labor. Those not assigned to the valued positions in the major workshops or the ammunition facility had to receive their work assignments from the Judenrat. The majority of the workers felt that as long as they were performing some productive service for the Germans their existence was relatively assured.

Other work patrols from the ghetto spent long days reconstructing the rail lines to transport the amazing volume of ammunition being produced to the front to the fighting forces. At the time they were performing the back-breaking labor they had no concept what the rail lines would eventually be used for. It was still impossible for anyone to conceive of what was to come.

FIFTEEN

THE FAMILY MANAGED TO experience a reasonable night's sleep on the wooden floor, the first they'd had since the relative warmth and safety of the barn in the countryside. They watched through the window as fellow residents of the ghetto traversed slowly toward their various work assignments. Hershel, Abraham, Zishe, and Moniek ventured into the street, again looking for any friends from Nowy Wisnicz or sources of food.

Hershel discovered in short time that the food distribution in the ghetto was totally controlled by the Germans. A person who was working was given a food rationing coupon which provided barely enough sustenance for one person. The quantity of food allocated was totally insufficient and many basic food items were not available or existent. Still, the meager food provided was nearly always divided into smaller portions and shared with other family members.

However, food was available for a price. Many local Polish residents would come to the fence of the ghetto under the darkness of night and sell flour, bread, milk, and other assorted food products. They also traded their food, which was still readily available to them, for articles like sheets, coats, or blouses, items which were difficult to obtain during the war. Very few purchases were transacted using money because for the most part Polish money was worthless.

Like Hershel had done many times in the past, some people would leave the ghetto at night and travel to nearby farms where they would trade, barter, or purchase virtually anything anyone could ever possibly want. This activity was exceptionally dangerous because if caught the perpetrators were executed on the spot. Nazi justice was swift and unforgiving.

Those fortunate enough to return to the ghetto would sell the items they had accumulated, many times for exorbitant prices to those who possessed a great deal of money or something which could be traded again for items of a higher value. For the most part it was only the wealthy who could afford to purchase their food in the shadows of what was referred to as the black market. Jewish laborers who worked outside the ghetto on road construction battalions or toiling in fields would buy or trade things for food items from local farmers near their work sites, bring the food back into the ghetto, and then sell or trade it for much more reasonable prices. Additional food was available if one had the means to purchase it.

Feigel and Nuta had a relatively quiet and comfortable day. Very few of the apartments or houses in the ghetto had indoor plumbing so the two of them would make ever so cautious trips down the street where they would visit the public restrooms. It was inconvenient but a great deal more acceptable than what they were used to while they were in the forest with no facilities at all.

The boys returned later that afternoon and again brought no information concerning any of their old neighbors or friends. While they were initially disappointed Feigel clearly pointed out that the population of the ghetto was growing on a daily basis and finding anyone in a town this size, even one which was enclosed by a wooden wall, would become increasingly difficult.

When Hershel arrived at the small apartment he might as well have been carrying a suitcase full of pure gold. Instead, he presented the family with two freshly baked loaves of bread. Feigel was astonished. "Where on earth did you get these?" she asked, her mouth wide open at the wondrous sight.

"One day a week they open just one bakery in the ghetto and people can bring their own dough to have it baked for them."

"But we don't have any dough," she countered. "How did you manage to...?"

"I bought it," he replied, cutting her off in mid-sentence. "We needed to have some food."

Feigel shook her head, not understanding. "Bought it with what?"

"As a precaution, when we left our home I brought along some folding money and also some jewelry in case we had to trade for things we might need. Right now we need food."

"Is that what you did with Mrs. Klein at the farm? Did you pay her to let us stay there?

"It's not important," he said. "It was only important that we had shelter over our heads and food in our stomachs. Let's have the bread now."

The family sat down on the floor and devoured the feast before them. Hershel had been wise in thinking ahead and planning for what they all hoped desperately would not be an extended stay away from their home. As they ate Hershel shared another piece of information with them. "The man I bought the bread from told me that just last month Germany invaded the Soviet Union. He said it was a thing called Operation Barbarossa."

"I thought the Soviet Union was on the same side as the Germans."

"So did the Soviet Union. The Nazis have clearly proven to the entire world that they can't be trusted by anyone." He offered a slight smile. "But tonight we have food. And tomorrow the boys and I will look for work so we can get some food rations and we'll all be just fine."

The boys quietly savored the delicacy, still warm from the oven. They were all too young to truly understand the potential ramifications of the news. Feigel just nodded slowly, her thinning face filled with apprehension, not quite sure how to take the information which had just been reported, but knowing deep in her heart that the news was not good.

What Hershel was not aware of was that also during the previous month Heinrich Himmler summoned Rudolf Hoess to Berlin to inform him, "The Fuehrer has ordered the Final Solution of the Jewish question. We, the SS, have to carry out this order...I have therefore chosen Auschwitz for this purpose." This order was further solidified within the following two weeks when Hermann Goering instructed Reinhard Heydrich to prepare for the Final Solution. The initial plan calling for the expulsion of the Jews from all Reich-controlled territory was not working as quickly or efficiently as had been expected and as a result much more drastic measures were being carefully and callously prepared.

Most people acknowledge and agree that the Holocaust actually began on January 30th, 1933, the same day Hitler became the chancellor of Germany. Surrounded by zealots and extremist anti-Semites and propelled dramatically by an enormously efficient propaganda machine, he converted the once vital and civilized society into a population based and energized purely by hate and revenge. His reign was supreme. His power was unchecked and never questioned.

The word "holocaust" was originally derived from the Greek word *holokauston*, meaning "a completely (holos) burnt (kaustos) sacrificial offering" or "a burnt sacrifice offered to God."

The Hebrew word *Shoa*, also spelled *Shoah*, meaning "calamity" and also used since the Middle Ages to refer to destruction became the standard Hebrew term for the Holocaust as early as the 1940s.

Hitler and his minions justified the Holocaust by claiming that the victims were subhumans who were both biologically inferior and in the case of Jews a potential challenge to the superiority of the Aryan race. They looked at their atrocities as a form of eugenics, the creation of a better race by eliminating the unfit. In their minds they were practicing nothing other than "racial hygiene" for the betterment of their country.

In a bizarre fashion, the Germans were constantly seeking more efficient ways of killing people. In 1941 after occupying Belarus, without compassion or concern, they used mental patients from Minsk asylums as guinea pigs. Initially they tried shooting them by having them stand one behind the other so that several people could be killed with one bullet, but the process was too slow. Then they tried dynamite and blew people up. But few were killed and many were left wounded with hands and legs missing so that the Germans had to finish them off with machine guns and bury them in open pits. In October of 1941 they tried the *Gaswagen* or "gas car." First they used a light military car and it took more than thirty minutes for those inside to die — again, too slow for their needs. Then they used a larger truck exhaust and it took only eight minutes to kill all the people enclosed. Their results, while effective, once again proved to be too slow for what they had in mind. Other measures had to be explored.

Jews were not the only victims of the Holocaust. The Germans also meticulously murdered Communists, homosexuals, gypsies, the mentally ill, the physically disabled, Soviet prisoners of war, Polish, Russian, and other Slavic intelligentsia, political activists, Jehovah's Witnesses, some Catholic and Protestant clergy, trade unionists, psychiatric patients, common criminals, and anyone else they wished to casually define as "enemies of the state."

The country of Poland in essence became a "laboratory" for the Nazis in the matter of Jewish extermination. Once Auschwitz was established, especially with the subcamp of Birkenau, other extermination camps soon followed.

"Tata," Moniek begged in the changing voice of a twelve-year-old. "Please let me go with you. I can work. I'm old enough."

Hershel smiled and patted his young son tenderly on the head, just as he had since he was an infant. "I know you are but the family needs someone here to watch out for your mother and your younger brother. Perhaps you can continue to try to find some friends of ours. That would be very helpful."

"I'll do that, Tata. I'll do my best. I promise."

"I know you will, son." And with that Hershel, Abraham, and Zishe were out the door. Feigel offered Moniek a slight smile.

"I wish I could fix you a decent breakfast," she whispered.

"I'd even eat your potato soup," he replied, returning the smile. "It was delicious."

Hershel and his two older sons went to the local Judenrat office and reported in. After waiting in a long and very quiet line they were greeted by clerks seated behind tables with a mood which was not hostile but certainly not cordial. The Polish clerks were highly militaristic and matter-of-fact. Hershel and the boys were asked their names, addresses, dates of birth, place of residence in the ghetto, and names of family members. They placed themselves within the rapidly growing Nazi system, one of immense record keeping and information gathering. For reasons no one could ever quite comprehend, the Nazis seemed to keep track of the most minute details. This was a fact which somewhat confused Hershel because all they were trying to do was get some place where they could work and receive some food rations for their efforts.

With his mother's permission Moniek left the apartment and began exploring their new surroundings. Of the few faces he saw on the streets none were familiar. He made his way to the far side of the ghetto, to the spot where they had entered, and peeked through the slats of wood to the market where his father was once a respected businessman. Now this once proud man, his hero, had been reduced to begging for work from the Nazis.

As he looked through the fence Moniek shuddered, reflecting on the day he'd heard the music coming from the occupied house in Nowy Wisnicz, watching the uniformed Germans having a party, and actually thinking for a moment that these people couldn't possibly be as bad as everybody was saying. He was angry with himself for even harboring that thought. Even for a moment.

A shoe store owner named Smychia Weiss was the head of the local Judenrat. A man named Dr. Rosen, who was actually a lawyer, was the chief of the Jewish Police Force. The Jewish Police Force was subordinate to the Judenrat but in reality received its orders directly from the SS. Weiss and Rosen, assisted by various personnel, provided Jewish manpower for forced labor purposes for anything the Germans required. The Nazis never requested. They insisted and their wishes were always carried out precisely and without question. Those who questioned anything for any reason disappeared and were never seen or heard from again. On a daily basis the local Judenrat, in essence the labor department, would draft hundreds of people for labor camp duties throughout the area as the German authorities found fit.

Unknown to the vast majority of the people confined in the Bochnia ghetto, they were all an integral part of the German war effort. While reasonably minor in its scale, the town, with the products and the ammunition it produced, added significantly to the German military-industrial complex throughout all of the Reich-controlled territory. As the workers performed only what was demanded of them for virtual scraps of food they were actually enhancing the probability of their own eventual annihilation.

Armaments, weapons, tanks, airplanes, ammunition, food, clothing, miscellaneous supplies, and fuel refineries were constructed and produced war essentials at an ever increasing rate. There were huge factories, many of them underground, to further the war effort. It began in 1933 and continued to grow on a massive scale. This scale was dramatically increased once the Nazis began to use prisoners in concentration camps and residents of ghettos for the purpose of forced labor.

Hershel and his two older sons were each given identification cards and ordered to report to a certain area. Having no idea of the geography within the walls of the ghetto they followed several others to the designated position. Once there they were separated and assigned to different work patrols. One worked on street maintenance, another worked in a stable, feeding and cleaning up after horses, and the third performed duties as a gardener, assisting in the growing of food which none of them would ever have the opportunity of tasting.

When their work patrol was completed they were each instructed to report to the same area the following morning. Then, according to plan, they were separately given the precious food ration coupons. The three of them met on the way back to their new apartment and together visited the food distribution warehouse where between them they managed to obtain two loaves of bread, a small section of cheese, and a tiny portion of margarine. While a meager exchange for what amounted to three full days of labor it would be viewed as a feast which would be shared by the entire family.

The following morning Hershel and the older boys prepared to return to their respective work sites. Once more Moniek pleaded to go with them and once again Hershel refused. Disappointed, the youngster made his way alone into the streets of the ghetto, still seeking anyone he might know or even recognize from his hometown. But like before his efforts proved to be unsuccessful.

As he walked down the street by himself he noticed two large trucks passing by and watched with interest. The trucks each had signs on their sides identifying them, their purpose, and where they were going. One seemed to be reserved for people who were being taken to a resettlement area. It was filled with people who were apparently off to a better location and a better life. The other one had a sign indicating "workers."

Moniek was fascinated in that many of the riders in the rear of the truck seemed to be not much older than he was. If they can do it, he thought to himself, there's no reason I can't. At that moment he made two decisions which would alter his life. One, he wouldn't say anything to his parents about his plans to go to work the following day. And two, that he would return to this exact same spot at the exact same time in the morning.

His life would never be the same.

Sixteen

Moniek could barely sleep that night, filled with anticipation, overflowing with an unbridled excitement only a twelve-year-old could even begin to comprehend. Tomorrow, in his young mind, he would become the man his father had professed him to be and actually do something productive and helpful for his family. He smiled to himself and somehow the wooden floor didn't seem quite as hard as it had been the previous night.

In the morning Hershel, Abraham, and Zishe left the apartment and returned to their assigned work sites. Moniek waited impatiently, pacing the floor of the small room, and within the hour also prepared to leave, supposedly still looking for old friends or neighbors. He kissed Feigel goodbye and gave her a tender hug.

"Why are you smiling?" she asked. "What are you up to?"

"Nothing, Mama," he answered, trying unsuccessfully to suppress the smile.

"I know you too well, young man. Tell me what's going on."

"What could possibly be going on?"

Feigel took a deep breath and hesitated for a moment. "Moniek, you're a very intelligent young man. Like the rest of us you've also been through a great deal since this all began. I want you to be aware that I trust you know exactly what you're doing. All I can tell you is that this is a very dangerous place and there are people here who want to hurt us."

"I know, Mama. Believe me, I know." And with that he tenderly kissed her cheek again, turned, and made his way toward the door. She watched as the youngster left, filled with apprehension, wondering what the coming day would bring. As always she hoped for only the best for all of them. But today her primary concern was for Moniek, traveling out into a strange place filled with untold danger, with an unexplainable smile covering his young face.

As Hershel and his two older sons returned to the same locations they had worked the previous day, Moniek made his way to the same street where he had seen the truck. He waited. Perhaps the truck wasn't going to come this way again. Absentmindedly he picked up a handful of rocks and casually threw them across the street and continued waiting.

A large truck eased its way down the street, swastika flags flying on each front fender, mufflers roaring. Moniek moved closer to the curb, anticipation rising, prepared to wave, step into the street, and stop the truck, until he saw the sign on the side of the vehicle. It was the truck carrying families to be resettled elsewhere, hopefully a better place. Hopefully a place where there would be food and even, if one could possibly imagine it, peace and tranquility.

The truck roared past and as Moniek watched it disappear down the road he considered that yesterday the resettlement truck had been the first one and the truck for workers followed closely behind. He casually threw another handful of rocks across the road and waited. Until he heard the sound of rumbling mufflers and his heart began to race.

It was the workers truck and he stepped into the street. He could see the rear of the truck filled with people, mostly youngsters, some as young as he was. Fortunately Moniek looked older than his actual age. He waved and to his astonishment the truck came to a stop. A soldier in the passenger seat of the cab said gruffly, "Get in the back. Be quick about it."

"Yes sir," he responded. Another youngster offered a helping hand and Moniek was in the truck with about twenty others. He had no idea where they were going or what they were going to do but he was confident that whatever the day would bring at the end of it he would be able to provide some food for his family, the most important thing in his life. In reality, family was the only thing in his life. His smile continued, confusing the rest of the riders.

The truck left the confines of the ghetto and after a few blocks stopped in front of a large, freshly painted house with trees and manicured shrubbery in the front. Children were playing in the yard, oblivious to the truck or its occupants. The soldier in the passenger seat pointed at Moniek. "You there," he announced. "This is where you'll work today. Go to the back door and be quick about it."

Even at his young age Moniek consciously reflected on the phrase, "be quick about it." The Germans always seemed to be in a hurry but there never seemed to be any reason for it. He walked briskly to the rear of the house as the truck pulled away. As he had learned well from parents who insisted on proper manners he knocked three times on the back door and waited.

The lady of the house, the wife of a Nazi officer, opened the door and invited him inside, just as she would any servant. She was in her mid-thirties, well-dressed, and wearing a sweet-smelling perfume. Moniek lowered his head, looking with great embarrassment at his filthy and tattered clothing. His smile dissipated and for the first time he could ever remember, felt shame, but he was there with a purpose, and he was not about to let his family down.

He looked up into the face of the lady of the house and smiled. It must have been contagious because the lady showed a degree of kindness and returned the smile. "I think you'll do just fine," she said. "First you need to do my husband's boots." She pointed to two pairs of black boots on the kitchen floor, the kind of boots worn by SS officers.

Moniek made the boots shine like never before. The lady nodded approval as he sat on the floor performing his duties. Her two children roamed in and out of the kitchen, grabbing snacks as they continued their play. For them it was as if Moniek didn't even exist. He was just another Jew, sitting on their kitchen floor, performing manual labor for the master Aryan race. They had been well-indoctrinated and would be the future of Germany. Moniek never spoke a word.

He contemplated their reality. There were ten of them, three families, stuffed into a small apartment in a ghetto, sleeping on a wooden floor. And here he was in the very lap of luxury. A large house which had obviously been stolen from someone, filled with fine furniture, well-dressed children with toys, and most of all, an endless supply of food.

While he couldn't help but envy their existence he also reflected on the tragic day not that very long ago when his father, assisted by his two older brothers, barely managed to make their way into the kitchen. The day he was taken to Gestapo headquarters just down the street from their own house and beaten senseless. He polished the boots harder, then harder. Taking out his frustration and anger but knowing with a certainty it would be impossible to ever utter a word about it. Not to these people. He had witnessed both sides of the Nazi mentality and couldn't really comprehend either. And this was clearly because neither of them made any sense.

He spent the entire morning polishing the boots and the lady was more than pleased with his efforts. As a reward she gave him a small piece of bread for his lunch. He continued to sit on the floor, not being invited to the table where the lady and her children enjoyed leftovers of beef brisket and cooked corn and beans. And, he was grateful for what he had. In the process he thought about his mother and younger brother and the distinct probability that they had nothing at all to eat. Guilt consumed him and while hungry to the core he placed half of the bread into his jacket pocket to take home later that afternoon and share with the family.

"You're a good worker," the lady said. "Not like most of the others. Tomorrow I'm going to ask that you come back again." Just as it appeared that she might actually be a decent human being she handed him a rag and some cleaning polish and said, "Now you can do the floors." Moniek nodded and began the task. He spent the entire day without saying a word. It wasn't that he was afraid, even though he should have been — he was just consciously reflecting on the treatment his father had received from the SS back in Nowy Wisnicz.

When he finished, the floors looked as if they were brand new. The lady nodded her approval but didn't say anything. Moniek hung his head, staring at the floor, awaiting his next assignment. He heard a horn honking at the front of the house but it didn't really register what it was for. The lady looked at Moniek and said, "That's your truck. It's time for you to go." He nodded and made his way toward the back door. As long as Germans occupied the house it was very clear that no Jew would ever enter or leave by the front door. "Wait," she said, as Moniek moved across the freshly polished kitchen floor. "I have something for you."

She opened a cupboard and handed him several small squares of hardened bread. He looked up and nodded his thanks, placing the pieces of bread in his pocket, but chose to not actually speak. "I'll see you tomorrow," she announced with authority.

Moniek exited the rear door, walked briskly around the side of the house and was helped into the rear of the truck by one of his fellow riders.

The rest of the workers all appeared to be bone-tired. There was no conversation. Moniek put his hand in his pocket, gently caressing the bread, enormously proud of what he'd accomplished, feeling certain that his parents and brothers would be proud of him. The very thought caused his smile to return and his fellow passengers just looked at him, shaking their heads in disbelief, wondering what on earth he could possibly have to be smiling about.

When he walked in the front door of the apartment the entire family was there. Feigel's eyes were red and puffy. It was clear that she'd been crying. She glared at the youngster and for only the second time he'd ever heard her raise her voice said, "Where on earth have you been? I've been sick to death worrying about you all day long."

Moniek was completely confused and didn't know how to respond. The very last thing in the world he ever wanted to do was to hurt any member of his family. His eyes showed his confusion and now his own pain. Embarrassed he stared at the floor, having no idea what to say.

"You've hurt your mother very deeply," Hershel said with authority. "I think both an apology and an explanation would be in order." And then he continued to stare at the youngster. Moniek was crushed. All he wanted to do was help them out, certainly not to hurt anyone. He reached into his pocket, produced the bread which he'd saved from lunch and also his daily wage which the lady gave him and placed it all on a small table for everyone to see.

"I worked today," he softly said, still staring at the floor, trying his best to avoid their piercing glares. "I got this for you. All of you." Tears began to roll down his cheeks and he wiped them away, trying his best to keep anyone else from seeing them.

Feigel rushed to his side and warmly embraced him, holding him tight, wiping away her own tears. "Why didn't you just tell us what you were going to do? Then we wouldn't have had to worry so much."

"I just wanted to help the family," he quietly replied. And then even softer, "I just wanted to help." He looked away, still embarrassed for the pain he had caused.

Hershel patted Moniek on the head and put his arm around the youngsters shoulder. "You've done a fine job, son. We're very proud of you and we all appreciate what you've done."

"Your father is right," Feigel said. "Just please let us know when you're going to do it again."

"I'm going back tomorrow," he said with resolve. "A German lady said I was a good worker and she wants me to return. Today I polished boots and cleaned their floors. She gave me the bread."

"But you're so young...," Feigel softly said.

"Today he's proven that he's old enough," Hershel quietly replied. "The bread you've provided will be a most welcome addition to our meal tonight."

On the way home from his work patrol Hershel had managed to obtain a small piece of meat which they cut into six small but equal portions. That, accompanied by the bread, and a tiny slice of margarine, provided a meal which was reasonably stomach filling for a pleasant change.

As they sat on the floor and slowly savored the food Moniek related his day's experiences. They weren't exciting by any stretch of the imagination but it was new information and the family listened with rapt attention to his every word.

Summer turned into fall. What few trees remained in the ghetto had leaves which changed colors and fell softly to the street. And, as night follows the day, the temperature began to fall. To make their existence even more unbearable the Germans had cut off all electrical power serving the ghetto. The residents, growing in number on a daily basis, had to result to innovative solutions. Coal and fuel for heating was not available so it was imperative that other means were sought before the vicious winter set in. In the beginning, trial and error was the order of the day, but then someone came up with the brilliant idea of burning wood shavings which were regularly discarded from the busy carpentry workshops. The shavings were abundant, easily accessible and relatively inexpensive. Small sawdust stoves were manufactured by hand and provided adequate heating, especially for a small enclosure like the Ebners occupied. While they had little else and their food supply was never adequate, at least they could now look forward to experiencing warmth during the coming winter months.

The Nazis knew no seasons. Those in the upper echelon of the Reich continued their mass-planning of eliminating all Jews and "subhumans" from their existence. While their entire military was bogged down in the war with the Soviet Union their plans to rid all Reich-controlled territory of Jews seemed to be more important to them than anything else. Their experiments of mass murder continued. It had been clearly determined that the Jews were not going to leave Poland or Germany of their own accord in numbers which were acceptable.

The "gas mobiles," while an acceptable form of execution, could not provide the Nazis the necessary numbers. Twenty people at a time were placed into the back of a truck, exhaust fumes were piped into the enclosure and in eight minutes they were all dead. Bodies were stripped, the clothing sent back to the military for redistribution, and they were unceremoniously dumped into mass graves and covered with mounds of dirt. But still, the means and the method of execution were too slow.

Zyklon-B, a commercial form of hydrocyanic acid, was initially developed as a powerful insecticide and rodent poison which was used primarily by farmers to exterminate roaming packs of vermin from destroying their crops. It was a crystalline form of hydrogen cyanide that turned gaseous when exposed to the air and was manufactured by a firm called Degesch (German Corporation for Pest Control) which was largely owned by I.G. Farben. After numerous experiments it was determined that by inhaling the pure vapors of the product the same effect could be equally effective with human beings. Testing occurred. Success was achieved. The results would prove to be devastating to an entire society of people.

On September 3rd of 1941, the first lethal gassing using Zyklon-B was done at Auschwitz, what would become known as the principal death camp. More than five hundred Russian prisoners and two hundred fifty sick prisoners from the camp hospital were crammed into an underground detention cell, the windows were covered with dirt, and SS men wearing gas masks opened the Zyklon-B canisters. What looked like blue chalk pellets about the size of peas created a cloud of poisonous gas and the people all died.

Its use proved to be effective. Hitler, Eichmann, Himmler, Heydrich, and all those under their command were enormously pleased. The answer to the Final Solution seemed to have finally been discovered. The Jews who had previously refused to leave their homes and their countries were now effectively destined for a reasonably swift yet agonizing death.

Moniek, his father, and brothers continued to work on a daily basis. Some of the clothing they had brought with them when they left their home mysteriously disappeared. It was assumed that Hershel traded various items for necessary food for the family. No one ever questioned the missing articles or ever said a word. They did the best they could, all arriving home to their cramped apartment and the hard wooden floors on a nightly basis, tired, worn out from a hard day's work.

Moniek toiled in several German houses, given recommendations from one lady to the next, always performing the required duties without complaint. Each night as the horn from the truck blew in the street he was rewarded for his services with a few scraps of bread which he shared with his family. While many others were literally starving on the streets of the ghetto, the Ebners seemed to make do. There was never enough to eat but on the other hand, compared to some of their neighbors, they had enough to get by. It was far less than an ideal existence but they had shelter, warmth, and while extremely limited an acceptable amount of food. Their family was intact and loving and helping each other every day.

People continued to disappear from the ghetto on a regular basis and almost everyone pretended not to notice. Everyone was much too concerned with taking care of themselves. Even so, the Jews of Bochnia did whatever they could to maintain a normal lifestyle within the ghetto. They established a hospital on Solna Gora Street within the ghetto boundaries, sadly without a surgeon who could care for those truly in need, which had forty-five beds, seven nurses, and a cook. The Judenrat provided medications whenever possible.

An elementary school was established, a Talmud Torah for small children, along with a bais midrash yeshiva for students who studied the Torah on a continual basis. The Germans seemed to be somewhat lenient in letting the Jews carry on a reasonable life even though they were confined within their limited boundaries. This attitude was generally viewed as a somewhat encouraging point until the end of September.

And then the deadly rumors became a harsh reality. Hershel had first heard it whispered from others on his work patrol. Several other men heard the same tragic story. At first it was impossible to believe, even after all they had been through and seen with their own eyes. But the stories and reports were far too numerous and consistent to disbelieve. They heard about an obscure ravine known as Babi Yar, near the Ukrainian city of Kiev.

With the initiation of Operation Barbarossa, Germany's assault on the Soviet Union, mobile killing units known as *Einsatzgruppen* followed the advancing troops and callously slaughtered countless groups of what they considered to be "undesirables" which included those who were referred to as political criminals, Polish government officials, gypsies, and mostly, Jews.

Kiev had a Jewish population of one hundred seventy-five thousand before the Nazi invasion. Many fled when the war began. Many others, just like the Ebner family, stayed behind, believing the Germans could never be as cold and vicious as they had been described in previous accounts. Those who stayed were proven to be wrong.

The German army invaded Kiev in mid-September and within two weeks, on the days and nights of September 29th and 30th, brought Jews from the town ghetto to a ravine known as Babi Yar. Here, like lambs to the slaughter, they were ordered to lie down on their stomachs in a large pit, which they had dug themselves and were systematically machine-gunned by the Nazis who were following orders. After the onslaught, soldiers entered the pit and using their pistols shot anyone in the head who managed to survive the machine gun bursts. Within the hour dirt was piled on top of the fresh corpses and another group was summoned to the site. Even though they had heard the gunshots they had no idea what their fate would be. It was the same as the first group. And then there was another. And then another. And then another.

Over a period of two days and nights the Nazis committed an orgy of execution and murdered nearly thirty-four thousand innocent Jewish men, women, and children for no other reason other than the fact that they were Jews.

Each morning Moniek continued to stand on the side of the street at the appointed hour and was usually selected for work. The few days he wasn't selected he normally explored the ghetto, just as any curious child of his age would do. He worked in various German houses for awhile and then was assigned to carry boxes of ammunition produced at the Klaj Camp from German trucks into small storage areas spread throughout the city.

It was during this work detail that he first heard from fellow workers about the atrocities which had been committed at Babi Yar and his little heart was nearly broken. He looked down at the heavy box he was carrying and wondered if some of the ammunition he was helping to transport had been used to viciously and mindlessly murder all those men, women, and children.

SEVENTEEN

WITH THE ARRIVAL OF winter, Hershel, Abraham, and Zishe were assigned the task of cleaning snow from the city streets. Moniek, still too young to obtain a work permit from the local Judenrat, continued to shuffle his duties between cleaning houses for the Germans to transporting boxes of ammunition for storage purposes. Each evening back at the small apartment they shared, they would tell stories concerning what they had experienced and seen during the course of the day. None of the stories were of a positive or hopeful nature.

One of the boys reported witnessing an elderly Jewish gentleman walking innocently down the sidewalk who had a long beard and sidelocks, long strands of hair replacing his sideburns and hanging in a curled fashion down to his chin. It was clear from his look and demeanor that he was a deeply religious person.

Three soldiers carrying submachine guns approached the man and stopped him. At first it was just a normal and regular interrogation, the kind most residents of the ghetto had experienced in the past: "What's your name? Where do you live? Where are you going? Where do you work?" And then they began their sadistic humiliation. "Why do you have such a long beard, old man? What's all that funny hair doing hanging off the side of your face?"

The old man stood as still as he was able and just stared at his three young tormentors with eyes which seemed to change from confusion to fear to an odd and unexplainable sense of compassion. The soldiers smiled, apparently amused by his silence. One moved behind him and took the submachine gun from his shoulder. "Tell us, old man, what are the stupid long sideburns for?"

The old man stared at the sidewalk, afraid to speak. The nineteen-year-old German standing behind him took his weapon and swinging it like a baseball bat smacked him in the small of his back, causing the elderly gentleman to fall to the sidewalk on his knees. Tears of pain entered his eyes and he looked toward the heavens, silently moving his lips in prayer. The soldiers merely laughed uproariously as other ghetto residents looked on from a safe distance on the other side of the street. "Is your God going to save the life of one miserable Jew?"

The people on the street were silent. Even traffic seemed to stand still. The old man just looked at the youngsters with the guns, wondering how such hate could possibly exist in the world. His eyes begged for mercy but no words would come from his mouth. "Pray out loud, you worthless, rotten Jew," the leader of the three shouted. He received only silence in response.

The soldier in the rear raised his gun again but the leader waved him off. Instead he produced a pair of scissors from his own pocket. "Hold off," he told the other soldier. "This'll hurt even more." The other soldiers smiled and nodded approval.

The old man remained on his knees as the German took the scissors and cut off each of the sidelocks which had been growing for literally decades. They were now gone. He gave one to each of his friends. "A souvenir for your children to learn how stupid and cowardly the Jews are. So that they will always know the truth." The other two soldiers placed the sidelocks into their pockets as their smiles continued.

"This is for me and *my* children," the leader said. Then, without anyone objecting, which would have proven to be fruitless and potentially deadly, he cut the old man's long beard off at his chin line while the others laughed. The old man stayed on his knees as tears continued to flow from his eyes which were still raised toward the heavens above. His lips continued to move but he never made a sound.

As the Germans walked away the leader of the group looked over his shoulder and proclaimed, "We'll be back for you later, old man. Your days on this earth are short. Enjoy what little you have left." The sparse but assembled crowd standing on the far side of the street watched in abject silence. They each knew that the parting message was also directed toward them.

These acts of mindless violence were commonplace in ghettos throughout Germany, Poland, and most other Reich-controlled territories. In most cases they were openly encouraged. In many cases they were actually rewarded in the form of days off from the war effort or bonuses. The bile which had been spewed forth in Hitler's *Mein Kampf*, and expanded exponentially by Goebbels' growing propaganda machine and the others heading the Third Reich served to nourish deep hatred for a group of people which had seldom been seen before in the entire recorded history of mankind.

Single acts of violence and tragic occurrences such as the one which transpired in Babi Yar were sadly only the tip of the Nazi iceberg. Not far from Bochnia, situated in the Lubin district located conveniently between the large Jewish populations of southeast Poland and eastern Galicia, was an area known as Belzec. On November 1st of 1941 a new camp was established there. It consisted of two camps divided into three parts: an administration section, barracks and storage for plundered goods, and a separate section designed specifically for extermination purposes. Initially it had three gas chambers housed in wooden buildings. Later those were replaced with six gas chambers enclosed in brick and concrete buildings. What began as a labor camp in April of 1940 was transformed into a center for death.

Moniek, his father and brothers, continued their various work assignments. Each day they would bring home their ration of bread and little more. Occasionally Hershel would be able to obtain other food items but those days were dwindling perilously. The workshops surrounding the ghetto continued to manufacture uniforms for the military and toys for German children and the Klaj Camp produced ammunition at an ever increasing rate.

On December 7th, Imperial Japan attacked the United States of America at Pearl Harbor. Later that same day Hitler issued *Nacht und Nebel*, the Night and Fog Decree. Its purpose was remarkably clear. Field Marshall Wilheim Keitel issued an order stating, "Efficient and enduring intimidation can only be achieved either by capital punishment or by measures by which the relatives of the criminal do not know the fate of the criminal. The prisoners are, in the future, to be transported to Germany secretly, and further treatment of the offenders will take place here; these measures will have a deterrent effect because (a) The prisoners will vanish without a trace; (b) No information may be given as to their whereabouts or their fate."

Most suspected offenders, real or unreal, were arrested in the middle of the night, dragged from their homes without mercy, transported to prisons sometimes hundreds of miles away for questioning and torture, and were never seen or heard from again. The deterrent effect proved to be remarkably efficient.

The next day the United States officially declared war on Germany and Japan. Two days later Germany and Japan formally reciprocated and announced their own declaration of war against America.

When the news became public, a glimmer of hope spread throughout the ghetto that with the United States officially entering the war effort, the conflict would end sooner than many had anticipated. These hopes were dashed just six days later when Hans Frank, the Governor of occupied Poland, stated in a speech:

> "One way or another — I will tell you quite openly — we must finish off the Jews. The Fuehrer put it into words once: should united Jewry again succeed in setting off a world war, then the blood sacrifice shall not be made only by the peoples driven into war, but the Jew in Europe will have met his end...
>
> "But what should be done with the Jews? Can you believe that they will be accommodated in settlements in the Ostland? In Berlin we were told: why are you making all this trouble? We don't want them either, not in the Ostland, not anywhere. Eliminate them yourselves! Gentlemen, I must ask you to steel

> yourselves against all considerations of compassion. We must destroy Jews wherever we find them, and wherever it is at all possible, in order to maintain the whole structure of the Reich."

There was no Chanukkah celebration that year at the Ebner place of residence. There was no great feast prepared by Feigel, no lighted menorah, and any prayers given were offered silently over virtual scraps of bread and whatever else could be obtained by trading in the street. Bonding and close friendships were never developed with any neighbors or fellow workers. This was primarily due to the fact that at any moment people would just mysteriously disappear. Becoming attached to anyone outside the immediate family inevitably proved to be a painful experience to be carefully avoided.

Hershel, the consummate businessman who at one time knew virtually everyone in Nowy Wisnicz, kept quietly to himself. Feigel, one of the few who would actually tolerate Mrs. Levy, the town gossip, generally stayed inside the small apartment they continued to share with the two other couples. The boys performed their assigned duties, but unlike days in the past never played with other children. There were no soccer or dodge ball games in front of where they lived. The majority of the other children were on the streets, begging for scraps of food for themselves and their families and doing their best to avoid the roaming Polish and Jewish police who continued to wield their brutal power within the ghetto.

It was a harsh winter with considerably more snowfall than normal. Hershel and the two older boys continued to shovel the snow so the truck convoys could keep delivering ammunition, uniforms, and other assorted clothing to the German army still fighting on the blood-stained front with the Soviets. People heard that the Nazi effort wasn't going all that well but from a realistic standpoint that mattered little if at all. For the most part the residents of the ghetto were bitterly cold, increasingly frustrated and frightened, and suffering from a continued severe shortage of food.

More and more people were seen on a daily basis, begging for food, clothing, anything. But there was little to be given. Over time the Nazis had made sure that was to be the case. As soldiers sat in warm shelters drinking hot coffee and eating snacks, they regularly commented on how the stupid Jews should have left when they had the chance. Now, as far as the Nazis were concerned, they could all die in one fashion or another and it was their own fault.

On January 20th of 1942, fifteen high-ranking Nazi party and German government leaders held a conference at an upscale and exclusive section of Berlin in a villa by a scenic lake known as Wannsee. Six months earlier, Hermann Goering charged Reinhard Heydrich, SS chief Heinrich Himmler's head deputy, with devising and coordinating an overall concept to execute the Final Solution of the Jewish Question. The conference was held to determine the most complete and systematic method of the total extermination of European Jewry.

Adolf Eichmann recorded detailed and extensive notes of the meeting as the party leaders, completely void of emotion or dissent, discussed various methods of liquidation and processes of extermination. In their conversations they were casually discussing mass murder on a scale which had never before been contemplated by a modern state, the murder of an entire people.

It was determined that 11 million Jews should be deported, many from countries not currently in a state of war against the Third Reich. None of the Germans in attendance objected to the policy.

Before the end of the month, killing of Jews began at Auschwitz-Birkenau using the poisonous gas Zyklon-B and in March the Belzec concentration camp became fully operational.

The snow disappeared slowly as spring arrived in the ghetto. More neighbors vanished mysteriously. As soon as they were gone others nearly instantly replaced them. More families were crammed into the already cramped and virtually unlivable spaces. Moniek fondly remembered the streets of Nowy Wisnicz and how much he had always enjoyed the coming of spring: the green buds exploding and filling out the barren limbs on all the trees, the blooming of countless flowers in front of all their neighbors' houses and gardens. However, there were few trees and virtually no flowers within the walls of the ghetto. The colors he saw all seemed to be a bland, depressing, and hopeless shade of gray. Little if any life was exhibited.

With the change of the seasons and weather, new work details were assigned. Hope of returning to their home had sadly all but dissipated. It was never spoken about. In fact the once vocal and outspoken family did very little talking at all. Each morning they'd wake up filled with aches and pains from sleeping on the hard wooden floor, make their way to their work sites with empty bellies, work all day without any food, and drag weary bodies back to the apartment with perhaps enough food to sustain them for one more day of ever-increasing misery.

During the spring and summer of 1942, the level of apprehension in the ghetto increased considerably. Rumors began to circulate that countless numbers of Jews were being rounded up throughout the entire area. There were also abundant rumors that mass executions were occurring on a regular basis during the various and assorted forced marches.

Many residents of the ghetto began to build and create hiding places, fearing the worst: that they'd be transported to an extermination camp, specifically Belzec which was very near Bochnia. Some constructed false walls for their families to hide behind. Others dug pits in their dirt-floor basements and covered them with wood planks.

On Friday evening, August 21st, all the Jews of the greater Bochnia district were rounded up and transported to the ghetto. Those who refused to leave their homes were shot on the spot. Those who tried to hide from the soldiers and were discovered were shot as well. Thousands of Jews in long convoys of horse-drawn wagons provided by non-Jewish peasants made their way toward the ghetto, guarded closely by Germans and assisted by Polish police forces. But the ghetto was already packed with people so the convoy made its way down the main street toward the train station where temporary housing had been constructed beside the train tracks.

Several people, risking life and limb and fearing the loss of both, jumped from the moving wagons and disappeared into the crowds watching from the sides of the street. Seeing this mass of people only served to heighten the panic within the hearts of the local residents. It was common knowledge that a major concentration of Jews into the central ghetto of an area was always a sign for a large and extended expulsion of the population. This panic deepened the next day when a huge, black steam engine flying numerous swastika flags and pulling a long line of boxcars arrived without ceremony at the station.

Many in the ghetto, as a result of providing bribes to the local SS, had advance knowledge of the planned major transport. Several were convinced they would be spared because they were employed at one of the workshops or in the ammunition factory. They felt a false sense of security because they believed the newcomers and those not providing beneficial products and efforts for the war effort would be taken first and they'd be spared.

Several of the ghetto residents were not as confident and began to secure themselves in the hiding places they'd constructed, taking what little food they had with them. Some fled into the nearby forests and fields. The wooden slats, which comprised the fence surrounding the ghetto, were not very difficult to dislodge, and did not present a deterrent from escape.

Moniek, like many of the others, had heard about the upcoming event and while not completely understanding the severity of what they were facing could clearly see the concern and fear on both of his parents' faces. The next day he chose not to go out on a work patrol and instead explored the perimeter of the ghetto. After several hours he achieved the success he'd desired.

He was greatly disappointed that he hadn't been able to provide any food for the family that evening but actually felt that he may have accomplished something far more worthwhile. With great caution he quietly broached the subject. "People are saying that the Germans are going to have a 'round up'..."

"It's called 'an Action,'" Hershel nervously corrected.

"What are we to do? What if we're separated and they take us to different places?"

"I don't know what to do. I don't know what any of us can do." There was a clear and certain defeatism in Hershel's voice. It was the first time Moniek had ever heard it and it troubled him deeply.

"We could go back to the forest," the youngster suggested.

"And just how would we do that," Hershel asked.

"Today I found a way out through the wall. We can all make it and then we'll be safe."

"Are you sure?"

"Positive," he replied with confidence.

"No soldiers roaming around?"

"None — I heard that they aren't coming until tomorrow morning."

The sky was dark that night as the family silently made its way to the spot Moniek had discovered earlier that day. It was near the area where they had entered the ghetto and the market where Hershel had done so much business over the years was also relatively close.

Moniek had been correct. One of the seven-foot tall boards was easily removed and the family slipped through, letting Hershel take the lead across the street and into the cover of more darkness. "Follow me," he whispered. They made their way into the market area where he was completely familiar with the surroundings. It was totally deserted which wasn't surprising in that it was late at night. Without further conversation he led them to the stalls where animals he had purchased in the past used to be sold on nearly a weekly basis.

Finding the empty stalls still filled with hay reminded them all of the months they'd stayed in the Klein barn. They stayed together, making themselves as comfortable as possible. At least with the August weather they weren't experiencing bitter cold. As they each closed their eyes the one prevailing thought in their minds was the fact that in the morning there would be no warm bread and cool water provided by Mrs. Klein and Rachel.

Moniek heard a voice. At first he thought it was someone talking in their sleep. Listening more closely he realized that it was Hershel. He was praying, under his breath, barely loud enough to hear and certainly not loud enough to wake any of the others. He was praying for their safety. Moniek closed his eyes and followed along with the prayer.

The loud, precise, and staccato clomping of boots outside startled them all. It was not yet sunrise on Tuesday, August 25th, 1942. They woke up, frozen with fear, waiting for instructions from Hershel. He waved for the rest of the family to remain quiet as he carefully eased his way to the front opening of the barn. He was only gone for a moment but when he returned his news was not good. "Nazis," he said. "They've surrounded the ghetto. No one else is going to get out as long as they're there. That's for sure."

If they'd stayed in the ghetto just one more night the chances of the entire family being transported to an execution center would have been all but certain. While their future was far from secure they still had each other and hopefully one more full day of relative freedom. Hershel looked at Moniek and the rest of the family followed suit. With a deep emotion he quietly said, "I always said that you were my lucky charm. Thank you, son, for my life, and for the lives of the rest of our family."

EIGHTEEN

WITHIN THE HOUR, LARGE troop transport trucks began pulling into the ghetto. Polish policemen patrolled the streets using bullhorns announcing repeatedly and calmly that all residents were to report to the Appellplatz, the roll-call square, by eight o'clock that morning. The announcement did not come as a surprise to most. Many people were prepared and actually packed suitcases and whatever meager food they had available for the trip they had been promised would be to a resettlement location. Things will be much better for all of you, the Germans assured them. You'll have better housing, good jobs, more food. It would be an ideal existence compared to the life they were now living in Bochnia.

Within a short period of time the streets were packed with people, old, young, men, women, children, even the sick and ailing. Some of them were pale as ghosts. They all moved slowly and silently through the ghetto, carrying their luggage and all of their earthly belongings. It was an eerie and sobering sight.

Initially there was only one ringing gunshot which captured their attention. Then there were more, then several more. The people began to move down the street at a faster pace, thinking logically that the gunshots were designed for them to pick up their pace. But such was not the case.

German soldiers had entered the ghetto and were going house to house, apartment to apartment, looking for stragglers and "encouraging" them to join the others. When residents refused, for whatever reason, they were executed on the spot in front of their families. There was no time allotted for mourning and those remaining knew their fate would be instantly sealed if they refused to follow orders.

Some people remained in the hiding places they had constructed, listening, like the others, to the nearby deadly gunshots. The Polish police altered the announcement from their bullhorns to explain forcefully, "All people going voluntarily on the transport will end up in a labor camp. All people caught in hiding will be shot." Many taking the announcement at face value came out of their hiding places and joined the others as they moved down the street. But the Germans knew with a certainty that there were many others who remained.

The Gestapo joined in the search and as was their trademark, were particularly vicious toward the Jews. Old and sick people were shot at point-blank range in their places of residence. Even those in the hospital too frail to walk were disposed of without thought or concern.

Each time a gunshot rang out on the other side of the fence it sent a shivering sensation down Moniek's spine. Feigel did her best to comfort all of the children but she as well was deathly frightened. "What if they come in here?" she whispered to Hershel, her voice filled with fear.

"They won't come here," Hershel softly replied, hoping he was correct. "They're dealing with plenty of people in the ghetto, plus all the new ones that just arrived. They won't have the time or have any reason to search here, at least not today."

"Should we be quiet, Mama?" Nuta asked with complete innocence.

"Yes, dear, be very quiet."

"What can I do to help, Tata?" Abraham asked, assuming by his age that he had become the second in command of the families safety and security.

"Nothing for right now. I'm assuming that since no one has brought any animals or products to the market it must be closed for the day. Perhaps it's been closed for a long time. I don't know."

"Is it safe to stay here?" Zishe asked.

"I think we'll be all right for the day but tonight we'll move back into the forest. Besides, we need to find some food."

It appeared that confidence and resolve had returned to Hershel's voice. Moniek noticed and it gave him reason to return his own level of confidence as well. As long as his father was in charge the family was somehow going to be all right.

The residents of the Bochnia ghetto were marched to the roll-call square, the gathering place, where the SS performed what they referred to as a "selection." The children, the aged, and the sick were separated from the others and all immediately marked for death. Those deemed to be physically fit were marked for hard labor. The first group composed of the children, women, numerous elderly people, and all the remaining patients of the Jewish hospital were transported by truck to the nearby town of Bochkov, about ten kilometers north of Bochnia.

Once they arrived they were marched in single file to the side of a large open pit which had been recently dug, as if in anticipation of their arrival, machine-gunned down in cold blood by the Nazis, and buried without the benefit of ceremony or even the slightest prayer. The Germans covered the mass grave and walked away, wiping their hands of the dirt, discussing the delightful meals they were all going to enjoy in the barracks or at their homes later that evening.

Those supposedly destined for hard labor were marched in military fashion, in columns of ten people abreast for the purpose of maintaining exact records, to the train station where they were crammed into freight cars once used to transport cattle, one hundred people per car. Their trip proved to be short. They were shipped north to the Belzec death camp where all of them were murdered by means of carbon monoxide poisoning in gas chambers.

Later that afternoon the gunshots emanating from the ghetto subsided and then ceased altogether. Another large train replaced the one which had recently left, prepared to carry another trainload of innocent Jews to their destruction. That night the ghetto was quiet. When the first train was filled and on its way, the people left in the ghetto were instructed to return to the gathering station at eight o'clock in the morning. They were assured that no harm would come to them.

Many knew this to be a lie since they had personally witnessed vicious, callous murders during the course of the day. Those believing they would be spared from the transport, as a result of having permanent status as a worker producing valuable items for the Reich, had their hopes dashed when Sala Grayver, the man who actually owned the two large workshops and had promised immunity to his workers, was shot to death in the street by the SS.

Still, even with what had been seen by the eyes of many, most still found it virtually impossible to believe the level of cruelty which the Nazis were capable of exerting. This feeling was somewhat astonishing in that they knew in their hearts that the Germans had lost all human understanding, all knowledge of the differences between right and wrong, moral and immoral. Remarkably the general consensus in the ghetto remained, mostly based on hope and little else, that the people who were shipped out on the transport would be taken to a labor camp.

Hershel led his family through the barns which once held animals and empty stands that used to sell produce and various cuts of poultry, cheeses, breads, and meats. Before they left their hiding place he carefully looked out the front of the barn: the soldiers were still there, still standing guard to make sure no one could escape.

In silence they weaved their way through the deserted, unlit streets until they came to the edge of the forest, ever watchful of patrolling Germans. Making sure the coast was clear the family eased across an open field and into the cover of the trees. They walked and walked. They walked until Feigel could walk no more. The area seemed secure enough and as Hershel gave them a silent hand signal they all stopped, sat down on the ground, and leaned against a large pine tree.

By now their eyes were all adjusted to the darkness and Moniek could clearly see the lush greenery which provided them cover. In the midst of their peril he took note of the leaves still covering the trees, the full bushes surrounding them, and even some nearby wild flowers. His nose captured the fresh and collective aroma they provided, one that his nostrils had not experienced for a very long time. Even so, he could still remember them as most pleasant and wonderful memories.

Hershel whispered to the others, "I know exactly where we are. I'll be back in just a little while with some food. The growing fields are just beyond that ridge of trees." Everyone nodded as he cautiously stood up and made his way into the darkness. For unexplainable reasons the rest of the family felt a slight sense of security, one which only could be provided by a confident husband and father.

They waited in silence for what seemed like hours but in reality was much less. Upon his arrival he presented them with his bounty: three potatoes and the same number of turnips. "I've stuffed my pants and jacket pocket with the same amount so we'll also have enough food for tomorrow."

"Will we stay here, Tata?" Nuta asked.

"We'll have to wait and see what tomorrow brings. For now, let's eat our food. It's been quite awhile." They each enjoyed the delicacy of a half a potato and a half a turnip. Compared to what they'd been eating lately this was an enormous feast. The best part of all was that it would be repeated tomorrow without either having to perform hard labor or beg for scraps on the street.

As the boys drifted off to sleep Hershel turned to Feigel and softly said, "It's ironic, isn't it?"

"What's that?"

"All these fields were once owned by Jews. Then they were stolen by the Germans to provide food for the Nazis. And now we're stealing from the Germans so we can stay alive. Don't you think that's ironic?"

"Yes, dear, whatever you say. Perhaps we should try and get some sleep now."

Hershel nodded, put his arm around his wife to provide some warmth and comfort, and closed his tired eyes.

The following morning produced more of the same within the confines of the ghetto. Residents slowly arrived from a sleepless and fear-filled night with their belongings at the roll-call square at eight o'clock and another selection occurred. The young, old, and infirm were separated from the able bodied workers. One group was taken away in trucks. The other group was marched to the train station and stuffed into cattle cars.

By mid-afternoon the gunshots began. Soldiers and the Gestapo had also returned and resumed their search for those in hiding or refusing to leave. The Polish police moved through the streets with their bullhorns announcing that those in hiding would be discovered and would be shot. Many were discovered. Many were shot. None were spared.

That night a new transport train arrived at the station and those who had not been selected were once again instructed to arrive at the roll-call square the following morning. As many of them returned to their places of residence they saw bodies in the street and on yards in front of houses and apartments. The assurances of their safety and relocation to a labor camp were ringing hollow. Nearly all of the people wanted to leave the ghetto, to somehow escape, but there was no possible way that this could happen. Anyone attempting such a thing would be executed on the spot.

Hershel led the family to another location to hide for the night, foraged for more food in the nearby fields, and they all just sat quietly and waited. They weren't even sure what they were waiting for. They just knew that dark had once again fallen and that they'd made it through another day alive. Based on that simple fact their fate far superseded that of many others.

The next day, much more of the same thing. Another selection, more executions, more trucks sent to Bochkov, another train full of people sent to Belzec. It was on this day, the third day of the Action, that the town rabbi, Rabbi Halberstam, and his wife were taken to the courtyard and murdered in front of their followers. The total population of the Bochnia ghetto had been dramatically reduced to less than a thousand people. They were understandably on edge, waiting nervously for their name to be called and then to be transported to a future unknown.

The following day, thankfully, all was quiet. The Action appeared to have ended. The selections and the transports which were carried out by the Gestapo, the SS, the German soldiers, the Polish police, and the Jewish police transpired between August 25th and 27th and decimated the population of the Bochnia ghetto.

Hershel eased his way to the edge of the forest and was relieved to see that the guards were no longer there. He chose to wait another day in their relative seclusion before making any final decision. Escaping through the forest was not an option. There were far too many soldiers on the surrounding roads and working in the nearby fields to even consider that. Continuing to hide in the forest brought back unpleasant memories of cold, wet, and freezing nights. Nights which Feigel could no longer realistically endure.

Under the cover of darkness the next night, their pockets filled with potatoes, turnips, and carrots, the family reentered the ghetto, figuring now that the three-day Action had come to a conclusion, they would be just as safe there as anywhere else, perhaps even safer. They returned to the same apartment they left just five days earlier and found it deserted. No words were necessary. It was clearly obvious that the other two couples previously sharing the apartment with them had been a part of the selection and had been taken away.

As rumors of the completion of the Action started to spread, thousands of Jews who had been sequestered in the surrounding vicinity began to arrive at the ghetto. The majority of those who had been in hiding in small communities came out of their seclusion and cautiously made their way through the gates and into what they hoped would provide at least a small degree of safety.

A German named Schomburg, the chief Gestapo officer in Bochnia, realized that the ghetto needed to quickly replenish its supply of forced labor. As a result he published and distributed special permits for all the arriving Jews who came out of hiding allowing them the privilege of living in the ghetto and working as slave laborers for the Third Reich. The workshops which had been closed for more than a week were reopened and production began anew. Where once they had two thousand workers they now swelled to more than three thousand. Over a short period of time the population of Bochnia increased to nearly eight thousand, far exceeding that which they had prior to the Action and selection.

Hershel and the two older boys received their special permits and continued the same work patrols they had been toiling on in the past. Moniek, still being too young, continued to wait on the street for the truck to stop each day, hoping he'd be selected and be able to provide some simple amount of food for the family.

The day was like any other late summer day, uncomfortably warm. Before he left that morning Hershel patted Moniek on top of his head and wished him a good day. He also, as was the normal routine, told him to be very careful. Feigel as well, wished him the same. Moniek said goodbye to his mother and, like so many other days, he walked down the street to the same spot where the truck usually stopped to pick him up on Leonardo Street, one hundred fifty feet away from where his mother stood.

But when the truck roared to a halt it was strangely different from all the others in the past. This particular truck did not have the familiar sign reading, "workers" on its side. It was completely unmarked. Moniek felt a queasy feeling beginning to swell up in the pit of his stomach but couldn't figure out why. A gruff looking soldier with a beard of stubble sitting on the passenger side of the cab shouted at Moniek, "Get in the back! Now!"

Moniek, without thinking anything of it, did exactly as he was instructed. The truck pulled away from the curb, filled with others who believed they were on their way to be deposited at various work locations where they would perform miscellaneous duties, be paid a few scraps of bread for their efforts, and later that afternoon return to whatever was left of their families.

The truck didn't stop at any of the regular places it had previously. It moved down the road past the fine houses Moniek had worked in and the storage areas where ammunition was kept. The queasy feeling deepened dramatically but he still couldn't understand why. Increasing speed the truck roared into the countryside, passing farms and fields filled with laborers. Moniek thought, perhaps today they're going to have us work in the fields. But the truck kept on moving, past fields, past forests, with no apparent destination in sight.

Moniek looked at the others riding in the rear of the truck and his eyes asked the question, "What's going on?" He was answered with a series of unknowing shrugs. And the truck continued to rumble on into the unknown.

Already he began to miss his family. Turning around, as the truck sped through the countryside, he could feel the presence of his mother and father and brothers, almost as if they were with him, sitting beside him. I'll come back to them, he thought, with a story of the day's adventure, with food in my pocket and we'll be together. It's little enough, but so long as we're together, we have all we need. He couldn't imagine being apart from them. They were his whole world.

NINETEEN

THE THIRD REICH'S MASTER plan for the elimination of all European Jewry was clearly defined and well-established long before Germany attacked Poland in September of 1939 and purposely began the tragic devastation of what was to become universally known as World War II.

The initial stage of the Nazi occupation concerned itself with denying the Jewish population of any benefits of the Polish economy. Money and possessions were randomly stolen, travel was restricted and eventually eliminated, businesses were confiscated at will, and houses were occupied by the Nazis. The entire Jewish population was virtually isolated from the general population. Where once they lived in relative harmony with their neighbors, they were now forced to be outsiders in their own community.

The SS engaged in senseless killing, the plundering of property, desecration and destruction of synagogues, and forbidding any religious practices. Their goal was to eliminate all traces of Jewish culture and history. Leaders and teachers and those considered to be intellectuals mysteriously disappeared.

There was a constant wave of deportations which served to undermine the morale of the people, drain their physical, mental, and moral strength, take away the last remnants of material security, and rob the Jews of their dignity and hope. By these acts, the Nazis assumed wrongfully, that the Jews would just leave on their own.

Moniek remembered those days well. The two events which stood out most in his young mind were the facts that his education was halted and he was no longer allowed to go to school, and also that the Nazis forced his father to cease his business operations. This alone caused enormous hardships on the family. For the first time in his life he had experienced not only the confusion of isolation and brutality without any justification whatsoever but also the pain of hunger.

The second stage of the German occupation was the establishment of ghettos. Their initial justification for this practice was twofold: to "protect" the Jews from the hostile local Aryan population and to protect the Aryan population from diseases and epidemics of which the Jews were the alleged carriers. By accomplishing the second stage the Germans had shut the Jews off from the outside world and placed them in the position of being easy prey for persecution, deportation, or brutal murder.

These days as well were deeply imbedded in Moniek's mind. Escaping into the forest for countless weeks, always hiding, moving every night from place to place, sleeping on the ground, and eating nothing but raw vegetables and berries. He remembered how difficult it had been for his mother and how badly he felt for her, always wishing he could do more. He remembered Mrs. Klein and Rachel and how kind they had been to them providing shelter and warm bread and cool water.

He also clearly remembered sneaking into the ghetto, living with nine other people crammed within the confines of a small apartment, working for the first time in his life, and honestly knowing what it was like to experience real hunger. Then there was the first major Action followed by the selection and thousands of people just disappeared by truck or train. Yes, Moniek was all too aware of the second stage of the German occupation. The sights, sounds, and feelings of the ongoing atrocity would never go away. They were permanently embedded.

Now the truck carrying an unknowing Moniek and the others was taking him toward the third and final stage of the occupation: the camps. By this time the Nazis had constructed camps of every imaginable description and name. There were Concentration Camps, Forced Labor Camps, Educational Work Camps, Jewish Camps, Jewish Work Camps, Community Camps, Prisoner Camps, Civilian Camps, Temporary Camps, Special Camps, Jewish Transfer Camps, Jewish Labor Camps, Exportation Camps, and many others.

Most of the major camps were supported by a series of subcamps in their surrounding area, sometimes as many or more than fifty different ones, each holding even more prisoners. Dachau, the first forced labor camp established by the Nazis, had more than one hundred subcamps which provided an assortment of munitions, clothing, food, and miscellaneous items to support the German war machine. The non-Jews who lived near or around the camps closed their eyes to the entire situation. It was as if the camps didn't exist or weren't even there. As towns, villages, and ghettos in the entirety of the occupied areas were emptied, their occupants were sent to various camps, the vast majority of them never to be seen again.

As a result of Goebbels remarkably effective propaganda machine thousands and thousands of people were so convinced the transports were taking them to resettlement areas and a life of freedom that they actually purchased tickets. They would stand in long lines at the train stations, chatting casually with others as fortunate as they, and discuss with great hope the brightness of their upcoming future. There was seldom any violence from the SS or soldiers at those particular stations. The Germans wanted everyone to remain as calm as possible so during the trip they would report back to friends concerning the fair treatment they were receiving and then others would purchase subsequent tickets and follow their lead.

When the whistle blew the people handed their passes to a German soldier and boarded the trains carrying as much with them as was humanly possible. The Jews carried treasured family heirlooms and items which would assist them in their trades or businesses as they began their lives in some distant, unknown place. Some carried sewing machines, others took tools of every imaginable configuration, there were scissors and other barbering equipment, pots and pans of every size and variety, a complete plethora of equipment. The vast majority of the possessions they brought with them were functional and in excellent working condition.

Within three days, at the very most, none of these people who had just paid handsomely for their own passage would ever see any of their possessions again.

As the truck slowed Moniek leaned over the side and looked up ahead. He saw a series of long buildings, side by side, most constructed of rough, unfinished lumber. The ground surrounding the buildings was hard caked dirt. There was no grass. In the distance he could see what appeared to be a town of some sort and they had trees there. *I hope that's where they're taking us,* he thought to himself.

The truck pulled through a large, wire, swinging gate and entered the compound. As they passed through the gate he could hear a low buzzing sound emanating in the air. "What's that sound?" he whispered to the man seated beside him.

"The wires," the man answered without emotion.

"I don't understand. Why would they make such a noise?"

"They're electrified. If you touch them, you'll die." The man looked straight ahead and didn't utter another word.

Moniek shivered at the thought and looked straight ahead as well. There were actually two rows of wires, separated by about six feet and each more than eight feet tall. A ditch filled with water ran between the two buzzing strands. As he looked in the distance it appeared that the fence went on for a very long way. Moniek resolved himself to the unpleasant idea that this was going to be the location for his work detail today. However, with an absolute certainty he looked forward to returning to the warmth and safety of his family later that evening. He also hoped desperately that he would not be selected for this detail again anytime in the near future.

The truck eased its way up a small incline and Moniek saw a group of four men struggling desperately as they carried a large and obviously heavy wooden carton. What caught his attention was that these men were wearing matching shirts, pants, and caps. The garb was striped, gray and blue. He turned to the man seated next to him but quickly decided not to say anything.

When the truck finally jerked to a halt soldiers lowered the rear tailgate and began to scream for them all to get out as quickly as possible. "*Raus! Raus!*" they shouted repeatedly. Moniek followed instructions along with the others but had a sense of confusion. He'd never experienced anything like this in Bochnia. In Bochnia he was dropped off in the morning, fulfilled his day's work at the assigned location, and returned to his family in the late afternoon. There was never any screaming and there certainly was never anything like the mass of soldiers holding rifles and pointing them at the new arrivals.

"Line up! Lines of five!" one of the soldiers shouted. "Quickly!" The new arrivals milled about, not really clear about what they were supposed to do. As the uncertainty continued for only a matter of seconds another soldier took a two foot long, wooden club and administered a mighty blow into the back of one of the new men. He dropped instantly to his knees, gasping for air, his eyes filled with bewilderment.

"Lines of five!" was repeated and this time there seemed to be no confusion. The order was instantly followed and still none of them had the faintest clue with reference to what was going on. Moniek, still remarkably innocent in the ways of cruelty the Nazis were capable of delivering, followed others as the lines were formed. Many of the men appeared to be frightened but Moniek was not. His natural curiosity dictated that he was considerably more interested in what was going on with all the people in striped suits walking to and fro, carrying things, and all the soldiers with guns.

"Forward!" another soldier shouted. Moniek thought it was somewhat unusual that for unknown reasons they seemed to yell all the time. There never appeared to be what would be considered a normal tone of voice. He wondered if they talked in that manner and volume when they were at home. Home, he thought, bringing an ever so slight smile to his face. Tonight I'll be home and all this will just be an interesting story for the others. He also thought that tomorrow he should probably look for another place to find work within the general area of Bochnia. As the columns of five marched forward he still had no idea where he was.

"Halt!" another soldier screamed. They were standing in front of a group of tables in what appeared to be a main courtyard of some sort. Construction was busily going on all around them. People were digging holes in the ground, pouring cement footers, raising walls for nondescript buildings, carrying long strips of lumber from open-sided rail cars located at the railroad tracks which ran near the front gate. It was logical for young Moniek to assume that this would be the crux of his day's work. Then, when his work was finished he would receive a few pieces of bread for his efforts and have some remarkable stories to share with his family.

The soldier screamed, "First five! Move to the table!" Moniek happened to be in the front group and did as instructed, anxious to get away from all the people with all the guns and just complete his work assignment and get it over with for the day.

He moved forward to a table where a man wearing one of the striped uniforms sat in a wooden chair. His middle-aged face was strangely blank, lifeless, and his shoulders were stooped over. Moniek looked side to side and following what the others were doing, brought himself to a rigidly straight position of attention.

"Name?" the lifeless man asked.

"Moniek Ebner."

The man, without looking up, wrote it down on a form. As Moniek was to learn, the Germans were fanatical concerning keeping records of virtually everything.

"Address?"

There was a slight hesitation and Moniek finally replied, "Well…I guess I still live in Nowy Wisnicz."

"Unlikely." The man muttered, still with no emotion or concern whatsoever. "Age?"

"Thirteen and a half," Moniek said. And now the man looked up. Then he looked from side to side to make sure they were out of earshot of the soldiers. For the first time his face registered a slight degree of compassion.

"You're Jewish, aren't you," the man stated quietly.

"Yes, sir," came the response, equally quiet.

"Faster! Hurry it up!" a soldier on the perimeter shouted.

The man looked deeply into Moniek's eyes and whispered, "I'm going to put down on the form that you're sixteen." He cautiously looked both ways again, returned his eyes to Moniek and said, "If anyone else ever asks how old you are tell them that you're sixteen. Do you understand?"

"Yes, sir," Moniek replied, but in truth he really didn't.

"Move!" a soldier shouted. "Over here!" Moniek followed the others as they moved to a nearby location where other men wearing striped clothing stuck what appeared to be a two-foot long metal wand down the front of each of their shirts, pressed a trigger, and released some sort of a powdery substance.

Moniek looked at the man beside him with eyes filled with wonder and even more confusion. The man looked back and shook his head at the youngster's naivety. "Delousing," was all the man said.

"For what?" Moniek questioned incredulously.

"For lice, kid," he answered in a matter-of-fact tone.

"I don't have any lice," Moniek replied with a sense of resolve and challenge.

"It's not for the ones you're bringin' in, kid. It's for the ones that are here."

"Over here!" another soldier shouted. The group was led to another area and reformed in lines of five, told to stand at attention, and waited. What did he mean, Moniek questioned. What did he mean about "the ones here"? It didn't make any sense. The powder which had been stuffed down the front of his shirt was now beginning to burn his chest.

Another soldier walked with absolute authority to the front of the group which now numbered close to thirty men. He stared at them as if they were pieces of dead meat, nothing more or less than a working labor force which was designed to assist the Third Reich in their total domination of the entire world. He looked like nearly all the rest of them. He was close shaven, had a well-trimmed haircut, and a uniform which fit perfectly. Indeed he was the textbook classic German doing his duty for the Fatherland.

The soldier held a clipboard and read off a series of names. Moniek's was among those called out. When the man finished he added, "You people whose names have been called have each been assigned to block 24. You will be escorted there and receive further instructions. Remember one thing clearly, you are now a part of group 150. Do not forget that number. After roll call and the morning count you are to report to this exact same spot for your work detail. Failure to do so will result in extreme punishment."

The soldier moved away and another replaced him, taking the clipboard and placing it under his arm. By waving his gun he made it crystal clear that the new arrivals were to follow him. Moniek walked along with the others but felt as if he had been strangely transposed into a different dimension. What on earth could that soldier have possibly meant when he said, "Report back here in the morning"? It didn't make any sense at all. *I'm going home tonight,* he thought to himself. *I'm supposed to go back to my family.*

Moniek looked to his right where he saw an open cart being slowly pulled down the street by two men wearing the unusual striped uniforms. The rear of the cart had four bodies piled unceremoniously on top of each other, all unmoving, all lifeless. Moniek's mouth fell open. It was the first time he had ever seen a dead person and it was understandably disturbing. The men pulling the wagon performed their duties as if it was just "business as usual." They each had hollow eyes and noncaring faces.

What is this place? Moniek asked himself. *Where am I? What's going on? All I want to do is put in a full day's work and then go home to my family.* The column arrived at block 24 and was instructed to enter, go to the front of the room, and stand at attention. The soldier handed the clipboard to another man and remained outside. The column of new arrivals did as instructed and waited. The interior of the barrack was quite large, probably thirty feet wide by close to seventy-five feet long. Wooden bunks, three tiers high, protruded from each side wall. Moniek noticed that they didn't look very comfortable but his primary thought was that this growing nightmare must be some sort of a mistake. He certainly wasn't supposed to be here.

Several of the men shuffled from side to side, foot to foot, whispering to one another, questioning their fate. "Shut up!" The voice was very loud, very booming, and very powerful. It belonged to the man who was standing outside the block and had been given the clipboard just moments earlier. "There will be no talking in my block unless I permit it. If you don't understand that I'll beat it into you with my stick." The man stared at the new arrivals with eyes that could pierce steel. He had a nasty looking scar on his right cheek that traversed from the bottom of his eye nearly down to his chin.

"My name is Feder," he announced with authority. "You will all address me as *Mr.* Feder. Failure to do so will result in instant and severe punishment. Do you clearly understand me?"

The men nodded in unison, their eyes fixed straight ahead. Moniek followed their lead automatically but was still enormously confused. *This is all wrong,* he thought to himself. *I'm supposed to go home tonight. Why are they keeping me here? I've done nothing wrong.*

"I'm your block senior," Feder continued in a gravelly voice. "When you're in here you will do exactly as I say. There will be no exceptions. I make the rules and if they're not followed to the letter you will pay dearly." After letting the words sink in and closely studying his new charges he began to slowly pace back and forth in front of them, looking for potential troublemakers. Each time he made eye contact the man on the receiving end of the glare lowered his own eyes toward the floor.

"You are now in a work camp called Plaszov. You are also some of the first arrivals and will be used extensively for construction purposes for others who will follow shortly."

Moniek had never heard of Plaszov, nor had most of the others. Rumors had circulated throughout the area that a labor camp was being built in close proximity to the city of Krakow but no one could substantiate them with first-hand knowledge.

Moniek only half-heard the information. He was completely involved in and consumed with a distant world of his own. If only Tata were there. Tata would know what to do, he always did. Always.

"For those of you who are not yet aware, the fences surrounding the camp are electrified. If you touch them you will die a very painful death. Believe me, I've seen it happen many times since the power was turned on. If you try in any way to escape from the camp you will be shot without any questions being asked. Do exactly what you're told and your life will be reasonably tolerable."

Feder passed out spoons and tin bowls to each of the new arrivals, instructing them they were to keep the items with them at all times. If they lost the spoons or bowls it was very simple, they just wouldn't eat. They would not be replaced. Even though his stomach was grumbling Moniek had little thought of food. His only thought was getting away from this place and going home.

Each person was then assigned a bunk which was to remain theirs as long as they were in the barrack. Feder looked down at the names on the clipboard. "Ebner," he said without feeling. Moniek stepped forward and was given a top bunk near the rear of the building. He walked toward the bunk in a state of complete disarray. The questions, why is this happening and how can I get out of here, would not leave his mind. He stared at the ersatz bed composed of little more than wooden slats and hoped that somehow the Germans would realize the incredible mistake they'd made and send him home.

"How old are you, kid?" It was a soft voice from another new arrival. The question was asked flatly, without emotion or any real concern.

Moniek hesitated but only for a brief second. Then he responded, "Sixteen."

The other man nearly broke into a smile. "No, you're not," he said quietly and with a degree of certainty. "You can't be more than fifteen if you're that."

"I'm sixteen."

The man looked around — it was a common trait. "Look, kid, I don't care how old you are. But I'll tell you what, you keep tellin' anybody who asks that you're sixteen and stick to it. Anybody who's younger than that doesn't last very long around here."

"I don't understand."

"Kids can't work. They send them all somewhere else. Nobody knows where. And they never come back. Just keep sayin' you're sixteen." The man moved away toward his own assigned bunk. As Moniek watched him walk down the aisle he reflected on the stranger behind the table when he first arrived earlier that day. In all probability the information which had been offered had proven to be life saving.

Darkness fell and the inhabitants of block 24 received a lukewarm bowl of foul-tasting turnip soup and nothing else. They ate in silence. Feder gruffly warned them again concerning the quiet he demanded and the penalty for violating his rules. The majority of the new inhabitants, including Moniek, crawled slowly into their bunks. They would not experience the comfort of blankets, mattresses, or pillows. They slept on the bare wooden slats.

After nearly a full year of sleeping on the wooden floor in the cramped apartment in Bochnia, Moniek, unlike many of the others, found a comfortable position. He used his jacket as a pillow and closed his eyes, pretending this whole thing was all some sort of a bad dream which would end at any moment.

Sleep would not come as he thought about his parents and how concerned they must certainly be by his absence. All he wanted to do was to go home, to be with his family. But reality dictated that wasn't going to occur this very night. *Perhaps tomorrow,* he thought. *Perhaps tomorrow they'll realize the mistake they've made and send me home to my family.* He tried his best to hold that thought but deep in his being he somehow knew that was not going to be the case.

As others in the barrack began to snore and make other vile sounds, Moniek could not sleep. For the first time since he could remember tears began to fall from his eyes. He wanted to be a man, the man his father had professed him to be. He wanted the tears to stop. But they would not. Most of all, he just wanted to go home, to be with his mother and father and brothers. He had never been separated from them before.

TWENTY

THE LONG TRAINS MAJESTICALLY flying the dreaded swastika flags on the front of their engines carrying the Jews who had purchased tickets for their own passage to a better way of life arrived in isolated places with names such as Auschwitz-Birkenau, Chelmno, Majdanek, Sobibor, Treblinka, and Belzec. None of the passengers had any idea where they were or what they were doing there. They clutched their precious belongings close to their chests and smiled nervously at one another.

They were instructed to exit the trains and place all their belongings and possessions on the railway siding. While many were hesitant to leave their luggage and everything else they owned, they were assured that it would all be returned to them later that same day. However, those who had experienced life in any of the ghettos knew that the Germans seldom kept their word. Nazi promises most always proved to be totally empty, without any sense of reality whatsoever. But there were many soldiers with many guns. Several of the soldiers restrained large, snarling German shepherd dogs on thick leather leashes, obviously eager to sink their gleaming teeth into the waiting skin of the new arrivals.

The majority of the people reluctantly did as they were instructed. The few who had the nerve to refuse were "nudged" along with the barrel of a rifle placed uncomfortably into the center of their backs.

Following this came a "selection." The new arrivals who were capable of working were separated from those who could not. As more and more of the people voiced their objections it was clearly and calmly explained that the ones who were going to be working were being taken to their new quarters so they could get settled in. The others, mostly women, the children, and the elderly, were going to a special area where they would all be provided with a nice warm shower.

Since this seemed reasonable and logical whatever grumbling which existed ceased and the people walked away in opposite directions, waving to each other, expecting to see their loved ones again soon.

When the columns were each out of sight trucks appeared at the railroad siding. Prisoners wearing striped uniforms climbed down from the rear of the trucks and began to collect the possessions which had been left on the ground. Every single piece of luggage, every sewing machine, every tool, every sack of food, everything, was thrown into the rear of the trucks and when the task was completed they fired up their engines and lumbered away.

Their precious and priceless possessions were all transported to large, open warehouses normally located outside the wires of the main camps where other prisoners would then sort through everything which had been accumulated and separate the items by category.

All German banknotes discovered were sent to the Reich Bank. Other foreign currency, gold, jewelry, and other valuables were sent to the SS Headquarters of the Economic Administration. Watches, clocks, and pens were distributed to troops in the front. Clothing was distributed to German families.

Much of the clothing was purposely torn apart by the prisoners in the collection warehouses because many items of great value were sewn into their linings for what the owner hoped would be safekeeping. These were items such as paper money and especially jewelry, most often in the form of loose diamonds. Many of these items were smuggled into the interior of the camps and were traded regularly on flourishing black markets where nearly anything was available for a price.

Inasmuch as the Nazis were fanatical concerning all sources of record keeping it was determined that by February of 1943 more than eight hundred boxcars filled with confiscated goods and materials had left Auschwitz and made their way toward Germany. Eight hundred boxcars filled with possessions stolen from the Jews made their way into the German economy — all this from just one camp.

A shrill, piercing bell shattered the stillness of the early morning hour. It was still pitch-black outside. Moniek sat straight up in his bunk, wondering what was going on, shaking the unpleasant cobwebs out of his head before sadly remembering where he was. He'd dozed on and off during the night, dreaming of home and his parents, jerking suddenly awake, then falling back asleep for just a few moments. He was still very tired.

"Outside! Rows of ten! Stand at attention!" It was *Mr.* Feder from the front of the barrack, once again screaming. The men all began to move quickly from their bunks toward the front door, not wishing to bear the wrath of Feder's stick. Moniek followed their lead and exited the room into the darkness of the morning. Once outside the men, now numbering more than one hundred, did their best to form the lines as ordered. After Feder joined them and administered several heavy blows to those who seemed confused, the task was accomplished with little further delay. They stood in silence, at attention, ten men to a line.

An SS man wearing a black uniform arrived, took the ever-so-important clipboard from Feder and studied it. They shared a brief, muffled conversation and then together walked down the rows of men counting each row carefully. Then they counted them again. The entire process took more than thirty minutes. The Nazis would not even consider the possibility of anyone ever escaping. They were completely able to shoot anyone who attempted such an unspeakable thing. While it was no longer a general topic of conversation between the German soldiers most still retained the thought, "Why didn't the stupid Jews just leave when they had the chance."

On the other hand, if the entire, sprawling system of camps throughout Europe had not been established, the soldiers who guarded them would no doubt have been at the front in a deadly and bloody shooting war. Guard duty was considered by the majority to be a plum assignment, one which was highly desired and once achieved seldom relinquished unless by direct order. In far too many cases their value to the Reich was judged by the amount and degree of brutality they were able to administer. Via their misplaced obedience to equally mind-numbed higher-ups they showed little if any mercy to the people confined inside the wires.

The SS man placed his signature on the clipboard, handed it back to Feder, and walked away into the darkness. Feder added his own initials to the form and announced, "The latrine is down there." He pointed. "You'll recognize it by the smell. You have fifteen minutes and if you're not back you won't get any breakfast." With that he returned to the barrack.

Moniek thought sadly about days long past when Feigel would prepare fine large breakfasts for him and his father and his brothers. He hoped from the bottom of his heart that they were all all right and not too overly concerned about his whereabouts. He was still hopeful that somehow the great mistake would be discovered and he'd be on his way home to a wonderful family reunion. He missed them terribly.

In this strange place he was not about to take the lead so he waited for others to begin the trek. The latrine was three barracks down the narrow road separating the barracks and Feder's description had been remarkably accurate. The stench from the building was appalling and actually sucked the breath from your lungs. The line of men waiting to enter was long, many of them choking and gagging from the smell. Some of them were throwing up uncontrollably on the road.

Moniek joined many of the others in the resounding chorus of coughing and choking and retching as he finally made his way into the latrine. He finished what needed to be done as quickly as possible and discovered that there was no toilet paper to be found. The Nazis were not about to waste anything of value on anyone as insignificant as a lowly Jew. In silence he walked with a few others back to his barrack for what he hoped would at least be a decent meal.

The decent meal consisted of a half a bowl full of watered down coffee made with an indescribable and foul smelling liquid. As Moniek sat on the edge of his bunk and slowly sipped the strange concoction he escaped in the thought of the first time he'd ever tasted coffee with his father that frigid morning at Mr. Cohen's farm. The pleasant memory was shattered as Feder began to yell at the top of his voice, "Outside! Everyone! Line up for work patrols!"

Moniek eased himself down to the floor, remembering to take his bowl and spoon with him, and exited the building. Once outside he waited for further instructions until a soldier approached and announced that all the members of group 150 were to follow him. Without thought Moniek did as he was told and he, along with nine others, walked down the street, still well before the sun would rise in the sky.

They marched in unison, two lines of five, to an area near the main gate where Moniek had entered only a day before but what now seemed like an eternity. He looked through the gate, now bustling with activity, people moving in and out, illuminated by brilliant floodlights, and desperately wanted to be on the other side of the wires. He was certainly not alone in his feelings.

When they reached their designated work area the group stopped and without instruction each were handed either a pickax or a shovel. They just stood there, confused, afraid to do anything until they were told exactly what to do.

A remarkably thin man wearing a striped uniform pointed at the ground. "Dig!" he commanded. And the men on the work patrol followed his orders. Those with picks swung them and broke the hard ground. Those with shovels picked up the dirt and threw it to another area. It was still dark and the new arrivals had no idea where they were or what they were doing.

As the sun slowly rose over the horizon the question was painfully answered. The work patrol was in the middle of a cemetery, destroying grave markers and exhuming buried bodies. It was a ghoulish thought and an even more ghoulish act. But there were soldiers standing nearby, all with guns. Moniek could tell from the names on the markers that they were desecrating a Jewish cemetery. Out of extreme pain and embarrassment he decided that he wouldn't tell his parents about this heinous act. It was too disgusting to ever mention to anyone.

A large tractor-like machine roared into their midst. It had hooks on the front of it and looked basically like a backhoe, normally used for digging purposes. Moniek stared at the strange looking contraption with bewilderment clearly covering his face. The man standing next to him gently poked him in the ribs and quietly said, "It's a 'bugger.'"

"What's a 'bugger'?" Moniek asked.

"You'll see. Just watch."

The machine moved forward and one by one picked up the grave markers with little or no effort, ripping them from the earth, and deposited them into a nearby wagon with a thud of finality. Moniek could not believe his own eyes but his astonishment was brought to an abrupt halt as the man wearing the striped uniform once again pointed toward the earth and shouted, "Dig!"

They followed instructions, digging deeper and deeper into the ground. Now there were open wagons placed beside the work areas and all excavated dirt was thrown into those and hauled away. As each wagon was filled up it was immediately replaced by another. This was to be the work detail for the day but the persistent thought remained that somehow, some way, when work was completed he'd receive a few scraps of bread and return to his family in the Bochnia ghetto. It was his driving, consuming thought, the only thing which kept him going.

There was a very loud *thunk*. Moniek lifted up his shovel and stood back, staring down at the loosened earth at his feet. He'd hit something very hard in the ground and wasn't quite sure what to do. The order, "Dig!" was again shouted directly toward him. And dig he did. What he discovered was disturbing to say the least. It was a leg bone, a human leg bone. Not all that long ago people were normally buried without the benefit of caskets. Sometimes they were wrapped in an ornate burial cloth. Other times the body was just presented to the earth. Moniek had just unearthed one of those bodies and his stomach was in a knot, retching from the experience.

"I said, dig! Get those bones out of there!"

With enormous trepidation Moniek picked up the leg bone and with a look of pure disbelief on his face showed it to the man doing the screaming. "Don't show it to me," the man said. "Throw it in the wagon." And he did. "Get the rest of them out of there! This area has to be cleared!" The balance of the work patrol stood by, silently watching the exchange. The man spun and with a rage shouted, "The rest of you, get back to work! Now!" And they did.

Moniek gingerly cleared the grave of the rest of the bones, carefully tossing the remains on the wagon, sick to his stomach, on the verge of throwing up. He'd never really been in a cemetery before. Less than twenty-four hours earlier he'd observed up close the first dead person he'd ever seen in his life and now this. It was all nearly too much for someone his age. He was thirteen and a half and had seen and experienced more despair and tragedy in the last day than the average person does in a lifetime.

This unpleasant exercise filled his remaining morning hours, grave to grave. Digging up one set of bones after another. Each time he tenderly touched one of the bones it seemed as if a small chunk of his own heart had been somehow painfully removed. He clearly remembered his late afternoons and evenings studying the Torah with the rabbi in Nowy Wisnicz and tried his best to offer a small prayer not only for the remains of those he was being forced to desecrate but also himself for the very act he was perpetrating. There was no justification for what he was doing. However, it was an absolute certainty that failure to follow orders would have no doubt resulted in extreme, violent punishment or even worse.

Lunch that very first day in Plaszov consisted of another half-full bowl of the foul tasting and foul smelling turnip soup. The workers sat on the edge of one of the graves they had just excavated, their legs hanging into the now empty crevice. By listening carefully to muted conversations from some of the men who had been there for awhile Moniek learned that parts of the Plaszow work camp were actually constructed on the grounds of two sacred Jewish cemeteries. They were both being completely destroyed so that additional barracks could be constructed to hold additional workers. Sadly, he was far too young to realize the extremity of that statement and that act. He just sat quietly and listened as the others talked in muted tones among themselves. Plaszow was actually within the Krakow city limits, on a site comprising the two Jewish cemeteries, community property, and the private property of Polish citizens who had been evicted.

He also discovered that the grave markers ripped from the ground by the "bugger" machine were actually taken away from the cemetery and used as foundations for either sidewalks or roads both inside the camp and around the city of Krakow. Roads upon which the German soldiers would march. Roads upon which German machines and equipment and armaments would traverse. It was a horrendous thought.

He also gleaned from the whispered conversations that Plaszow was a large place and growing at an alarming pace. The camp had numerous production barracks which housed various workshops, storage areas, and administration facilities. There was a tannery, a harness shop, a building for tailors, knitting shops, carpentry shops, and a large kitchen which to date, in his limited experience, had not produced any real edible food.

Jews confined to the camp also worked in other facilities outside the wires including a large cable factory in the town itself, a brickyard in nearby Rakowice, and other companies located in Zablocie. Others worked in arms factories in the nearby subcamps of Mauthausen and Gross-Rosen. The workers were marched to their various assignments by a contingent of armed guards, watched closely all day long, and then marched back to the camp under the same armed supervision.

There was another factory in town which was in very close proximity to the front gate of the camp. A very special factory, the company name was Emalia. The facility which produced enamel goods in the form of pots and pans was initially owned by Jewish businessmen but was confiscated by the Nazis when the Germans occupied Poland. Later they converted the operation to manufacture mess kits for the German army.

It was commonplace that when businesses and especially manufacturing facilities were taken over by the Nazis they were sold at bargain basement, dirt-cheap prices to industrialists who could produce needed items for the ever-continuing growth and needs of the war machine. And always at a price which was acceptable to the Germans. In virtually all cases Jewish forced labor was used to keep the facilities producing. As such, factory Emalia was sold to an ethnic German who had wined, dined, and entertained nearly all of the higher-ups in the Reich throughout the surrounding area. He did his homework well and it paid off quite handsomely.

The stranger, who was born in 1908 and grew up as a child of privilege in Austria-Hungary, had become both the coveted friend and the darling of the Nazis. As such he was accorded great lenience in both his business and hiring practices. His name was Oskar Schindler and his life was chronicled many years later in a riveting book written by Thomas Keneally. That enormously powerful book later became the basis of Steven Spielberg's Oscar-winning film, *Schindler's List.*

Twenty-One

After the Jewish families were separated, marched in different directions and all of their earthly possessions hauled away to warehouses for redistribution, the trains left their various sidings on their way to pick up more unsuspecting and innocent passengers. Goebbels' plan of alleged resettlement had proven to be remarkably successful and thousands upon thousands of people had contributed to the German war effort and, in the process, tragically signed their own warrants of death.

Those deemed able for work were assigned to various barracks remarkably similar in size and design to the one in which Moniek was presently residing. They went through a series of indoctrinations with reference to camp rules and were calmly reassured that they would be reunited with both their families and their possessions later that day. It was yet another Nazi lie.

The balance of the train passengers, most of the women, all the children, the old, the frail, and the sick, were marched or transported by trucks to areas which were always on the outskirts of the camp, sometimes even outside the wires. Once there they were led into a changing area, told to remove their clothing, hang them on hooks on the wall, and remember where they were so they could be retrieved when the shower was completed.

It was common for soft, soothing music to be playing on loudspeakers throughout the enclosure. While many objected to disrobing in front of others, especially total strangers, they were assured that this was an absolute necessity before they would be reunited with their families. The Nazis also told them the showers were for their own health purposes as well as that of the entire camp. Children began to whimper and cry and mothers did their very best to calm them. "Everything's going to be fine," was a frequently offered phrase, passed from mother to child.

Generally men wearing the striped uniforms and exhibiting blank, sad faces would assist those who needed help and directed them into the communal shower area. Few if any words were exchanged. The men were aware of what they were doing and what fate awaited those expecting a nice, warm shower. Many of them painfully bit their tongues and the inside of their cheeks, wanting to scream out warnings of what was to come. But they knew that by doing so would only have created an unnecessary panic within the confines of the room and most likely would cause their own deaths. The people taking off their clothing were doomed and there wasn't anything anyone could do or say to save them. Let them go as peacefully as possible was the tragic but universally accepted mindset.

Once the assembled multitude was inside the shower area a thick metal door was closed and securely locked. The men looked at one another with a sense of desperation and resolve. They'd performed this most horrific task often enough that tears would no longer come to their eyes. One shook his head slowly from side to side and slowly offered to no one in particular, "The children are the worst. No matter what, I'll never understand that."

Another man softly answered. His words seemed to come from a place far away and expressed a combination of hatred mixed with enormous sadness. "Hitler," the man quietly said. "Hitler not only wants to kill all of us, he has to kill all the children so there will never be any more Jews."

The other men nodded and slowly left the area, realizing based on what they had seen while working at this particular work patrol that the statement was painfully accurate.

Two soldiers made their way across the roof of the shower area, each carrying a bag. As they did so the inhabitants of the shower area tried desperately but in vain to turn on the nozzles of what they all expected would be warm refreshing water. They were packed into the area body to body. Many were embarrassed. Then, when no water appeared, most of them became frightened. The soldiers on the roof opened canisters and emptied green pellets into the air ducts.

When the Zyklon-B came in contact with the open air its poisonous gasses were instantly released. The women, children, old, and frail began to gasp for air but there was none to be had. Then the screams began. Screams for precious air. Screams for life itself. But no one was there to care about their screams.

The men wearing the striped uniforms heard them. They heard them several times a day for days on end. As the screaming continued the men collected all of the clothing left behind on hooks hanging on the wall. It would all be redistributed into the German economy. Very little was wasted. Except life.

Within fifteen to twenty minutes the screaming thankfully ceased. Large fans were turned on which forced the remaining poisonous gas out of the area and into the relative safety of the atmosphere outside. The shower area now contained little more than a pile of naked, dead bodies, all Jews. The most unpleasant work for the time being was done. Done at least until the next train filled with those seeking safety and security arrived.

Within the short span of that fifteen to twenty minute timeframe, Hitler, Eichmann, Goebbels, Goering, Heydrich, Himmler, and their minions and followers had routinely eliminated more than one thousand Jews in cold blood. Tragically this procedure was repeated over and over, night and day, day and night, in each of the six specifically acknowledged extermination camps throughout Poland.

The mistake Moniek so desperately hoped would be discovered unfortunately never materialized. His days turned into nights and then even more days into more nights. The weeks evolved into months and not a day passed that he didn't think often about his family and how much he wanted to be with them. For the most part he kept to himself, remembering the lesson Hershel taught him in the ghetto: don't get too close to anyone outside the family. It was a well-learned lesson in that often during his work patrol or even worse, in the dead of night, people would just mysteriously disappear and were never seen again. It was his thoughts of his wonderful family that kept him going and kept him hopeful. He knew that, someday, they would all be together again. This thought kept him alive, day after day.

He continued to toil at the increasingly depressing job of exhuming bodies in the cemetery during the relentless, driving, late fall rains which chilled the air and cut through to the very bone. Each evening following the work detail Moniek would return to his barrack covered with mud from the day's task. Also, each evening, just like every single morning, while standing at attention in lines of ten, there was a roll call and count.

Feder, with his ever-present clipboard and an SS man, were exacting and making absolutely sure all of the workers had returned. This exercise only served to add to Moniek's discomfort. Many evenings Moniek would make the most unpleasant trip to the latrine, the only nearby source of water, and clean himself as best as he could, remembering the times in the forest when at the insistence of his mother he'd done exactly the same thing.

The rains were not a deterrent to the constant construction going on within the camp. Barracks, roads, streets, factories, and workshops were built at a steady pace. Carpenters, bricklayers, locksmiths, electricians, and all construction workers were housed and sequestered in the same area. Moniek saw several people on a regular basis but words were seldom exchanged.

From his vantage point on his work patrol he could also see the front gate of the camp and the constant infusion of new people, new workers all. They came from everywhere, near and far, and spoke a myriad of languages. None of them were prepared for what lay ahead of them.

As the brutal winter approached the effort of digging became increasingly difficult. Such minor details never bothered the Germans.

They were dressed in warm clothing with long woolen overcoats while Moniek and most of the others on his patrol still wore the very same clothing they had arrived with.

For all practical purposes the food in the camp remained the same, the weak, strange tasting coffee in the mornings and the turnip soup occasionally mixed with potatoes as an alternate for the other so-called meals. They were normally served with a small crust of bread which for some reason never seemed to be fresh. On very rare occasions Moniek and the others would receive small portions of cheese which never seemed to taste quite right or a miniscule sliver of horsemeat which didn't appear to be exactly the correct color and presented an unusual, pungent aroma. Whatever they were given was eaten without complaint. No food offered was ever returned.

Whenever Moniek tasted and thankfully devoured one of those oh-so-rare potatoes he recalled their final weeks in Nowy Wisnicz when they virtually lived on potatoes and the delightful, family-filled evenings prior to the Nazi occupation. The precious days when he would refuse to eat Feigel's delicious potato soup and the ever-patient father, knowing his trick all along, smiling to himself and paying him a few pennies to eat. They were fine childhood days which would never be forgotten. It was on these special days when Moniek tried his best to get any sort of a communication smuggled outside of the camp and to his parents. Sadly every attempt he made was unsuccessful.

The winter months proved to be exceptionally harsh. There was one small wood-burning stove in the center of the room which provided not nearly enough warmth to adequately heat the entire barrack. The men assigned to sleep in these chilling surroundings did whatever they had to do in order to survive. They stole clothing from the new arrivals. They smuggled in blankets and even sheets of paper from their various worksites to wrap themselves in during the cold winter nights. The miniscule portions of food, while obviously and certainly not abundant, proved to be barely adequate for most of the men and provided just enough energy for them to complete their work assignments.

During those first winter months no additional clothing was provided. All clothing confiscated by the Nazis was redistributed to families residing in Germany and if applicable to soldiers fighting on the Russian front. There was absolutely no concern for the workforce providing the very backbone of their war machine. Without exception all Jews and workers were expendable at any time and for any reason. They were still considered to be subhuman.

Camp block seniors, normally referred to as kapos, all possessed the capacity for remarkable brutality and unquestioned authority to administer punishment. Many of them were former political prisoners who had been transferred from prisons in Germany and were already intimately familiar with incarceration. Their new positions gave them power and privilege. They were given extra food rations and had the capability to steal whatever they wanted from anyone staying in their barrack. Because of the responsibility they assumed the kapos were also excused from work patrols. Moniek was most fortunate in that *Mr.* Feder seemed to have a somewhat reasonable temperament and only expressed any degree of violence when in the presence of an SS man, and then only for the purpose of impressing the Nazi that he indeed was doing an acceptable job.

However, for the most part, Plaszow seemed to have a little less extreme violence than other camps, though Moniek had no way to make a comparison. There were occasional beatings and miscellaneous punishment such as forcing men to stand outside at attention in the freezing temperatures until icicles formed on their extremities, which usually resulted in frostbite. Whenever this occurred the man was normally taken to the camp infirmary and never returned. Only the newcomers ever asked questions about such things and were generally met with blank stares or bland explanations such as, "You'll learn."

There was an open-air area called *Hujowa Gurka*, a sloping hill inside the wires but overlooking the rear of the camp. There were two sets of three large and sturdy four-by-four pieces of lumber planted deep into the ground and supporting a crossbar of another four-by-four beam about ten feet in the air. The space between the two holding poles on each end of the contraption was more than fifteen feet across. Hanging from the crossbar were nooses, nooses to be used to hold necks, as many as six of them at the same time. It was a hanging station for the ultimate punishment and fortunately Moniek had not witnessed the apparatus in action. A similar device was located near the front gate of the camp and equally fortunate, this one as well, to the best of Moniek's knowledge, had also not been utilized.

Via his longevity Moniek was now virtually considered to be an "old-timer." He'd been in the camp for several months and in that time, unlike the majority of the others, had never been beaten or punished for anything. For the most part he continued to stay to himself and never caused trouble or created any disturbances. He remained in the background, never asking anything of anyone, and just doing the job he was assigned to do.

It would have been logical to assume that because of his youthful appearance and relative naivete in the ways of the world, especially the ways of the new world in which they were being forced to exist, others would take advantage of him whenever possible. But quite the opposite proved to be the case. Because of his relative exuberance and willingness to do whatever was asked of him without complaint the others left the youngster alone and on rare occasions even offered words of encouragement.

Late one night, while the others were asleep and the barrack was quiet with the exception of the ever-present snoring and offensive noises, Moniek's lips began to move uncontrollably. He found himself whispering the very same prayer his father had offered the night they were hiding in the marketplace in Bochnia while escaping the first major selection of the ghetto. It was the prayer delivered for all, for their safety and well-being. Midway through the prayer the words ceased. They would no longer come.

It wasn't because he had forgotten the words. Rather, it was because he no longer believed the words or their power. The months of restricted confinement and painful separation from his family had diminished his faith. No facet of love or compassion existed anywhere in this place. Tears had fallen from his eyes the first few nights he was in the camp and then they stopped out of necessity. But this night the tears returned and he was embarrassed. He looked toward the roof of the barrack and whispered, "I'm sorry, Tata. I wish I were there to help you and mother and my brothers."

Moniek had lost his faith in everything...except his family, and his belief that they would all be together again.

Twenty-Two

Moniek's world had been altered dramatically over the last two and a half years. Traversing from an idyllic life in the peaceful town of Nowy Wisnicz, to one in which he was a virtual prisoner in his own home, to hiding in the forest and the shelter of a barn, ever conscious of German soldiers searching for them, to a cramped existence with strangers in a small apartment in the ghetto and severe food shortages, and now separated from his family and exiled to a forced labor camp. On February 11th, 1943, his life would be distorted further than he ever thought possible.

Prior to that date Plaszow had no official instructions or specific regulations for any of the people incarcerated there. The condition of their life was basically in the hands of their block senior and the kapo in charge of their work patrol. If those two people were reasonable and normal, not necessarily prone to abject violence, their life and existence could, considering the surroundings and the food allotted, be merely horrible...but it could get a great deal worse.

Moniek was one of the fortunate ones. Feder usually held his temper in check with the exception of when people violated his barrack rules or whenever he was trying to impress as SS man for the purpose of securing his own position. Strangely enough Moniek seemed to blend somewhat comfortably into the background. He did exactly what he was told, never bothered anyone, never caused any trouble, and never complained about anything. As a result, both Feder and his kapo on the work patrol never seemed to bother him and, more importantly, never caused him any physical harm.

Others were not anywhere near as lucky. Many of the block seniors and work patrol kapos took great pleasure in causing and inflicting pain. One such example was in a nearby granite quarry, one of two in the immediate area, where prisoners were forced to carry extremely heavy rocks removed from the ground and place them into waiting trucks. After two or three hours of such literally back-breaking work many would often collapse from sheer exhaustion. When that occurred it was not uncommon for the SS guards to beat them senseless, kick them mindlessly, and in many cases just kill them outright.

Even though these tragic events occurred on occasion both within the camp and in its surrounding confines, the constant threat of death and execution did not hang over the heads of most of the prisoners until February 11th when a new camp commandant arrived. His presence was not publicized to anyone residing in the camp but rumors, just like always, persisted. The "new man" was said to be an exceptionally vile person, capable of inhuman treatment the likes of which none of them had ever seen or could even comprehend.

The new commandant carried impressive credentials with him. He had previous experience in various management levels at three death camps in eastern Poland: Sobibor, Treblinka, and Belzec. Being placed completely in charge of a camp with the size, scope, and importance of Plaszow constituted an impressive promotion and was the pinnacle of his career. Those higher up in the Reich were impressed with what they judged to be his remarkable accomplishments and considered him to be a rising star.

Amon Leopold Goeth was born on February 11th, 1908, in Vienna, Austria. He came from a family that was well-established in the printing industry. At seventeen he joined a Nazi youth group.

Upon his arrival in Plaszow, Goeth summoned all of his senior officers together and made it crystal clear that he was now the one, the only, and the complete authority in the camp. He would issue all orders, make all the decisions, and had the first and last word in the selection of prisoners either for their life or death. At his insistence the camp speedily increased its construction and size. Additional grounds were added in order to house the soldiers who guarded the camp, the administration of the camp, the estate of the new commandant, and the residential quarters for the officers.

Moniek continued to labor on the same work patrol but the freezing February temperatures were taking their toll on many of the others. Like before, when they were too sick or frail to work, for whatever reason, and missed the morning roll call they were transported to the infirmary and never returned.

As soon as Goeth took over the management of the camp the conditions worsened dramatically and took on radical changes. The methods employed by the new commandant were characterized by completely willful administrating of brutal punishment and death. Executions became a part of the daily routine. At Goeth's insistence and encouragement people were beaten or shot for the slightest deviation from the new camp rules he had established. Sometimes, again at Goeth's insistence and encouragement, people were beaten or shot for no particular reason at all.

One evening, while returning to his barrack from yet another foul-smelling and gut-wrenching trip to the latrine, Moniek heard an unusual sound coming from an area between two nearby barracks. While the condition had mostly dissipated he still retained a small degree of the childlike curiosity which once consumed him and once even, in all probability, saved the lives of his entire family.

He eased his way around the corner of one of the buildings and could see the outline of a man lying on the ground, trying his best yet unsuccessfully to protect himself. Three Ukrainians in ill-fitting uniforms who worked for the Nazis as guards within the wires were beating the poor man without mercy with their two-foot-long wooden sticks.

Moniek felt as if his legs were frozen. He knew with a certainty that this was the wrong place to be. Even in the dim and muted light he could see blood coming out of the man's mouth and nose.

"Please," the man on the ground pleaded, barely able to talk, begging for his very life. "I didn't do anything..."

Before he could finish the sentence he was struck forcefully in his ribs with one of the lethal sticks, effectively capturing the last of his breath. "You're nothing but a dirty Jew!" the Ukrainian soldier shouted. "Worthless slime like you isn't going to live that much longer anyway!"

Another one added, "We're probably doing you a big favor." And the three of them laughed boisterously. Moniek slowly backed into the road, back into the mainstream of others returning to their barracks from their evening trip to the latrine.

At first he marched along in step with the others, slogging as best they could through the frozen mud beneath their feet, freezing their toes and ankles more and more with each step. Snow began to fall covering each of the men and the ground. It created a strangely peaceful picture of pristine white, a delightful contrast to the normal bland grayness of everything in the camp. But this night the cold and the accompanying snow, for reasons Moniek could not begin to understand or explain, didn't seem to bother him all that much. He moved faster in the column, passing others who looked at him with questioning eyes. He eased his way through row after row of men who were so remarkably weary from their daily work patrols that they could barely make the trek.

In his heart he felt like running but that was not allowed within the camp and if detected would most certainly bring forth harsh and painful repercussions. The last time he actually ran was when the family safely made their way through the Bochnia ghetto fence and into the livestock area of the market where they hid during the major selection which took countless people to places no one really wanted to know about.

Within moments Moniek reached his barrack, walked quietly to his bunk, staring at the floor, never making eye contact with anyone. This was not a difficult task in that few others were in a talkative mood. At this moment they were only interested in warmth. After he climbed up and wrapped his coat a little tighter around his neck he realized that the wanting to be as far away as possible from that horrible scene he'd just witnessed was motivated by fear. Fear was certainly not anything new. In this place it was something you sadly learned to live with on a daily basis. But Moniek had been strangely exempted from actually viewing such acts of brutality and savagery.

He closed his eyes but the words he'd heard just moments before would not leave his mind. "You're nothing but a dirty Jew." He repeated the phrase over and over. He'd heard the words before from a personal standpoint on several occasions but the time which stood out most clearly in his mind was the afternoon when he, his brothers, and a few of their friends were walking home from school. It was a day not unlike today. It was a crimson dusk and the sun was falling, a brisk cold temperature permeating the air. And then his good friend Jacob called him a dirty Jew which resulted in a fight which for all practical purposes meant little to anyone. That was just the way it was in Nowy Wisnicz so very long ago but it was certainly not the way it was in this place.

As he twisted and turned and finally fell asleep he felt a sad sense of remorse because try as he might he could not remember Jacob's last name. The good times, the peaceful times, the childhood times. They all seemed to be such a pleasant yet vague and rapidly fading memory.

No one in the camp was allowed to have a clock or a wristwatch. A timepiece of any variety was considered to be contraband and discovery would always result in extreme punishment. Nor were any calendars permitted which meant that the task of keeping track of days and even months had to be done for the most part by memory. The people interred in the camp knew when it was hot, when it was cold, when the sun came up, and when it went down. Other than that they had very little concept of time.

When Goeth arrived at Plaszow there were less than two thousand people in confinement. Under his direction more than one hundred people a day were steadily transferred from the Krakow ghetto into the camp. The majority of these new arrivals was assigned construction details and worked diligently through the freezing weather expanding the size of the camp for reasons none of them could begin to understand.

The reasons became explicitly clear to everyone on March 13th and 14th when Goeth, assisted by the SS, the Gestapo, and a large contingency of Ukrainian soldiers stormed the Krakow ghetto for the express purpose of liquidating it completely. Their rationale for this unexpected move was to transfer all its inhabitants into the camp where those who were able would be utilized as slave labor for the Nazis. The fate of those who couldn't work was undetermined.

Like Bochnia many people tried to hide or escape. The scene was remarkably similar to the one which transpired in Bochnia but on a considerably larger scale. The armed military swept through houses and apartment buildings, rounding up everyone, shooting in cold blood those who refused to leave or didn't move fast enough. The massacre, in essence, became sport to many of the sadists with the guns. Murder was indiscriminate. Age, sex, and physical condition had no bearing on whether or not anyone was selected randomly as a target. Sick people in the hospital were shot as they lay helplessly in their beds. Even the infants didn't escape the murderous wrath of the brave and mighty Germans.

The streets of the ghetto ended up covered with blood and the Nazis showed no remorse whatsoever for their actions. Goeth, who personally led both days of the purge, was pleased with their results. More than eight thousand Jews were marched to the camp and Jews from outside the city were rounded up as well.

Within a very brief period of time the new arrivals were all assigned work details in various functions to produce necessary materials for the continually expanding war machine. Those who were unable to work were placed into boxcars at the train siding, unceremoniously hauled away, and never returned to their families and loved ones.

Conditions of life at Plaszow were made even more dreadful upon the arrival of Amon Goeth. A prisoner was considered to be extremely fortunate if they survived there more than four weeks. Collective punishment and torture became a frequent exercise. There was a complete and willful administration of brutal punishment. Executions became part of the daily routine of the camp. There were some attempts of escape from the camp but during Goeth's administration anyone who was caught was immediately executed.

One evening while Moniek was on his way back to his barrack with the others in his work detail they were stopped by an SS man and instructed to report to the *Appellplatz,* the open-air meeting area near the main gate. They did as ordered and once they arrived discovered a large group of prisoners, all standing at attention in the always-present lines of ten. They were all facing the same direction, toward the feared gallows. A man in a striped suit, his hands tied securely behind his back, was standing on a chair, a noose firmly cinched around his neck. His face was understandably shrouded in fear.

The audience of the other prisoners was eerily silent. There was no talk and no shuffling of feet. There was apprehension mixed with abject fear and a sense of relief for the majority of them knew with a certainty that it could just as well be them standing on that chair. Nearly all of them had seen the exercise before. For Moniek it was his first time.

Goeth arrived majestically riding a white horse and dismounted. He was tall, reasonably handsome, and heavy-set with blue eyes, thin legs, and unusually large ears. As was the custom he wore a black leather jacket, held a riding crop in one hand, and a short automatic rifle in the other. There were two large dogs accompanying him named Ralf and Rolf, each taking a position on either side of the new commandant. The dogs both growled at the columns of people facing them, baring teeth and anxious for the command to attack, but that was to be held in check for another day.

There seemed to be armed guards everywhere as Goeth moved with complete authority to the front of the assembled multitude. With eyes of steel he examined those facing him with complete disdain and announced, "This man attempted to escape last night. You have all been told, clearly forewarned, that there will be no escape from my camp." Without expression he kicked the chair out from under the helpless man and his neck snapped violently as the rope jerked him to a halt, leaving him swinging gently in midair, legs twitching, and eyes bulging.

Once all movement ceased Goeth walked behind the dead man, pulled out his pistol, and shot him in the head. Blood splattered several of those standing in the front row. Again, without emotion he explained, "This is what will happen to any of you if you try to escape." With that he climbed back on his horse and rode away, followed by the two dogs.

The prisoners forced to watch the execution were dismissed and instructed to return to their barracks. Moniek was transfixed, staring with disbelief at the lifeless body hanging from the gallows. Since he'd first arrived in Bochnia he'd seen brutality and beatings and certainly experienced much verbal abuse himself, but this was the first time he had actually seen another human being murdered in cold blood.

A bony elbow gently punched him in the ribs, bringing him back to whatever sense of reality there was in this place. "Move, kid," the voice softly but strongly suggested. "This is the last place in the world you want to be." Recognizing the certainty of the statement Moniek moved along with the others. It seemed from their facial expressions few of them actually cared about what they had just witnessed. They were all just dead tired from a long day's work and knew clearly that another one stared them in the face and then another one after that. They looked forward to being inside. They even looked forward to the foul-smelling turnip soup. They mostly looked forward to just being left alone.

Following the evening count which lasted much longer than normal, adding to their already bone-freezing existence, the men made the unpleasant trip to the latrine. While the vile smell and stench was never something they actually got used to, it was something they just grew to accept. The "old timers" dealt with the situation as best as they could and the newcomers were the ones retching and throwing up on the road.

Moniek ate his soup without comment or complaint and crawled into his bunk, away from the others, trying desperately to be away from everything in this hell of a place. As others shuffled throughout the barrack he closed his eyes, reflecting on the night the family had escaped from Bochnia, wondering if those caught in their attempt had suffered the same fate as the one he just witnessed. And in that reflection, thoughts once again returned to his family. Where were they? What were they doing? Were they still together?

While the events of the day had greatly disturbed him and his mind offered alternate opinions, he still believed from the bottom of his heart that somehow, someway, this madness would all end and he would be reunited with his father, mother, and brothers. It was the very last thought he treasured each night before much needed sleep would finally come and provide a very small degree of much needed escape.

He heard a low muffled sound from the corner of the room, opened eyes which were nearly asleep, and looked in the direction of the disturbance. The lights had been turned off but he could see through the darkness that it was a small group of men, sitting on two lower bunks, facing each other. It was a group of ten men, in the Jewish tradition referred to as a minyan, the number required by Jewish law to formally offer a prayer.

They were quietly praying for the soul of the man who had been executed earlier that evening. They were praying for the souls of all those who had been mindlessly persecuted and murdered for absolutely no reason. They were praying for peace.

Moniek turned over in his bunk and looked away. Then he closed his eyes again. After what he'd experienced at his young age he seriously questioned the value of prayer. Most difficult to comprehend and what kept him awake the remainder of the night was that he was also beginning to question the very existence of God. In pained silence he apologized to his parents for harboring the thought.

Twenty-Three

Amon Goeth lived in splendor in an exquisite villa at the top of a hill overlooking the camp. When he wasn't brutalizing prisoners he enjoyed a life of luxury and entertained his officers and guests with great charm and the finest of food and liquor on a regular basis. Many evenings people who were living in abject squalor and slowly starving to death at the bottom of the hill could hear gay music drift through the air from the outside terrace. It was common for those to think about the food and drink barely yards away while they mostly existed on scraps of bread and lukewarm, foul-tasting turnip soup.

Occasionally when Goeth would rise in the morning after an evening of hard partying and equally hard drinking he would take his high-powered rifle with a long range scope out on the terrace with him. He would begin shooting prisoners below at random as they made their way to their respective work details. He referred to the exercise as target practice and showed no remorse for his murderous actions.

As Moniek and the others on his work detail slowly marched back toward their barrack they were ordered to report to *Hujowa Gurka*, the rolling hill which overlooked the rear of the camp. This place also had a large and very sturdy gallows. Other prisoners were already there, thousands of them, standing at attention, facing the gallows. There were many well-armed guards.

Three men with their hands tied behind their backs and nooses around their necks were standing on chairs. As he had often done, Goeth arrived on horseback accompanied by his vicious dogs. Upon his appearance those wearing caps removed them. Failure to do so nearly always resulted in several vicious strikes from the sticks. Flogging, normally twenty-five but sometimes as many as one hundred strokes administered to the small of the back, was a common punishment for any violation of camp rules.

Goeth dismounted and stared coldly and blankly through the prisoners standing at attention as if they weren't even there, as if they didn't even exist. "One of these men tried to smuggle food into the camp. This is against the rules. For his crime two others will be executed as well. Keep this in mind if you should see anyone breaking any camp rules. If they're not reported you may be executed as well." He nodded and three guards pushed the chairs out from under the helpless victims — only one of them had actually been trying to obtain some food and extend his life a little further.

The prisoners were not dismissed as Goeth mounted his horse and rode away. The three hanged men were lowered from the gallows to the ground and a man in a white coat approached them and placed something inside their mouths. Moniek was too far away to see what was really happening. In a few minutes the men were all ordered to return to their barracks.

As they walked Moniek turned to the man beside him and asked, "Who was that man in the white coat?"

"Dentist," was all the man said.

"Why?" He quietly questioned.

"They rip out all the gold fillings from the men's teeth, melt them down, and send them back to Germany so they can buy more guns to kill more people."

They walked in silence for awhile. Then Moniek cautiously asked, "What do they do with the bodies? I mean the dead people."

"There's an open pit behind the camp. They take the bodies there, pour gasoline on top of them, and light them. When the wind is just right you can smell the burning flesh. Of course the Nazis don't burn them. They make prisoners do it." Following that there was no further conversation.

Over the next few months Moniek viewed several such executions, standing at attention with the rest of the prisoners. Sometimes as many as six people were murdered at the same time. Executions by pistol or rifle were also a matter of increasing regularity. Life wasn't just cheap, it was insignificant and irrelevant.

Late one night while Moniek lay in his bunk he felt something stinging his chest. It was a few pesky lice, doing their best to bore their way under his skin and to suck away his precious blood. He carefully picked them from his skin and held them in his hand, studying them. He reflected on the days and nights the family had spent in the forest with the lice a constant source of discomfort, especially for his mother. He hoped beyond hope that wherever they were their conditions were better than his own.

He watched the lice as they crawled back and forth in the palm of his hand. It occurred to him that these vile and insipid insects had but one purpose in their lives and that was to suck blood from others, if necessary until those others died. Then it also occurred to him that the Germans were doing exactly the same thing.

Just before sleep came he thought he heard a voice. It was muffled and soft and he couldn't quite make out who it was or where it was coming from. The voice calmly said, "Moniek, don't sleep in your bunk tonight." He opened his eyes and there was no one there. The voice resembled that of his father.

"Tata?" He whispered. "Is that you?" But there was no answer. Only the regular sounds made by the others as they slept. Was it all just a dream? Was he really asleep and just imagined the voice? Now wide awake he decided he shouldn't ignore the words whether he'd really heard them or not.

Silently he crawled down from his bunk, moved to the rear of the barrack, and slid across the floor under the bottom of one of the other bunks. No more than five minutes passed by before the front door opened and he could hear heavy boots traversing across the floor, coming in his direction. Moniek held his breath and didn't move a muscle. A gruff voice said, "His bunk's empty. Where is he?"

Another voice answered, "I don't know. He probably went to the latrine." Moniek could recognize the voice: it was Feder, the block senior.

"We'll go there and we better find him," the first voice said with authority.

The sound of the boots moved away and left the barrack. Now at least Moniek could breathe but he still refused to move. He stayed on the cold floor the remainder of the night, waiting fearfully for the door to reopen and the boots to return. It was clear they were looking for him and hiding anywhere was enormously difficult at best. There was no place to go which would provide any degree of safety.

In the morning when the bell rang he crawled quickly from under the bunk and joined the others for the roll call outside the barrack. He stood at attention and imagined himself to be invisible so that no one would notice him. But such was not to be the case. Feder approached, a serious scowl covering his face. "Where were you last night?" he hissed.

"I was in bed, sir," Moniek replied earnestly.

"I checked your bed and you weren't in it."

"Oh," he replied innocently. "That must have been when I went to the latrine."

"I checked the latrine too. You weren't there either. How do you explain that?"

Moniek hesitated momentarily, thinking as fast as he possibly could. "I guess somehow we must have passed each other on the way."

"That's impossible," Feder replied. He was about to continue speaking when the SS man arrived at the front of the group to conduct the count. As Feder moved away he looked over his shoulder and casually replied, "You were lucky last night." It was too dark to tell for sure but it almost appeared to Moniek that the block senior had a slight smile on his face.

The count that morning went as well as could be expected and best of all, no one came looking for him, which offered a tremendous sense of relief. Following the count they were all ordered to report to the *Appellplatz* near the front gate. As they had done so many times in the recent past the prisoners stood at attention facing six men standing on chairs underneath the gallows, nooses securely around each of their necks.

While he never considered himself to be particularly wise in the ways of the camp, Moniek did his level best to do what was asked of him and stay out of people's way, especially the SS and the brutal Ukrainian guards. However, he had been around long enough to have a general idea of how things worked. And that was that there was little sense to anything the Nazis ever did. While on one hand they were exceptionally organized and could manufacture and produce enormous amounts of products, materials and armaments for the war effort, they seemed to be systematically killing the very workforce that was responsible for the majority of the production.

A man wearing a black uniform at the front of the column calmly announced, "One of these men tried to escape yesterday and five more are also being punished." He nodded casually, the chairs were kicked out from under the men, and their necks were snapped. Those being executed never seemed to shout out or beg for mercy. They were resigned to their fate. Most of those watching knew it was only a matter of time until they themselves met their own demise as a result of starvation, being transported to another place perhaps even worse than this, diseases such as typhus and dysentery which permeated the camp, or just a random, mindless, senseless murder committed by anyone for no particular reason.

It was at that very moment that Moniek realized how fate had remarkably stepped in and saved his life. He was convinced that the people looking for him last night wanted him to be one of the six men hanging dead in front of the assembled multitude. It was not uncommon at all that people would be selected at random for execution. It didn't matter in the very least if you were a good and efficient worker.

The only thing that mattered, from the German perspective, was that they had six fewer Jews to kill.

Moniek spent the entire day on his work detail filled with apprehension, wonder, and worry. His time could come at any moment. Perhaps he'd been spared. Perhaps he'd been forgotten. He didn't know. As was always the case, no one knew anything. But there was an exception to this generally accepted rule of thumb. He knew with a certainty that he had heard a voice last night and that it had saved his life.

After the evening count, the trip to the latrine, and the soup accompanied by a crust of bread, he passed block senior Feder who made no comment about the previous night. It would appear as if it never happened and at the very least had been completely forgotten. But that was something which could not be taken for granted.

After the lights had been extinguished he lay in the dark, wondering about the voice. The more he thought about it the more his reflection seemed to tell him that it had been his father. He missed them so much. They were constantly on his mind. Wondering, always wondering, where they all were and what they were doing. More amazing, he still believed that someday they would all be reunited.

From his work detail during the day Moniek had noticed a large pile of furniture stacked near the front gate of the camp. In all probability it had been confiscated from Jews and was awaiting transport and distribution to German families who had done nothing to deserve the hard-earned possessions of others.

Fearing that his days on this earth might be numbered he eased his way once again out of his bunk. But this night, rather than heading toward the end of the barrack and hiding on the floor, he cautiously and as quietly as possible moved toward the front of the enclosure. Very carefully he opened the front door, concerned about waking Feder and ruining his plan, which at this point was not really all that well thought-out. All he really felt with a certainty was that he had to get out of this place and wanted to be back with his family.

Watchfully and slowly weaving his way in and out of the lights illuminating the compound he managed to maneuver the short trip to the area where he worked on a daily basis, well in sight of the front gate up ahead. The pile of furniture was still there. There were always guards patrolling, both day and night. He had observed them every day he was at work. They exercised great regularity, as if they were controlled by an unseen timepiece. Moniek figured the nighttime patrols would function with the same degree of regularity.

He was correct. As he concealed himself in the shadows, a pair of guards passed in one direction and within three minutes another pair passed the other way. Then, there was a lull until they crossed again. Moniek waited patiently, his heart pounding, until the guards had passed each other once again. Then, it was time for him to make his move.

There were searchlights mounted on poles at the front gate, weaving slowly to and fro, watching for anything and everything. Moniek waited until there was a small break in the light covering the ground between him and his objective. When the tiny shred of darkness pervaded he dashed across the open area to the pile of furniture. Once there, undetected, he quickly crawled inside the mound of chairs, couches, and tables and studied everything around him: the lights, the patrolling guards, the guard towers, and the gate itself.

After catching his breath, he determined that his best chance for escape was when the searchlights passed one another, leaving a blind spot. However, for success to have any remote chance this would have to occur when a vehicle was entering or leaving the camp and the gate was momentarily opened. The odds against all of this happening at exactly the same time were undeterminable. Still his hope was alive that freedom was within reach and, beyond that, reunification with his family.

While waiting and watching patiently for the perfect opportunity he couldn't help but reflect on the last two years of his life. He remembered Nowy Wisnicz but the memories seemed to be fading. His childhood had been stolen for absolutely no reason. The Germans could have just as well fed the workers a reasonable amount of food and left them alone. The work would have been completed. There was no earthly reason for this kind of treatment to anyone. It still made no sense to him at all.

"Don't move or I'll shoot!" The deep German voice was commanding and authoritative.

Moniek froze, awaiting either further instruction or death.

"Get out of there! Slowly! Keep your hands where I can see them!"

Moniek, terrified, did as he was instructed until he was facing the guard who couldn't have been more than nineteen years old. The guard had a rifle pointed directly at his chest. "What are you doing?" the guard asked.

"Nothing," Moniek answered. When the searchlights passed in front of them the guard could see the young face of his captive for the first time.

"You're nothing but a kid," the guard said with a genuine degree of amazement. He slowly shook his head from side to side and said quietly, "If you were about three years older, I'd have shot you on the spot. Do you understand me?"

"Yes, sir," Moniek answered, keeping his eyes focused on the ground.

The guard shook his head again and looked from side to side to make sure they were alone. "Go back to your barrack and don't ever try this again."

Moniek nodded and moved quickly through the shadows, ever watchful for other guards on patrol, clearly and most thankfully aware that his life had been spared two times during the course of the last two days. His only thought was that he had been incredibly fortunate, terribly lucky. And when the word "lucky" entered his mind he remembered the several times his father had referred to him as his "lucky charm." He thought about the times he spent fishing with his father, then he silently entered the front door of the barrack and slipped quietly and unnoticed to his bunk.

Twenty-Four

Months passed slowly with more public executions and at Commandant Goeth's encouragement the levels of brutality increased. Moniek, now well accustomed to witnessing death on a regular basis, miraculously continued to escape vicious punishment from either his block senior or work detail kapo. People continued to disappear from the barrack and his work detail with regularity and were instantly replaced with others.

Whenever Goeth appeared the prisoners became even more fearful than before. The men would take off their caps and stare at the ground, refusing to make eye contact or do anything which might be remotely considered to be provocative. On occasion, for no particular reason, Goeth would give the attack order to Ralf and Rolf and watch with amusement as the dogs viscously ripped skin from their innocent victims, sometimes leaving them dead. Sometimes leaving them barely alive for Goeth to finish the job with a bullet from his pistol.

Moniek knew fear intimately, with an absolute certainty. He lived within it and was surrounded by it on a constant basis, day and night, even while sleeping. Occasionally he'd overhear whispered rumors about the progress of the war. From his perspective none of it sounded very positive or encouraging. While basically resolved that this existence was going to continue for a very long time he still held a glimmer of hope that either the Germans would finally come to their senses and discontinue their madness or that the Allies fighting the Nazis would defeat them and return all those held as captives to the freedom they once so preciously enjoyed.

Some evenings after a hard day of completely exhausting work and not nearly enough to eat Moniek would lay motionless in his bunk and think about his childhood. At least the days of his childhood leading up to the time they escaped into the relative safety of the forest. He remembered attending school and playing games and studying the Torah and even the delightful taste of the sugar cookies his loving mother used to prepare for him. He longed desperately for those days and somewhere deeply imbedded in the bottom of his heart he kept the feeling that somehow, someday, they would all magically return and take place once again.

He also was sadly aware that his youth had been cruelly stolen from him and could never be returned or restored. Since the German occupation he had been humiliated, robbed, and imprisoned. But through all of this Moniek was still alive. That was his quest, his ultimate goal, to return to and be reunited with his family. During all this time in this absolute living hell he managed to be a survivor which at this point, compared to so many others, had to be considered a blessing. Just before sleep finally came that night he thought to himself, maybe Tata was right. Maybe I am good luck.

The following day while still digging up graves on his work detail, an SS man approached. All the workers stopped what they were doing and stood at attention, eyes directed toward the ground. The SS man moved toward where Moniek stood until they were virtually face to face. Moniek's knees were trembling, shaking uncontrollably. As his heartbeat increased rapidly he felt that his recent thoughts concerning being lucky had not been accurate after all. Perhaps, after making it this far, his time had finally come to be transported elsewhere for reasons unknown.

The SS man looked at a clipboard and without expression simply said, "Borowitz."

"Yes, sir," the man standing next to Moniek softly replied. The SS man moved in front of the other prisoner and Moniek felt an enormous sense of relief.

"Follow me," the SS man said dryly. "You're being transferred to a new work detail."

"Please, sir," the man pleaded. "Can't I just stay here? I'm a good worker. You can ask anybody."

"You say you want to stay here?" the SS man asked.

"Yes, sir. Please."

"Fine, then you can stay here," he said without emotion. With that he removed his pistol from its holster and shot the man in the head. He dropped like a rock and rolled into the same grave he had recently been excavating. The SS man looked at the rest of the prisoners who for the most part had seen such acts before. They were not all that uncommon. "Does anybody else want to stay here?" His sarcasm was answered with complete silence. "Then get back to work."

Late one evening Moniek woke up to the dreaded sound of leather boots marching across the floor, coming toward his bunk. On this night, the one he had feared for so long, there was no time or place for him to hide. He held his breath, pretending to still be asleep, hoping the boots would continue down the aisle. But they stopped directly in front of him.

"Ebner," the voice in the dark said.

"Yes, sir," he quietly replied.

"Come with me. Be quick about it." Moniek crawled down from his top bunk and stood at attention, waiting for further instructions. The SS man carrying his ever-present clipboard called off the names of several others who left their own bunks and stood at attention as well. When the Nazi finished reading off the names on his list he announced, "Follow me. Outside. Lines of five."

The men were intimately familiar with "lines of five." Other than the morning and evening counts and when they were forced to witness executions and stand in perfect lines of ten each, every time they moved or went anywhere it was always in "lines of five." And it seemed like everywhere they went there was always someone counting them.

Always making sure everyone was accounted for. Always making sure there would never be an escape to the outside world to tell people what Goeth and the other Nazis were actually doing in this place so filled with senseless violence and mindless murder.

Once outside and standing in formation the SS man, who was now joined by two other armed guards, waved his pistol for the men to follow him. The prisoners, totaling nearly fifty, in complete silence, complied and they marched away in the darkness. Several of them would look at others alongside with deeply questioning eyes. The gesture was always answered with shrugging shoulders. Since September of 1939, no one had any idea what was going on, where they were going, or what their eventual fate would be. It was the same now.

They marched past the cemeteries where Moniek had worked for nearly a year, through blazing summer heat and freezing winter cold, through the main gate with the sweeping, blinding floodlights and more guards appearing. They ended up at the train siding where boxcars with open doors awaited them. The guards began to shout for the men to enter the cars and, as was always the case, they did as they were instructed without question, pause, or objection.

Once inside the boxcar the door was slammed shut and they could clearly hear it being securely locked from the outside. No one had the nerve to check and see if they could still open the door because they knew with a certainty what waited on the other side. There was adequate room for nearly all of them to sit on the floor. A few of the men quickly fell back asleep. Others rocked back and forth in silent prayer. Moniek just leaned against the wall and watched the others, wishing desperately that the train would miraculously return him to his family.

They spent the balance of the night in total darkness other than the occasional beam of floodlights from the main gate in the distance. The sounds were the normal and regular ones: an occasional whispered prayer, someone softly weeping, others cursing the Nazis under their breath. The night became morning and the summer heat finally began to take its toll.

None of the people seated in the boxcar were given anything to eat or drink. They waited, an occasional question quietly asked to no one in particular, but no answers were provided. None were available. The heat began to slowly rise and some of the men began to remove layers of clothing, trying to escape the temperature. The effort offered little degree of help. And they continued to wait.

Darkness finally fell which at least provided a slight reprieve from the heat. But by now, after sitting in the boxcar for nearly twenty-four hours without food or water, the turnip soup and crust of bread sounded like a treasured delicacy. The far corner of the boxcar was used as the latrine facility. They were provided no other choice. As a result the rancid aroma which permeated the enclosed area caused many of the others to throw up violently. Once this began it created an involuntary gagging reflex and many others followed suit. The stench within the boxcar equaled that of the latrine in the camp.

The train finally lurched forward. For reasons no one could begin to comprehend the trains in and out of Plaszow nearly always seemed to arrive or leave under the cover of darkness. Perhaps there were Allied planes overhead, searching for targets. No one knew, certainly no one within the foul-smelling confines of the traveling boxcar.

It proved to be a very long night. Some slept. Most couldn't. The train rocked to and fro, back and forth in a constant, rhythmic, droning motion. The unvarying sound of the wheels beneath the train began to sound like a dull announcement of doom, taking all of the passengers to their demise. More questioning eyes roamed back and forth, expressing hopelessness, and more shrugs provided more nonanswers.

As the sun finally appeared the train thankfully slowed to a halt and the door was jerked open with a crashing metallic sound. The occupants were ordered outside and as always was the case, it had to be as quickly as possible. Those not quick enough to satisfy the waiting German guards were met with the savage sting of the sticks. In a matter of seconds they realized that whatever this place was it was probably not going to be any better than Plaszow had been.

They were marched in the familiar lines of five to a wooden barrack, remarkably similar to the one they just left, and unlike before, instructed to find their own bunks. Several other men were already in the barrack, just rising and preparing for their own morning count and yet another day of slave labor for the Nazis.

Moniek and the other new arrivals were issued bowls and spoons with the same instructions as before and after a day and a half of having nothing to eat looked forward to whatever food scraps they might receive. The morning coffee tasted better than what they were familiar with. It was hot and unlike before actually had a taste to it. While it seemed like a simple thing it was a pleasant and refreshing change. Most surprising, the coffee was accompanied with a slice of bread which was eagerly devoured by all.

The youngster sat on the edge of his bunk across from a man who was there when they arrived little more than an hour ago. Moniek was understandably hesitant at first but his curiosity overwhelmed him. "Excuse me, sir," he politely said.

"Yes," the man softly replied. He was middle-aged with kind eyes which over the years of imprisonment seemed to somehow sadly express a dulling of the mind and heart.

"I don't mean to bother you."

"No bother, young man," he quietly answered. "You're new. I expect you have questions. We all did when we got here."

"Where are we?" It was an honest question and several others seated nearby listened with careful attention to the hushed conversation.

"Just outside a town called Kielce, about seventy-five miles north of Krakow."

"Why would they bring us here?" he asked with genuine innocence.

The man slowly shook his head from side to side, and then patiently looked directly into Moniek's eyes. "Why would they do anything?" he answered. "We're here to die. We're all here to die. That's why they brought you here. That's why they brought us all here."

Throughout the course of the conversation and others over the next several days Moniek learned that Kielce was actually a combination of three labor camps. One was designated for workers to toil in a nearby quarry, various workshops, and a facility which produced ammunition. Another held prisoners who worked exclusively in a foundry. The third, the one which Moniek was assigned to, was a good-sized carpentry shop. The prisoners were all segregated according to their work assignments and as a result had no real knowledge or concept of what any of the others were actually doing or the work they were performing.

Like so many other cities and towns throughout Poland, following the German invasion in September of 1939, Kielce was turned into its own repressive ghetto where conditions and depravity were the same as that which Moniek experienced. The ghetto was established in April of 1941 and liquidated in August of 1942. At one point there were twenty-seven thousand Jews in the ghetto and when it was liquidated, with the exception of two thousand healthy people who were sent to the various labor camps, the vast majority of the balance of them were transported to Treblinka and, for the most part, were never seen or heard from again.

Moniek also heard that the Germans had surrendered at Stalingrad, Russia, in the first major defeat of Hitler's armies. He was told that hundreds of thousands of people had perished but it really didn't register with the youngster. He saw death on an up-close and personal basis but thankfully not as much as that which he witnessed at Plaszow. The concept of death on that massive of a scale was literally beyond his perception.

Others listened in as the same rumor was shared and hushed conversation was optimistic that the Germans were losing the evil war they had begun and it was only a matter of time before the Allies would free them all. The majority of those who still survived held the hope that somehow lives could be restored and futures could be rebuilt. Some were not as optimistic.

"None of us will ever be free," whispered a raspy voice. It was the man Moniek had first spoken with when he arrived at Kielce. The man stared at the floor and slowly shook his head as the others listened attentively. He had been there longer than most and as such commanded a certain degree of respect. He pointed toward Moniek.

"I told this young man when he arrived that the only reason we're here is to die." His voice lowered to the point where it was barely audible. "Nothing has changed. We're never going to get out of here. Not alive." His comments were followed by silence as men returned to their respective bunks.

What they had not heard while confined in the Kielce labor camp was that the Germans had constructed gas chambers/crematoriums II, III, IV, and V at Auschwitz-Birkenau. With the completion of these four new facilities the Nazis were now able to execute and dispose of a daily capacity of 4,756 bodies in every twenty-four hour cycle, the vast majority of them, Jews.

While for the most part, from Moniek's perspective, conditions had been tolerable, if only barely, in Plaszow, Kielce proved itself to be considerably more acceptable. The food was a little bit more plentiful and normally warm with nearly each serving. The daily soup actually contained recognizable traces of potatoes. The kapos seemed to be more tolerant and punishment was meted out much less frequently than when commandant Goeth was in complete control of Moniek's life. Beatings and mindless murders, while they still occurred on a random basis, were at a minimum compared to what he'd recently experienced.

His primary assignment was in the carpentry shop, which produced wagons expressly used for transporting ammunition and supplies to the front lines of the war. On occasion Moniek would work inside the facility alongside about a hundred other prisoners but most of his time was spent at the railroad siding where he and three others would unload a constant barrage of lumber arriving by trains and then push heavy carts into the factory where it would be unloaded and used in the construction process.

His hours each day were very long and the constant lifting was understandably exhausting. However, none of what he was doing carried the repercussions and mental anguish that digging up graves had taken over the past year. For the most part it was just the same boring routine over and over. The morning count, the latrine, coffee usually accompanied by a crust of bread, and a full day's work. Once work was completed it was back to the barrack, the evening count, the latrine, a bowl of soup, and then well-deserved sleep.

As a result of the minimal diet and daily hard labor many of the other prisoners lost considerable amounts of weight, strength, health, and in some cases even the will to live. Strangely enough Moniek seemed to be almost revitalized as a result of working outside and not in an environment which was surrounded by death. While he never actually gained weight he also never lost an appreciable amount. From all of the heavy lifting he was forced to do his young muscles essentially developed during the course of his incarceration.

During the scorching summer months Moniek was always careful to take his jacket with him to the work detail and kept a close eye on it. It wasn't because he needed it. It was because if he left it behind there was an excellent probability that it would be stolen. Theft among the prisoners was commonplace and newcomers not familiar with the ways of the camp were taken advantage of on a regular basis. They had virtually no possessions, only the clothing on their backs, and even that was ripe for the pickings of many of the others.

During that summer Himmler ordered the liquidation of all of the Jewish ghettos. The Jews were uncaringly ripped away from their meager existence and taken by force to a variety of camps, the majority of them, tragically, to one of the extermination camps. Prisoners who were aware of this information and had been in the camp system for awhile sat in small groups and quietly questioned why the Germans would do such a thing. It didn't make any sense. That observation was always followed with the normal response of, "Nothing they do makes any sense."

As the men carried out their hushed conversations it seemed to them to be increasingly clear that the Nazis were expending a great deal of time, manpower, energy, and effort in moving the Jews around and continuing to make their lives miserable — energy and effort that should have gone into the actual war effort, which, according to more rumors, continued to go badly. Trains which normally would have been used to carry supplies, ammunition, and even troops to the front were being diverted to transport Jews, hundreds of thousands of Jews from the ghettos, to various German camps where they would be prisoners. The fortunate ones would become slave laborers, at least for awhile. The less-than-fortunate would become catastrophic statistics, an integral piece of the Final Solution.

On occasion Moniek would have his labor detail altered and be assigned to work on the night shift in a place they referred to as "the steam room." Wearing gloves and using tongs the men would place steaming hot metal spikes into the center of the wagon wheels and as they cooled they expanded, holding the wheel tightly together. The heat was oppressive, nearly unbearable. Men who had worked on this detail for any appreciable amount of time discovered that their skin turned yellow. Those who complained in any manner, no matter how small or seemingly insignificant, were transferred somewhere else and like so many others before them, never seen or heard from again.

On the first chilly day of that fall Moniek and several of the others in his barrack were ordered outside. As always, standing at attention in lines of ten. The anxiety level was at an all-time high. Their day's work was completed. Now what? Whispered possibilities were all of a negative nature. Surrounded by armed guards they were marched to a building near the far side of the camp.

Once inside they were surprised to discover a pot-bellied stove emitting a great deal of warmth. The men were ordered to remove their clothes, hang them on hooks lining the walls, and remember where they left them. The first person who hesitated was beaten with a stick. The others moved quickly. Once naked they were all directed into an attached enclosure. The door behind them was shut and locked from the outside. Again, more looks composed of questioning eyes and more shrugging of the shoulders.

They could see nozzles in the ceiling of the room. Someone began to whisper that they'd heard this was what they did to the Jews in Auschwitz-Birkenau and the other extermination camps. The buzz of, "They're going to gas us," instantly permeated the room. But they were trapped. There was no way out. A controlled panic set in and the men began to shuffle against one another, trying to maneuver their way closer toward the securely locked door.

They heard a hissing sound. Many of them hung their heads and began to pray, believing they were facing their final moments. To their delightful surprise the nozzles in the ceiling began to spew forth streams of water. Certainly not hot but warm nonetheless. In ecstasy they basked in the liquid warmth. There was no soap but that mattered little. Some of them actually smiled.

This was the first shower Moniek had experienced since the last few days at his home in Nowy Wisnicz. That was why he smiled to himself, remembering. The warm water, for just an instant, carried him back to the warmth of his family. Just as his mind recreated the smiling faces of his mother, father, and brothers the door jerked open and a shrill voice shattered the memory.

"Out! Out! Everybody! Put on your clothes as quickly as possible!" Guards were in the dressing area, only too eager to assist the men in their quickness. There was a great surge of bodies pressing against one another, trying to reach the wall and get to their clothes. In the mass of humanity Moniek was pushed away from his objective and toward the pot-bellied stove. He tried to hold his ground, fearing what was coming, but his best efforts proved to be fruitless.

As his naked skin touched the glowing stove he cried out in pain but no one offered assistance. They were all too busy taking care of and trying to protect themselves. In agony Moniek managed to ease his misery-filled body away from the stove toward his clothes hanging on the wall. No towels were offered. That would be an unnecessary expense the Germans would never tolerate.

As he put on his pants and shirt there was a burning sensation in his side, the place of contact where he had been forced into the stove. The eight-inch long burn had already turned red and was beginning to form blisters. The pain intensified and he bent over to compensate for the intense discomfort. When he touched the inflicted area it only magnified the throbbing tenderness.

Sleep that night was very difficult because each time he rolled over trying to find any degree of comfort the tenderness and soreness from the burn would instantly remind him of his painful experience. Work the following day was unusually difficult as a result of stretching the very tender skin. Fortunately that evening when the soup was delivered to the barrack along with a crust of bread the meal was accompanied by a small portion of margarine.

Instead of applying the margarine to his bread, like the rest of the others, he gingerly rubbed it onto the stinging burn on his side. The prisoners received the margarine treat on an irregular basis, usually every three or four days. After denying himself of the treat which others savored and several self-applications the blistering subsided, the redness went away, and the pain finally diminished. Against all odds Moniek had once again prevailed.

One morning, following the count, the prisoners were marched to the general area of the camp, the area in which the gallows had been constructed. As the vast majority of them had seen all too many times three men were standing on chairs with their hands tied behind their backs and nooses around their necks. No one questioned what they were about to witness. Some considered the exercise, "old hat," just something which the Nazis perpetrated on a regular basis. For others, viewing cold-blooded murder was never something which could be tolerated or accepted and it turned their stomachs. No matter what their feelings were, they were still forced to watch the proceedings.

An SS man in his crisp black uniform marched smartly to the front of the three doomed prisoners. He cleared his throat and pronounced, "There was a fire in the carpentry shop last night." This was news to all of the men present. They had been asleep and had no knowledge of the event. "These are the three men responsible for starting the fire. There will be no sabotage within this camp."

Whispers began to spread among the prisoners. They passed along the word that the fire was very small and relatively insignificant. There wasn't even enough damage to halt the daily production of the shop. But to the Germans it was a major attempt at sabotage and in addition to not being tolerated would be severely punished.

The SS man nodded to three of his associates but before they kicked the chairs out from under the condemned men one of them, a man named Jacob Silbering, a person Moniek knew casually, shouted out, "Take revenge, guys! Whatever..." And before he could finish the comment the chair went flying from beneath his feet, his neck snapped, and he hung helplessly, swinging gently as the morning wind came over the hill.

Twenty-Five

Moniek crawled into his bunk that night and thought long and hard about Jacob Silbering. Even at his young age Moniek was aware that there were rules and courts where evidence is presented in front of a jury of ones peers before a life is taken, but not here in this place. Here the only rules were the Nazi rules. They had the authority and the ability to kill on a moment's notice without rhyme, reason, or any justification whatsoever.

The front door of the barrack burst open. Several sets of boots stomped in screaming, "Out! Out! Everybody out!" Moniek and the others left their bunks as quickly as possible and rushed outside, forming the lines of ten and standing at attention, having no idea of what was happening. They were marched to the front of the camp, through the gate, and toward the rail siding where a train with many boxcars waited.

While sticks were swinging wildly in all directions the prisoners were forced into another cattle car. More and more people and then still more and more. When the door was finally slammed shut and locked they were packed so tightly that they could not move. They were body to body, literally mashed against one another. Unlike the last time he had been on a train there was no room to sit down. There was actually no room to even turn around.

Unlike the last time he was on a train, as disgusting and unpleasant as it was, there was no corner of the boxcar which could be used as a latrine facility. When the men had to relieve themselves they had no choice but to do it in their trousers where they stood. The aroma in the enclosed cattle car was far beyond pungent, and in many cases caused uncontrollable gagging which sometimes was then followed by throwing up. Because of the close proximity of the prisoners whenever someone threw up they had to do so literally on the people standing around them. It was common that a chain reaction followed.

Like the last time he was on a train there was no food or water offered. Like before, they waited as the sun came up, as more people relieved themselves, as more people threw up, and as the stench intensified. There was a small window with bars in the top left corner of the cattle car. Those closest to it would shout out, begging for water, but none was ever delivered.

It was late afternoon when the train, now composed of more than twenty cars, left the siding and slowly pulled away into the setting sun. The men were so tightly packed in the enclosure that when the train jerked forward they didn't even move. Someone quietly suggested that they were packed like sardines in a tin can. Sadly the observation was accurate.

The train moved slowly across the countryside making many stops along the way. At each stop the men could hear the heavy metal doors opening and closing. They didn't know if current passengers were getting off the train or if other new ones were getting on. They didn't know anything.

Darkness fell along with the temperature. No one felt the chill in the air because of the body heat which was generated inside the boxcar. Some of the men fell asleep, standing up, supported by the others surrounding them. Even packed in as tightly as they were, surrounded by a sea of bodies, Moniek felt an incredible sense of aloneness, abject isolation. He closed his eyes, trying to emulate some of the others nearby who were asleep.

It was not to be. As the train edged ever forward, leaning to and fro, and the wheels beneath them clicked out a constant yet curiously unpleasant rhythm, his mind drifted back to days when he experienced freedom: to the days when he played soccer with neighborhood friends on the street in front of his home, to studying Torah with his Rabbi, to home-cooked meals with his family that his mother so deliciously prepared. He would see them all again, he knew. For what seemed like only a moment he escaped from the abject misery surrounding him.

While sleep never actually came, the moments filled with pleasant memories turned into hours until the train once again jerked to a violent halt. As had been the case before the doors were ripped open and many well-armed soldiers began screaming for them to leave the car as quickly as possible. Three by three by three they jumped out of the car and onto the siding. Without instruction the new arrivals formed the familiar lines of five.

Far in the distance Moniek could see the outline of a very wide, two-story brick building. The center of the building was actually three stories high and had a large opening at its bottom on the ground. The men waited for the unknown, clearly uncertain as to what was going to come next. Many of the soldiers guarding them had snarling German shepherds on leashes, anxious to get at anyone who made the slightest move which might be considered to be irregular or threatening. Once the train had been emptied the men were ordered to march forward at a very slow pace. At the front of the line was an SS man in his perfectly tailored black uniform.

The man would briefly examine each prisoner as they passed and wave his finger either to the right or to the left. Those waved to the right kept marching forward, surrounded by guards. Moniek was among this group. Those waved to the left were ordered to stay behind and stood off to one side. Far more men stayed behind than were selected to move. Everyone was filled with questions but none were asked openly. They knew better. In time, as was generally the case, most of their questions would be answered.

As they marched forward through the opening at the bottom of the brick building Moniek finally took his eyes from the ground and realized several things. The first was that this place, wherever it was and whatever it was, was absolutely huge. Looking in all directions for nearly as far as the eye could see there were endless rows of barracks. There seemed to be hundreds of them, which just went on and on.

There appeared to be several different areas, which were segregated, separated by the electrified double wire fences.

The second thing he noticed was while he could see trees far off in the distance, well beyond the outer limits of the wires, past the guard towers, there didn't appear to be any bird songs in the air. There didn't even appear to be any birds. It was as if this place, isolated as it was, had somehow transformed nature into an evil repository of silence. The only sound was that of the shoes as they slowly moved across the hardened red clay beneath their feet.

The third thing, the thing which bothered him the most, was the smell that hung in the air. It was indescribable. Over time he'd learned to sleep with aromas which would keep most normal people awake at night. He'd just spent two days and one night and one hundred miles packed into a boxcar surrounded by the most unimaginable smells known to man. But this smell was different. Completely unlike anything he'd ever experienced.

The column turned left, marched through a set of the double wires, and entered a barrack which resembled all the others. A sign over the door identified the building as "the Central Sauna." They were ordered to undress, this time without any instructions as to keeping track of their clothing. No one argued. As Moniek removed his clothes he looked at the torn and tattered items. They were filthy, covered with dust, dirt, and mud which had accumulated since the day he and his family left Nowy Wisnicz.

They were then ushered into a separate room where nozzles hung menacingly from the ceiling. Like before many of the men in the room were very concerned that the nozzles would soon release poisonous gas and end all of their lives. Others had no other choice but to wait patiently, silently. There was no possible means of escape and panic would have proven to be fruitless. Unlike before every third man entering the room was handed a bar of soap and told to use it. Several thought it was just a ploy to achieve a degree of calmness.

And they waited. Some murmured, some prayed openly, some stayed silent. And they waited some more. Within moments the nozzles in the ceiling erupted with a surge of warm water, drenching all those below, bringing smiles of relief. They lathered themselves as quickly as possible, sharing the bars of soap with each other, having no idea of how long their moment of pleasure would last. In truth it lasted about three minutes.

But those three minutes proved to be absolutely heavenly. During the fleeting one hundred and eighty seconds most of the men had the opportunity to briefly forget the pains they had experienced, the countless hangings they'd witnessed, and the vicious cold-blooded murders that they'd seen. Moniek, actually clean for the first time in nearly three years, could not think about what lay ahead. He captured the moment and relished in it. But in the back of his mind, based on what he had experienced, he knew that when the delightful shower was finished the cruelty would once again most certainly begin.

The remarkably pleasant stream of water ceased, the door was jerked open, and the men were led into an adjoining room where other men wearing striped uniforms stood behind a long row of chairs. They each held strange looking instruments in their hands. The new arrivals were instructed to occupy the chairs. The other men were barbers and each new arrival was completely shaved of all hair, everywhere. The clippers were dull from constant usage and while one man's pubic area was being shaved he shouted out in pain. For his understandable outburst he was rewarded with a sharp strike from a stick. There were no more vocal complaints.

Once completely hairless they were shuffled back into the dressing area where all of their clothing had been removed. In its place, stacked in pile after pile, were striped uniforms: shirts and pants. Underneath the tables holding the uniforms were wooden clogs. "Pick out a uniform and get some shoes!" one of the guards shouted. With mass confusion the men complied with the instruction. No underwear or socks were offered.

It created a rather hectic scenario with men exchanging clothing back and forth which was either too small or too large for them to wear. All the while the guards continued to scream at them to hurry. It was a constant matter of hurry, hurry, hurry. In a very short period of time the task was accomplished and while many of the threadbare uniforms were ill-fitting their new clothing was now in order and would continue to be that way for a very long time.

As they filed outside into the afternoon air with the strange smell wavering through and hanging in the wind. Moniek looked down at the stripes now covering his chest, sleeves and legs — he same uniform that he had seen others wearing for nearly the last three years. While he had been under Nazi control, literally since he was twelve years old, he never actually felt as if he were a prisoner. Today, this day, this very moment, for the first time in his life, he felt the pain and abject sadness of being a prisoner of people who hated him for no reason, and wished him harm.

The group was marched into another barrack where other men wearing striped uniforms sat behind long rows of tables. The majority of them seemed to be bored, bothered by the necessity of having to be there but equally thankful that they weren't somewhere else. Wooden chairs were lined up in front of each of the men behind the tables. They reminded Moniek of the many times he'd seen the same type chairs with people standing on them, their hands tied behind their backs, a noose firmly around their neck.

A metal tray was on the table in front of each of the men and beside them lay what appeared to be a needle of some sort. While anxiety increased tremendously among the majority of the men Moniek continued to stare at the striped uniform he was now wearing and the reality that he was now a prisoner. The severity of the feeling, which should have been felt and acknowledged over the last three years, superseded his surroundings and left him in a state of enormous confusion.

"Take a chair!" one of the lead guards shouted. The men forming the front of the line did as instructed. Moniek sat across the table from a man whose face showed no expression. No compassion, no understanding, no caring, no nothing. He stared at the needles in front of him as if Moniek didn't even exist. He represented less than just another body. His eyes were dark, deep-set, without feeling, and he was remarkably thin.

"Roll up your sleeve," the man with the dark eyes said. Moniek did as he was told. "Arm on the table." Again Moniek followed instructions, exactly like all of the others in the room. The man with no expression on his face picked up one of the needles in front of him. He dipped the needle casually and uncaringly into the metal tray which contained a black liquid and gripped Moniek firmly by the wrist. "Don't twist too much or it'll hurt more." He delivered the line as if he'd repeated it many times.

He tightened his grip and jabbed the needle into Moniek's forearm. Initially there was a sharp stinging sensation and he jerked involuntarily. "Try not to move," the man softly offered. Moniek looked into the empty, deep-set eyes and could sense that the man was only doing his job as directed by the Nazis. If he didn't do what he was told... well...who could guess what the outcome would have been for him.

Moniek looked away as the man continued to dip the needle into the black ink and jab it into his arm. He flinched each time the needle penetrated his skin but kept as immobile as possible. The pain shot through his arm and into his brain. He wanted to scream out in pain and to beg them to stop whatever they were doing but knew that any such outburst would only cause more pain for himself. So, he bit down on the inside of his cheeks until they literally bled and held the pain within.

Briefly, thankfully, the ordeal was completed. The man behind the table said, "Name."

"Moniek Ebner." The man wrote it down on a list attached to a clipboard and placed a number behind it.

"Next." the man calmly announced. Moniek left his chair, another prisoner quickly replaced him and the same procedure followed.

"Outside! Lines of ten!" a guard shouted. The first group of men moved through the front door, formed the lines of ten, and waited. Once settled, Moniek rolled up his sleeve and looked down at his forearm, still stinging from the constant jabbing of the needle.

The vile, black mark on his arm said, "B2992." It was permanent, applied with indelible ink. Try as hard as he might Moniek could not rub it off. A man standing next to him whispered, "Don't even try, kid, that number will be on your arm till the day you die. You don't have a name anymore. That's who you are now."

Moniek stood in silence, staring at the tattoo on his forearm. *I am not B2992,* he thought to himself. *I am Moniek Ebner and some day, somehow, I'm going to get out of this evil place and be back with my family.*

They waited, standing at attention, until more than one hundred men had been assembled. Together they marched past several other barracks until they were ordered by the guards to enter one that seemed to be marginally separated from the others. The room was quite large with rows of bunks lined up against each wall. Moniek guessed that the room could hold more than five hundred men.

After they were all inside the men assumed the position of attention. And they waited. The block senior, also wearing a striped uniform, stepped to the front of the group. "This is a quarantine barrack," he announced. "You will be kept here for about a week to make sure you don't bring any diseases into the camp. You will not be allowed to mix or congregate or have conversations with any of the other prisoners."

Moniek was more than confused. His skin had been viciously tattooed against his will, his very identity had been stolen, and now he was a prisoner within what he logically assumed was a prison camp. In time, he further assumed, they would be assigned work details and like before many others would perish as a result of the hard labor imposed on them by their captors. In addition to the hangings, the beatings, the murders, the starvations, and the rampant diseases which took lives on a daily basis, many others merely died from being overworked literally to the point of complete exhaustion. Why would the Nazis care whether they brought sickness into the camp? Why would it possibly matter? It made no sense.

Bowls and spoons were distributed and they were all assigned bunks. There were five men in each bunk with a thin straw mattress and one threadbare blanket, which had to be shared. They were told that they could go to the latrine later that evening. The men sat on the ends of their bunks and stared at one another, waiting. Later that evening, after the sun had gone down, they could hear a great cacophony of sound, wooden clogs marching on the cement-hard, red dirt ground outside. Without giving the appearance of rushing in any sense or manner, several of the men walked to the front of the barrack and looked out through the front door and a small window.

Those fortunate enough to have secured a view saw fellow prisoners returning from various, countless work details throughout the vast area. The column marching by in their carefully constructed lines of five seemed to go on forever. There were thousands of men wearing the striped uniforms. Perhaps tens of thousands. There were far too many to count, but the Germans counted them. They knew exactly how many were incarcerated and by the numbers applied to their arms knew exactly where each and every one of them was. No one was going to slip through the cracks and with an absolute certainty no one was going to escape.

After an hour or so a wooden cart pulled by two prisoners arrived at the barrack. It carried a large tureen delivering the evening ration of soup. The soup was doled out, the men returned to their bunks where they sat back down, and the wagon pulled away toward its next stop. Moniek looked at the man across from him as they each slowly slurped the liquid. The man was older by perhaps twenty years. You could somehow clearly tell from the expression on and the lines in his face that he had been around for awhile.

Moniek had the usual questions running rapidly through his mind but didn't say anything, just occasionally stealing a casual glance at the man sitting across. The man finally caught the stolen glance and quietly offered, "You look like there's something on your mind."

"I'm new," was all Moniek could think of in response.

"I know. It shows. Most of you are. I've been in and out of here for a few months and perhaps I can answer some of those questions running around in your mind."

"What do you mean, 'in and out of here'?"

"They transferred me from one camp to another and this is the first time they've ever really gotten around to officially registering me." The man picked his teeth with a dirty fingernail. "We have some time before we go to the latrine. What's your first question and I'll do the best that I can."

"What's your name?" the youngster asked.

He looked down at his forearm, frowned sadly, and replied, "My name is B2654 until this madness is over, one way or the other." He looked at the floor, a sense of resolve on his face.

"Why do the block senior and some of those other men have the triangles on their uniforms?"

"You're a Jew, aren't you?" Moniek nodded. "You'll get your own triangle soon enough. It'll be yellow."

"Why yellow?"

"No reason. It just means you're a Jew and should be dealt with appropriately by the soldiers and guards."

"But our new block senior has a green triangle. I don't understand."

"Green means he's a common criminal and usually given special privileges over others in the camp. He has a lot of powers over the other prisoners, especially the people in his own barrack."

"You mean there are others?" And Moniek learned that there were several categories of triangles identifying the various prisoners in the camp. Red was worn by political dissidents including Communists. Purple was primarily worn by religious fundamentalists, most notably Jehovah's Witnesses. Blue was for immigrants. Brown was for the Gypsies. Black was for lesbians and those considered to be antisocials such as alcoholics and those who refused to work. Lastly, the pink triangle was worn by gay men.

Because of his age and his years of isolation and confinement Moniek had never heard the expression or the term "gay men." When it was explained to him it mattered little. The only terms and labels which mattered were, "Germans" and "Nazis," and "the Gestapo." Those were the terms and those were the people who had the power to end his life at their smallest whim.

The block senior announced that it was time for the first group of them to go to the latrine. The prisoners left their bunks and walked toward the front door. As they slowly shuffled along the man Moniek had been speaking with looked in his direction and said, "Something else is troubling you."

Moniek took his time and finally asked, "What is that strange and unpleasant smell that seems to be in the air?"

They walked in silence for a few steps until they finally moved outside and the aroma in question became even stronger. Finally the man slowly and sadly replied, "You haven't heard the rule yet, have you?"

"What rule?" Moniek softly asked.

"You enter by the gate. You leave by the chimney."

Twenty-Six

Moniek lay quietly in his bunk with four other men beside him. They were packed so tightly into the cramped space that if one of them rolled over the rest were forced to follow suit. Floodlights from a guardhouse in the distance would pass by their windows with regularity. Suddenly he heard a noise in the distance. It was a foreign sound, something he hadn't heard in a very long time. He opened his eyes, turned his head, and listened with increased attention. It was music. Light, happy music played by guitars, mandolins, and violins. He was quite sure he was hallucinating.

The man beside him was also still awake and noticed Moniek's questioning look. "It's the Gypsies," the man quietly explained.

"What do you mean, 'the Gypsies'?" Moniek asked.

"There's a Gypsy camp right across the way, separated from everybody else. The Germans let their families stay together and do pretty much whatever they want. Most every night they play music. It's nice." The man closed his eyes and went to sleep. But Moniek's eyes remained open, listening, remembering how his mother used to sing and hum seemingly all day long as she prepared fine meals and cleaned their house. The music had a haunting resonance to it that hung in the air like a heavy and somehow plaintive cloud. It was pleasant and at the same time enormously depressing.

The following morning was much like those Moniek had grown used to: Early morning bell shattering the stillness, block senior screaming for everyone to hurry, hurry, hurry, quick trip to the foul-smelling latrine, morning count in the lines of ten. Except for something Moniek had never seen before. Several lifeless bodies lay beside the front door of the barrack. They were naked, their clothes had been stripped. Moniek looked at the man standing beside him with an intense questioning look on his face.

"Died last night," the man said without emotion. "Still have to be counted. Everybody has to be counted."

And when the SS man arrived for the count he carefully checked the numbers on the forearms of each of the dead men on the ground and recorded it on his clipboard. The man standing beside Moniek had been correct. Everyone was counted. The Nazis knew where everyone was at all times. On occasion, if the block senior was in good stead with the SS man he'd be allowed to keep the bodies for a day or two so the barrack could receive the food portions allotted to the men no longer with them. Naturally it was the block senior and his favorites who enjoyed the additional portions.

They were finally released, returned to the barrack, and the cart carrying the large tureen arrived with food for the morning distribution. As usual they were each provided with a bowlful of the strange tasting coffee and this day they were each given a medium sized slice of stale bread. Moniek eagerly chomped into the morsel and a fellow prisoner nearby quietly warned, "You might want to save some of that for later. That's all you're going to get today." Moniek took his advice and stuffed the balance of the bread into his pocket.

The work patrol that day consisted of carrying large rocks from one side of their enclosure to the other. As soon as that task was completed they turned around and carried them back to the other side. Back and forth and back and forth. Those who collapsed from exhaustion were beaten with sticks as they lay on the ground. A few perished during the ordeal. Their pockets were searched quickly by other prisoners looking hopefully for a scrap of saved bread and then their clothes were removed and treasured by those fortunate enough to get them.

That afternoon those bodies would be taken back to the barrack and in the morning they would lay outside the front door for the SS man to check each of their forearms and write his information down on a clipboard.

Another bell resounded throughout the camp and it was time for their very short but much needed lunch break. Each of the men carried his bowl and spoon with him at all times because those who didn't have them didn't eat. It was a simple yet well-enforced rule. There were no exceptions and those who forgot theirs just went hungry until the evening meal was delivered. Of course, that was assuming that their bowl and spoon hadn't been stolen by someone else to use as a trading item, perhaps for an extra ration of food itself.

The wagon carrying the tureen appeared and the prisoners each received a cup full of soup, nothing more. Those who had devoured their bread earlier that morning watched jealously as those who didn't had a bite or two of their own along with what the Germans ridiculously referred to as a meal.

While seated on the hard dirt Moniek learned from others whispered conversations that the isolation area they were being held in was generally designated for prisoners who were going to be sent to other nearby camps for the purposes of slave labor. No one seemed to be quite sure but in reality the Auschwitz complex actually had three main camps and contained fifty-one subcamps throughout the surrounding area. A sampling of these included camps such as Rajsko, an experimental agricultural station, one of hundreds used to produce food for the armies and the growing cadre of prison guards. Another was Gleiwitz, a coal mine which produced energy to help fuel the ever-growing war machine.

The majority of the subcamps were self-contained and had their own well-guarded barracks surrounded by the electrified wires but a few were close enough so that prisoners could walk there in the morning for their work detail and return to the camp in the evenings.

After just one morning of back-breaking work Moniek determined that he wanted to be transferred elsewhere. But of course, he had absolutely nothing to say in the matter. He also learned that he was now confined in a place referred to as Auschwitz II, Auschwitz-Birkenau — "The Death Factory."

In April of 1940, Rudolph Hess, who was to become the first commandant of the camp, recommended that the town of Oswiecim be considered as a possible site for a concentration camp. It was centrally located in Poland and a series of rail lines connected the area to virtually all of Europe. On April 27th of that same year Himmler approved the recommendation and ordered construction of the camp. Poles were evicted from the vicinity of the barracks and work crews began expanding the existing structure.

The following March, Himmler ordered that the camp be enlarged even further and that the capacity be increased from twelve thousand prisoners to one which would hold as many as thirty thousand. By design it had developed a reputation for torture and mass murder. During that same visit Himmler also ordered the construction of a second camp for as many as one hundred thousand prisoners to be located on the site of the village of Brzezinka (Birkenau), located roughly four kilometers from the main camp. This is the camp that would be known as Auschwitz-Birkenau, or Auschwitz II.

More Poles were evicted from their homes and the huge area was completely leveled, not just the main area of the camp but for well more than a hundred yards beyond the established perimeter. This was designed to guarantee privacy so that no one could possibly realize what was occurring inside the double wires and also to absolutely prevent anyone from escaping and sharing the horror stories from this tragic place of hell.

Soviet prisoners of war and local Poles provided the initial construction effort but as the camp took shape and security became more efficient more prisoners were transported to the area to build more barracks. This was followed by more prisoners and more barracks until it reached the point that Himmler's command had been actualized: Auschwitz-Birkenau was capable of holding one hundred thousand prisoners who would be used as slave labor for the Germans. Birkenau was formally established on October 8th, 1941 as an extermination camp. But it was not until the autumn of 1942 when it seemed clear that the SS planners and civilian contractors were intending to construct and operate a plant that was specifically designed for the express purpose of mass murder.

During this same time frame and with the clear understanding that a massive labor force was going to be available, I.G. Farben, the chemical giant who produced synthetic fuel, rubber products, and vast amounts of materials for the Third Reich and the national economy, expressed interest in building a manufacturing facility in the vicinity and utilizing the prisoner labor force as well. Because of their close relationship with the masters of the Reich, and because Farben's was one of the biggest industrial projects of the war, permission was granted and construction proceeded at a rapid pace on a third major camp which would be officially known as Auschwitz III or IGF Buna.

To provide support for the main Auschwitz III factory a series of twenty-four subcamps was eventually established within the general vicinity of the camp. The majority of them were relatively small and self-contained but the living arrangements, the limited food provided, and the working conditions varied little from the other two main camps. Those conditions were deplorable, and would have shamed any decent human being.

For the next four days Moniek woke up to the piercing bell and followed the daily routine. As had been the case for several years, he adhered to his father's advice, and because he expected that he and his fellow prisoners were going to be separated soon, he chose not to develop close relationships with anyone. Like before he got up before the break of dawn, did his day's work, and returned to the barrack in the evening for what he hoped would at least be a peaceful night's sleep. Those continued to be few and far between.

During those few days he was in Birkenau he was told the express purpose of carrying the heavy rocks back and forth from side to side of their electrified enclosure was merely to keep the men completely exhausted and prevent them from causing any sort of disturbance. In the process of carrying out this exercise several more men perished. They ended up naked in a pile in front of the barrack and few if anyone gave it or them any thought at all. Many became numb to the process. It just sadly became a part of the daily way of life and death.

During his days carrying the rocks back and forth Moniek could see a separate women's camp inside the main enclosure which held thousands of prisoners dressed in plain, drab gray garb. Like the men they as well had been completely shaved from head to toe. Another camp held families, a facility that was separate from and in addition to the Gypsy camp.

Throughout his brief stay in Birkenau Moniek continued to be bothered by the unusual aroma which never seemed to leave the air. On his last evening there he finally summoned the nerve to approach one of the men delivering the soup from the large tureen to the bowls and silently asked, "Can you tell me what that strange smell is? Please."

The other prisoner looked from side to side, as was the custom, and nodded to Moniek's left, toward the far end of the massive camp. There was a glow in the night sky and ashes made their way into the drifting wind, some toward the heavens and some toward the ground. "I don't understand," Moniek said.

"The chimneys," the man replied quietly and nothing more.

"What about the chimneys?"

The man continued to ladle the soup and asked, "How many of the men who came with you on the train are still here now?"

"Most of them went somewhere else," was his response.

And again the man nodded toward the far side of the camp. "That's where they went, to the chimneys. They were gassed and then they were burned. That smell you're asking about? It's human flesh burning."

"B2992," The block senior announced without expression. Moniek's number was called out along with several others who gathered up their bowls and spoons, quickly left their bunks, and congregated outside. As was always the case, they waited. After the numbers on their arms were carefully checked a soldier, assisted by several others, instructed the prisoners to move forward.

The column left the confines of Birkenau, which pleased Moniek greatly, and proceeded to walk on a dirt-covered road in a northerly direction. That day they did not have even a crust of bread for breakfast. During the midday sun there was no lukewarm bowl of soup offered. They just kept on marching. While the walk was enormously draining on all of the men, it was much less so than carrying the heavy rocks back and forth as many of them had done for the better part of the last five days. Someone silently estimated that they had walked nearly fifteen miles.

The sun was falling in the distance as they entered their new confines. The sign above the main gate said, "Trzebinia," and it was, by comparison, a very small facility. There were only about a half dozen barracks, a kitchen, and by its familiar aroma, a latrine. The prisoners were directed into a barrack that was somewhat smaller than the one they left that morning in Birkenau.

The new block senior assumed all of his control and went through the now familiar explanation, "This is my barrack, you will follow all my rules, there is no chance of escape," etc., etc., etc. The new arrivals listened carefully, clearly aware of the punishment that would be delivered should they not. After bunks were assigned the wooden cart arrived carrying the tureen of soup. The men were eager for any sort or degree of nourishment. Someone commented that he felt it was odd that after being interred in several different camps the "food" they received always seemed to be the same consistency.

On the other hand the SS and supporting soldiers experienced a rather different fare. The countless farms which had been confiscated and created by the Nazis produced vast amounts of food for the troops. Enormous facilities, maintained by prisoners, produced all forms and varieties of livestock which were butchered and consumed. Tens of thousands of acres of farmlands, again maintained by prisoners, produced a continual array of vegetables and fruits. Millions of people had to be fed to keep the armies moving, and conquering other countries.

For the most part, the guards at the growing number of concentration camps ate very well. And while this abundance of food could have been shared with their captives, it never was. The principal idea was to keep all of the prisoners as weak as possible for two specific reasons: One, due to their lack of strength there would be little if any possibility of revolts or revenge. The second reason was a systematic plan, whether written or not, to gradually starve the prisoners to death. The final thought being, "one less Jew for them to kill." So, while the majority of the Germans ate well the prisoners in nearly all of the camps were treated to a menu of turnip soup, occasionally laced with a potato or two, and on a good day, a small portion of bread.

The next morning, following the trip to the latrine, the morning count, and the coffee, thankfully with a slice of bread and actually a small portion of honey, Moniek was marched with several others to another enclosed facility a little more than a half a mile from their camp. It was a petroleum oil refinery that produced raw fuel for various vehicles including the deadly German tanks that caused such unimaginable devastation throughout all of Europe.

Initially Moniek worked inside the relatively small building in one of the pump rooms, constantly wiping dust and oil from the sensitive equipment. While the work itself was tedious and mindless it was a world away from carrying the rocks at Birkenau.

Trzebinia was one of the twenty-four subcamps in the Auschwitz III complex. Materials manufactured there were sent to the main facility and the final refining was completed before it was used in the war effort. Few if any of the prisoners had any idea what they were doing or why. They only knew what would happen to them if they didn't comply with each order.

They had their afternoon lunch break, another bowl of soup, and then back to work until well after dark. Following that they marched back to Trzebinia for the evening count, the trip to the latrine, and the evening ration. While the work itself was tedious it was not that physically demanding. The guards, for the most part, generally left the prisoners alone, comforted in the fact that they had relatively easy jobs, were being fed well, and most important of all, were not assigned to the front and the real war where their lives would be in a constant state of peril.

While usually not all that unpleasant a work detail there were occasions when violence would flare up for no apparent reason and a prisoner would be beaten to the point of unconsciousness without explanation. Whenever this happened the others were just forced to stand helplessly at attention and watch the senseless carnage.

In the fall of 1943 airplanes began to appear in the cloud-covered sky. The prisoners outside the facility stopped what they were doing and looked upwards. They were initially punished by the guards because they stopped what they were supposed to be doing. Then small black things began to fall from the airplanes. They were bombs. The refinery was under a full-scale attack, bombs exploding everywhere. The guards and the prisoners ran desperately for cover.

While understandably terrified, the prisoners, for the most part, were thrilled that someone had finally arrived to rescue them from their captors and hopefully return them to freedom and the lives they had once known. Everyone was rushed inside the main building and remained there, huddled under tables and various pieces of equipment and machinery. Another bombing run took place and the building shook violently but did not experience a direct hit.

Then, silence. No more airplane sounds. No more bombs exploding. Everyone held their breath for what seemed like an eternity. After another three minutes or so, after hushed consultation, the guards determined that they should all return to the camp, which apparently was not on the target list, at least not yet.

The prisoners double-timed their way back to the camp and everyone waited anxiously for the planes to return. Inside Moniek's barrack there was a continuing hushed conversation concerning the day's activity. Some whispered that the planes were American. Some said they were British. Like so many other things, it mattered little. The only thing which truly mattered was that someone was finally aware that they were in this evil place and they were doing what they could to free the prisoners. At least that was the common perception.

The hushed conversation lasted late into the evening until sleep finally came. But nothing would stop the pre-dawn morning bell, and the count, and the trip to the latrine, and the strange tasting coffee. Their German captors, with their traditional swagger, appeared and acted as if the bombing raid had never occurred. But the prisoners knew better.

The column was marched back to the refinery site but this day instead of working inside Moniek, along with several others, was handed a shovel and ordered to fill in the bomb craters that pockmarked the surrounding area. The work was considerably more difficult than he was accustomed to and his muscles ached by midmorning. The midday soup, tasteless as it was, was a pleasant treat. Not so much the soup itself but just the opportunity to sit down and relax for a few precious minutes.

After lunch they heard the sound again and looked into the sky. The planes were returning. Knowing what would most certainly follow, the prisoners were rushed inside and took cover. It was ironic that the prisoners were in some senses a precious commodity because they could work and provide benefit to the Third Reich but at the same time they were also completely expendable. The bombs began to explode nearby.

Twenty-Seven

"It is actually true that the Jews have, so to speak, disappeared from Europe and that the Jewish 'Reservoir of the East' from which the Jewish pestilence has for centuries beset the peoples of Europe has ceased to exist. But the Fuehrer of the German people at the beginning of the war prophesied what has now come to pass."

The above quote was printed on November 4, 1943, in the Nazi newspaper, *Der Sturmer*, published by Julius Streicher.

The Jews were disappearing to be sure, but rather than to other countries, as was the original plan, they were disappearing to concentration and extermination camps spread mostly throughout Germany and Poland where they were systematically destroyed in numbers which were so overwhelming they were literally impossible to comprehend. The public announcement in the newspaper and the fact that the Jews were disappearing was considered as remarkably good news to the majority of the German population who followed and adhered to Hitler's line of bizarre reasoning.

In mid-December of that same year the chief surgeon at Auschwitz reported that 106 castration operations had been conducted on Jewish "patients." This barbaric procedure, performed without the benefit of any anesthesia, was yet another attempt designed to contain the further growth of the Jewish population. Understandably it was a remarkably painful and humiliating experience for those forced to experience the practice. These atrocities were carried out in addition to other grotesque medical experiments.

After hundreds of additional "operations" were performed it was determined that the procedure was far too slow to be effective for their stated purposes and it was just easier and considerably quicker to direct the prisoners toward the gas chambers where they would die a gasping death. Efficiency was thought to be important to the Nazis.

And the bombing raids continued. And each time they did Moniek and the others filling in the craters were rushed inside the refinery. And they waited. While cowering underneath a table one of the prisoners whispered, "Isn't it odd that they can target this place and never seem to hit it. They just blow up the surrounding area."

"And why," another man finally said, "if they're this close and they know what's going on, don't they just bomb the camp?"

"They probably don't want to kill any of the prisoners," came a reply from the other side of the table.

"What's the difference," another man offered. "The Germans are going to kill us anyway. If some of us die in a bombing raid that'll probably mean some others will live." Moniek hoped that the raids would continue, because it meant that he'd be reunited with his family that much sooner.

When the guards determined that the raid was over, they could all return to work. Moniek's shovel was in the same place he'd left it barely a half hour before. While understandably terrifying, the bombing raids provided a chance for the prisoners to escape the bitter winter cold and experience a degree of warmth provided by the equipment and machinery in the refinery. Back outside was a bone-chilling reality.

They shoveled the exploded dirt back into the craters, one by one, for no particular reason. Later that afternoon they were thankfully ordered away from the mindless task and moved closer to the outside of the refinery itself. Several carts filled with bricks and bags of cement awaited them at their new worksite as the men stood by, waiting to be told what to do next.

They were told that to better protect the main building they were going to construct a thick brick wall surrounding it. Other prisoners appeared with wheelbarrows, trowels, and pails of ice-cold water. None of the men were experienced bricklayers so more instruction was clearly in order. Once that was accomplished the men set about their new task. Moniek was assigned the job of mixing cement in one of the wheelbarrows. The constant activity, stirring back and forth, actually provided a degree of welcome warmth. But the best part of all was yet to come.

The cement bags were discarded on the ground as they were emptied and Moniek had a flash of genius. The cement bags were double sided and could provide an additional degree of warmth. Cautiously, carefully, he placed two of the empty bags inside his shirt and further, kept his actions to himself so as to not expose his thievery of what would most certainly be considered to be contraband and if discovered would have carried a most severe punishment.

The walk back to their camp that evening was filled with great apprehension. What if he was caught? What would they do to him? To provide additional warmth against the falling temperatures he felt it was a risk which was most definitely worth the taking.

Occasionally there were random searches as they entered the small camp but fortunately tonight that was not to be the case. The cold the prisoners were experiencing was intense, all-consuming. Because they had no socks the cold began literally at their toes and proceeded upward throughout the entire body. When the snow came the pain only intensified. And the Germans showed no concern or regard whatsoever for their captives, innocent people who had done nothing against them. For the most part their only crime, in the eyes of the Third Reich, was that they were Jews and must all, eventually, be destroyed.

After the evening soup and while the majority of the other men visited the latrine, Moniek finally took the treasured cement bags out from under his shirt and stared at them as if he had discovered pure gold. In fact, from a practical standpoint, he had. Obviously there were no scissors, knives, or cutting instruments of any kind inside the barrack. Creativity was the order of the day. With his teeth he ripped the bags into smaller pieces, two of them which he wrapped around his feet to protect them from the cold. If noticed by the guards they would most likely be viewed without reprimand.

Next he ripped and shaped two layers of the bag to fit around his chest. While scratchy and remarkably uncomfortable at first he clearly understood that when the work patrol began the following morning he would be far better protected against the bitter winter elements. One of the other prisoners nearby noticed what he was doing and watched with a degree of jealousy. It was clear he was envious of the creative youngster and at the first possible opportunity would do everything in his powers to replicate his actions.

Soon, on a daily basis, the cement bags began to mysteriously disappear from the work site. No one was really sure if the guards were merely being duped or if they had gotten to the point where they just didn't care anymore. Because of the situation in the war and the fact that the Germans were being forced to retreat on several fronts the majority of them were far more concerned with being transferred from their cushy jobs to real combat and actually having to fight the Americans, the Russians, the British, and the other Allies.

Spring came and then summer and the bombing raids continued. And with each raid the men would be hustled inside to the protective custody of the main building which never experienced a direct hit in all of the air raids. It almost seemed, some of them theorized, as if there was some sort of a master plan to avoid destroying the main plant. However, it was just theory and as was always the case, no one had any real idea of what was going on. The only thing they knew, at the end of each day, was that they had survived another day.

Earlier that year the Soviet troops reached the Polish border and were pushing forward at a slow yet deliberate pace while the Germans gradually retreated. Even losing ground the Nazis deployed troops and occupied Hungary which had a Jewish population of seven hundred twenty-five thousand. Two months later those same people would experience their first of many deportations to Auschwitz-Birkenau where their death was a certainty.

While President Franklin D. Roosevelt issued a statement condemning the Germans and Japanese for their ongoing "crimes against humanity," it did little to ease the burden of Moniek and the others still alive and in confinement. They carried out their daily work assignments and hoped against the fateful moment when their number would be called and they'd be transported back to Birkenau and the gas chambers for their own demise. The fear factor was ever-present.

In April of that year at least three prisoners managed to miraculously escape from Auschwitz and made it safely to Czechoslovakia where one of them, a man named Rudolf Vrba, submitted a report to the Papal Nuncio in Slovakia that was forwarded to the Vatican in mid-June. No official response to the report concerning conditions and treatment at Auschwitz was ever recorded.

While the deadly war raged on, tens of thousands more lives were lost and while the Germans were vocally condemned for "crimes against humanity," in June of that year Auschwitz-Birkenau recorded its highest ever number of persons gassed and burned. More than nine thousand people perished in one twenty-four hour period. Six huge pits just outside the wires of the camp were used to burn the majority of the bodies as the number far exceeded the capacity of the crematories.

There were thousands of guards throughout the massive concentration camp complex. While they could have been utilized in the war effort, which Germany was slowly losing, Hitler chose to keep them in place, terrorizing the growing prisoner population, and executing the prisoner population. It seemed, clearly to many, that Hitler was far more concerned with eliminating the entire Jewish population of Europe than he was with winning the world war he had started or protecting what he pronounced as his treasured Fatherland.

B2992 did exactly as he was instructed, never caused any trouble to or for anyone, and never complained about anything. More rumors spread throughout their small camp, increasing on nearly a nightly basis. They heard that in late July the Soviets had actually liberated the first concentration camp at Majdanek. While a seemingly obscure place in the middle of nowhere, it was later estimated that more than three hundred sixty thousand people had been murdered there.

As the Soviets continued their push forward, Hitler was still adamant in his ultimate goal of achieving Aryan Supremacy. As more and more major battles were lost to the Allies, the Germans liquidated the last Jewish ghetto in Lodz, Poland. Sixty thousand Jews were forced onto boxcars and sent to Auschwitz-Birkenau. They had managed to survive this long and now this trip would be their last.

For unknown reasons more information seemed to be available and transferable between the prisoner population. The guards, and even the SS, while not humane in any sense of the word, began to let many things slide which normally would have carried severe repercussions and severe penalties. They were looking out for themselves, certainly not willing or wishing to go to the front and face the enemy on an up close and personal basis. After all, they had their sticks and their guns and a captive audience which they could abuse as they wished. The actual thought of having to enter a real battle, a shooting war, to protect their country was not appealing in the least.

Moniek heard yet another of the countless rumors floating about near the end of October. This one most definitely caught his attention. Someone whispered late one night that they had heard that the concentration camp at Plaszow had been liquidated and all of its survivors were being transported to Auschwitz. It was indeed a double-edged sword. On one hand Moniek's heart swelled with the possibility that he would once again be able to see his family, that once again, finally, they'd all be reunited. On the other hand, he knew that only a very few who entered the main gate of Birkenau left in any direction other than through the tragic ashes of the chimneys.

He tried as best as he was able to get word into the camp but it was all in vain. There was never a response and in all probability his efforts were never even delivered. By this time the majority of the remaining camps mostly seemed to be in a mass state of confusion. The Soviets were advancing, the Americans and the other Allies were advancing, and the Germans seemed more concerned and preoccupied with killing Jews than anything else.

For no logical reason the prisoners continued to construct brick walls around the main refinery. On days when the sky was clear, the planes would return along with their bombs. Each time this happened the men rushed inside to the warmth and protection of the building. On cloudy days there were no planes and the men were forced to stay outside in the freezing temperature the entire day. Some without the benefit of additional protection against the cold experienced frostbite, some so severely that they could not walk. Those who could not walk could not work. Those who could not work were of no use to the Nazis and were transported by wagon back to Birkenau; everyone knew with a certainty what their fate was going to be.

One day a man from Moniek's barrack was carrying a heavy armload of bricks to the site of the wall and he tripped on the icy ground and dropped them. Several of them shattered on the frozen earth. A guard approached, his wooden stick ready, and began to beat the man. He fell to his knees, his eyes begging for mercy. And the guard continued to beat him. Others wanted to assist, to stop the mindless viciousness, but other guards trained rifles at them as they watched helplessly. And the guard continued to beat him. The man fell flat on his stomach, trying his best to protect himself, to no avail.

And the guard continued to beat him. After a few moments the man's arms fell at his side, no longer able to even make the pretense of trying to protect himself. As he lay lifeless on the cold, hard ground, the guard continued to beat him. He was beating a dead man for no reason. No reason at all.

The Germans continued to lose ground to the Allies. Their war was most certainly being lost and almost everyone was aware of that fact. All men between the ages of sixteen and sixty were drafted into the army, barely trained, and instructed to fight to the death to protect the Fatherland, which was diminishing in size on a daily basis.

The evil Nazi regime and Hitler's madness, especially concerning the concentration and extermination camps, were universally viewed with great disgust. In a final effort to at least try and protect their rapidly dwindling reputation, the Third Reich determined that they must physically erase all evidence of their massive crimes against humanity and Jews in particular.

On November 26th Himmler personally ordered the complete destruction of the gas chambers and crematoriums at Auschwitz-Birkenau. The instruction was that there should be nothing left in the entire camp that could provide proof that they were the mass murderers that they most definitely were.

While the war, for all practical purposes, was over and lost, the Germans persisted in their cruelty toward humanity. In mid-December the Waffen SS murdered eighty-one United States military prisoners of war at a place called Malmedy. There was no more reason for this than there was for the unimaginable carnage carried out in the extermination camps. It was madness personified and executed by underlings who later professed that they were only doing their jobs — they were only following orders.

Many of the soldiers perpetrating these acts of insanity and violence were the same ones who came home from what they considered to be a hard day on the job, kissed their wife, had a hearty and hot meal, read their children a story, said prayers, and tucked them safely into their beds for the night. While this continued to occur, the Jews were being moved in mass volumes, away from the approaching Allies, away from their own liberation and from life itself.

In early January of 1945, Moniek and the others in the barrack were greeted by the familiar, piercing sound of the bell. By now their routine was well established. But this day would be different from all the rest. This day, when the morning count was completed, they were marched out of the camp and rather than their normal direction, moved toward the south. Moniek was especially pleased on this day that he had used the cement bags to create additional warmth. Others who had followed his lead were equally pleased. Those who had not had icicles form on their lips and hair as the march continued.

By nightfall they reached their destination. They had been marched back to Auschwitz. Except this time they were entering Auschwitz

I, the initial and the principal camp of the enormous complex. As they passed underneath it the sign above the main gate proclaimed, *Arbeit Macht Frei,* translated as "Work Will Make You Free." This phrase had, over the years, proven to be one of the greatest and most tragic lies recorded throughout history.

Twenty-Eight

The main camp of Auschwitz was unlike anything Moniek had ever seen. It was austere and remarkably clean. The roads were paved and the two and a half story tall brick barracks resembled collegiate dormitories considerably more than places where both men and women were mindlessly tortured, had horrendous medical experiments performed on them, worked literally to death, or just senselessly murdered.

They were marched to a barrack in the middle of the camp which initially seemed to be about half full of other prisoners. For the most part the men were sitting on the ends of their bunks, staring blankly into a dark sea of nothingness. They generally appeared to be somewhere between young and middle-aged. Their common trait was that they each, to the man, looked to be semiemaciated and nearly starved to death. They were bone-thin, eyes hollow. Moniek tried to quietly initiate conversations with some of the men but it was to no avail. The men he was trying to speak with were men who were waiting to die. Their demise would be their escape from this place which had created so much evil and inhumanity over the last several years.

A block senior appeared and addressed the new arrivals but his message was nothing like the ones Moniek had heard in the past. This particular speech was low key, actually reserved, as if he didn't want to be there any more than any of the rest them. But he had his job to do and it was done by rote, without compassion but also without the vile and ominous threats Moniek was so familiar with.

In time several others entered the barrack from their various work patrols outside the main compound. They were normally considered to be the lucky ones, the ones who were still alive. Work details that particular day and for several days preceding it were lax to say the very least. Punishment seemed to strangely ease for no apparent reason and the enormously ridiculous work schedule was virtually abandoned. There was most definitely something going on and none of the guards or anyone else was talking about it.

Moniek and the other new arrivals were each given new bowls and spoons. As always they were treasured items, closely watched, and protected above all other things. Which in fact was reasonably ironic because those simple things, a tin bowl and a rusty spoon, were the only possessions they had in this bizarre world that had transformed all of their lives.

The evening cart arrived with the tureen of soup and it was understandably devoured with haste but not by all. Some of the men, some of the ones Moniek had seen when he first arrived, appeared to have no appetite at all. Others, presumed to be friends, collected their soup and brought it to their bunks where they sat in silence but they expressed no interest in eating. They continued to stare into a world that only they could see. And again, like so many times before, Moniek was confused.

Why weren't these other people eating, Moniek asked himself? Their tins, filled with the soup, were soon taken by others and eaten without comment. The people the food had been stolen from continued to stare at the walls with no expression on their faces. They were too weak to work. They were too weak to eat. They were too weak to do anything but die, once again saving the Nazis the expense of gas or a bullet for their ultimate demise.

"Musselmen," a man seated beside Moniek calmly stated.

"Excuse me," Moniek responded.

"Musselmen," the man repeated. "They're what we call Musselmen. You're looking at them with wide eyes like you don't know anything."

The youngster, too wise beyond his years, said, "You're right. I don't know anything." And then he looked at the floor.

After a few seconds the man said, "The people who don't eat are what we call the walking dead. They are just waiting for their time to end."

"But why?" Moniek questioned.

The man slowly shook his head and softly replied, "Because they see no reason to live, no reason to go on. They've seen too much death over the long, painful years. They've lost their entire families. They've been worked beyond the capacity of human capability. A person can only take so much."

"And this is their choice? To starve to death? As near as we probably are to being liberated?"

"Some of them will die from starvation. Others will go to the wires. All of them will die." The man spoke with no trace of emotion as he slurped his soup. He was merely stating facts, a reality which he had witnessed all too many times.

The building had its own running water and restroom facilities, considerably different from what Moniek had experienced over the years. And, like the outside of the building, the floors and the walls were exceptionally clean. That evening as the lights were extinguished the youngster didn't hear the familiar sound of tiny feet, scratching their way across the floor: the rats.

In the past he had seen other people occasionally catch rats, prepare a small fire, cook them and then eat them. However, as hungry as he normally was, he could not bring himself to eat the disease-infected vermin, which proved to be a wise decision on his part. The diseases carried by the majority of the rats normally quickened the death rate of those who ate them. In many cases it was basically the same as eating poison.

Being in a clean place with indoor plumbing, even knowing that he was still a prisoner, proved to be a delightful treat. Moniek hoped silently that in spite of all he'd heard perhaps this place would be different from the others he'd experienced. Just before he fell asleep he thought about Plaszow and what he'd heard about all its inhabitants being transferred to Auschwitz. If, he thought, his parents and brothers had come to a place like the one he was presently in, they would most certainly still be alive. As he drifted off to sleep he actually had a small smile on his face. It was the first time that had happened in a very long time. He knew he would see his family again; he had hope.

The following morning the all too familiar bell rang, but instead of the normal and usual panic as all the men ran to and fro, there was a bizarre sense of calm. The prisoners who had been there previously went to the lavatory and actually took their time about it. They relieved themselves. They washed their hands and faces. The block senior was not in the room screaming at everyone to hurry, hurry, hurry. The entire general attitude was altogether different from what he had experienced in the past and he found it to be confusing.

After grabbing his bowl and spoon Moniek stood at attention at the front of the barrack. He was soon joined by several of the other new arrivals. The prisoners who had been there for a while just shook their heads. "Sit back down," one of them said. "The coffee'll be here in a little bit. Then you can relax some more."

"What about the morning count?" Moniek asked. It was a logical question considering the fact that he had been counted every single morning while he was a prisoner in Plaszow, Kielce, Birkenau, and Trzebinia. What had happened to the meticulous recordkeeping of the Nazis?

"Stopped having the count two days ago," the man answered.

"What about our work details?" another newcomer asked.

"Pretty much stopped those too. Mostly we just stay inside and try to keep warm. At least they still bring food."

Moniek was stunned. "What's going on?"

The man shook his head. "No one knows, not even the block senior or the guards. Everybody seems to be really confused."

No count, no work detail, the ability to stay inside and keep out of the freezing temperatures. It all sounded much too good to be true. An inner voice told him that this treatment couldn't possibly last but he was more than prepared to take advantage of it for as long as it did. Moniek looked outside the front door and saw other prisoners milling about. There didn't appear to be any organization and no one was marching in the familiar lines of five. It was all very strange. It was an unexpected and unusual sight.

"Are we allowed to go outside?" Moniek asked the man.

"If you want. You can't get out of the camp but from what I hear you can go anywhere on the inside. One thing though…"

"What's that?"

"Stay away from the wires. If you get too close to them, you'll be shot."

Moniek took the advice to heart though he'd heard it before in other places. With the rest of the prisoners he waited patiently in the warmth of the barrack until the morning coffee was delivered. It was brought with a crust of bread and like before he saved a portion of it for later in the day. After a brief rest and while others sat on their bunks or returned to sleep, Moniek decided to venture outside and explore this infamous place for himself.

Many other prisoners were milling about apparently without supervision. There were no block seniors shouting instructions or any sign of uniformed guards or SS men. After a few minutes Moniek did witness a series of what he felt were truly unusual sights. He saw an occasional SS man entering a barrack and then quickly leaving carrying handfuls of paper.

These pages were taken away and burned along with thousands of other pages, cabinet after cabinet filled with files which the Nazis had accumulated over the years in their attempt to maintain perfect records concerning everything they had done and the successes they had achieved since the Third Reich came into control over the entire country and virtually all of Europe. The Nazis had been pathologically diligent in keeping their records, and now they scrambled like rats to hide their sins, burning all the meaningless records.

Burning paper, files, and records of all sorts and variety was not enough to disguise, diffuse, or diminish the tragedy and unbelievable pain the German army had inflicted in six agony-filled years on an entire continent. Tragically, other burnings were also taking place. In many of the camps when prisoners would perish from starvation, exhaustion, suicide, medical experimentation, or just a series of mindless murders, their bodies were placed in large open holes dug in the ground until the pits were filled. Once the maximum level had been achieved the pits were covered over with dirt.

Naturally this labor was carried out by other prisoners. Shovel after shovel filled with dirt, covering up an open pile of dead bodies. But on rare occasion someone would still be alive, screaming or moaning through the surrounding pile of cadavers. The workers who reported this miracle and begged for the mercy of life were generally rewarded with a bullet into their head and thrown into the pile themselves. Since the bodies had not had time to decompose the Nazis at the highest level decided that the mass graves must be reopened, dug up. Once that horrendous task was completed they were forced to pour gasoline on the bodies and set them on fire.

The sickening aroma from the burning flesh in the raging blazes spread throughout Europe's countryside. It was not uncommon that many of the prisoners who had participated in the digging and the burning were subsequently executed and thrown into the burning pyre as well. The actions of the Nazis were all designed to erase all traces of the tragedy they had personally created. They didn't want to leave any evidence. No witnesses were to be left alive. Beneath their arrogance and madness at least some of the Reich's leaders still knew shame, seemingly.

Moniek moved cautiously through the compound, occasionally nodding at other prisoners as they passed. There was little if any conversation. Most of the others he saw were very thin, thin to the point that it must have been an effort for some of them to even walk. The well-kept camp was fairly large. It had twenty-eight barracks which were each capable of holding up to one thousand prisoners, a laundry facility which not long ago provided clean uniforms to the prisoners on a weekly basis, and a large kitchen right beside the main gate. Moniek was told that until recently this was the area where the camp orchestra would perform every morning as the prisoners marched out toward their various work assignments and then again in the evening as the men returned.

He could easily smell the food being prepared from the kitchen area as he passed by. He stopped long enough to savor the aromas, wishing he were inside surrounded by the volumes of food, remembering the kitchen where he grew up, and the meals his mother used to prepare, still hoping and expecting that they were all still alive and that they'd somehow be reunited.

That evening he ate his soup and chose to remain inside while a few others ventured out into the confines of the camp. He didn't ask where they were going or why. Even though the guards and the SS had virtually vanished from inside the wires they were always there, always lurking, always willing to end a life for no reason at all. He felt safer inside and that's where he stayed.

Just before sleep came he heard the violent burst of a machine gun. Very few of the others in the room seemed to be startled. It was almost as if it was a commonplace sound and occurrence. The man in the next bunk offered without expression or concern, "A musselman."

"What about it?" Moniek innocently asked.

"Usually the guards let them get to the wires where they'll be electrocuted. While they're hanging there on the wires, still alive, they shoot them." Then the man rolled over and went to sleep. From all the places he'd been and all the things he'd heard about, and all the things he'd personally seen, this was among the cruelest and most sadistic of the stories which had ever entered his still very young and impressionable ears.

The following morning, thankfully, was the same as the previous one. No screaming block senior, no hurry, hurry, hurry, no count, no work details. While enormously delightful, it all seemed very strange. A few SS men were walking inside the camp, for a pleasant change not delivering punishment to any of the prisoners who happened to be on the roads between the barracks.

The SS men appeared to have no real focus, no certain direction. One could ascertain that they were confused and not clearly sure as to what they were doing. However, as long as they weren't mindlessly beating people for no reason, it was a blessing that many of the prisoners were more than glad to receive.

After the coffee and a slice of bread Moniek continued his exploration of the enclosed facility. He went to the far corner of the camp, a location most people dreaded and feared. It was here that the infamous blocks 10 and 11 were located. Block 10 was the hospital barrack which in truth was actually more of a torture chamber. It was here that many of the heinous medical experiments were conducted on completely innocent victims.

Block 11 was the prison facility within the prison facility. Here people were tortured beyond any rational person's imagination. Among other devices they utilized an apparatus referred to as *der baum* or, "the tree." It was a crossbar about six feet in the air. Prisoners, after constant, vicious beatings during interrogation, would have their hands tied securely behind their backs. Then their hands were tied to a rope hanging from the crossbar and pulled tightly until their feet left the ground.

Once hanging in the air the weight of their body would normally dislocate both of their shoulders. Following this it was normal for most people to pass out, the only way the intense pain could possibly be relieved. Attempts were made to revive the suffering agony, but only for an even worse and more tragic event which was soon to follow.

The prisoner being interrogated would be taken outside, in most cases they literally had to be dragged. Outside was "the Wall." There was a brick wall constructed between block 10 and 11 near the outside wall of the camp. This place was most usually referred to as "the Wall of Death." The prisoner, with dislocated shoulders and in most cases barely able to walk, was stood against the wall and shot. It was common to hear gunshots ringing out throughout most of every day. Once the executions were completed the bodies were transported to Birkenau where they were cremated and their ashes would be distributed into a large marsh behind the gas chambers and crematoriums.

That day Moniek also returned to the front gate by the camp kitchen. Through the wires and on the other side of the road he could see a very large brick building to his left. A passerby explained that that place was the main administration building for the camp. It was normal that when new prisoners arrived they would go through the administration building to be showered, shaved, deloused, tattooed, and officially registered onto the ever expanding roll of men who would never know or experience freedom again.

Across the road from the administration building was a series of other well-kept buildings. These were production areas and workshops. For the most part these were light manufacturing facilities where among other things a machine shop produced gun barrels for the German army on a series of lathes. When work and production this critical was necessary, the prisoners were usually supervised by a small number of skilled civilian employees. Very few if any of these "civilian employees" ever divulged the truth about Auschwitz or what was going on there. They did their jobs, got paid, went home, and slept well.

Later that evening Moniek learned that there was a large construction site behind the manufacturing facilities. Several of the men in the barrack where he was now incarcerated had actually been assigned to work on the project but for unexplained reasons the construction was mysteriously halted. From the cement footers and foundations they were preparing it was fairly common knowledge that the additional construction site was actually for the completion of another twenty barracks. Rumor had it that the majority of these barracks were going to be utilized by women. If this were indeed the case the facility known as Auschwitz I would have had the capacity of holding up to fifty thousand prisoners at any one time.

Because of the continuing advancement of the Soviet army and what seemed to be the confusion of the SS and the other guards, all construction in the entire area came to an abrupt halt. For this the prisoners, especially the ones doing the back-breaking work in the freezing temperatures, were greatly relieved. They were inside, they were reasonably warm, they were being fed; unfortunately they were still prisoners of the Third Reich and had no idea what their fate was going to be. Based on the confusion surrounding the camp itself it seemed that no one else had any idea either. Like so many of them had done for so many years, they waited.

Twenty-Nine

All three of the camps, Auschwitz I, Auschwitz II-Birkenau, and Auschwitz III, the production facility for the I.G. Farben factory which created synthetic fuel and rubber, were surrounded by what the Nazis referred to as an "Interest Zone." The zone was well patrolled and no one without an official reason and well-documented identification papers was allowed anywhere near any of the camps. Their security system was virtually impenetrable. The nearby town of Oswiecim was completely off limits and the residents insisted that they had no idea what was occurring within the walls of these sprawling compounds.

Several subcamps within the Interest Zone provided a variety of goods and services for the prisoners, the guards, and the German army. Among them was Budy, which was an auxiliary camp for men; a women's camp; and a punishment facility, as well as vast agricultural products, including several large fishponds. Harmense and Plawy also produced agricultural products and contained many fish farms and livestock breeding areas as well. Rajsko was an SS Hygiene Institute which had a woman's labor camp and an experimental station where unspeakable atrocities were performed on prisoners on a daily basis.

While Auschwitz I was very large with its twenty-eight barracks, laundry and kitchen facilities, manufacturing facilities, and ongoing construction, it paled in comparison to the dimensions of Birkenau. The camp known as Birkenau consisted of more than three hundred buildings. The vast majority of them were barracks for prisoners, several were separate latrine facilities, and thirty composed the area known as Canada where stolen clothing and personal possessions were separated and stored until they were distributed to troops on the front or sent back to Germany. Birkenau, the Death Factory, also had five gas chambers and crematoriums which operated twenty-four hours a day. Behind the wires of the enclosure were several huge, mass graves, many of them still engulfed in flames from the burning bodies.

In addition, an attached facility was well under construction. By the end of 1944 sixty-seven new buildings were in various stages of completion. When completed the buildings were designed to reach a total of one hundred and eighty and effectively would have doubled the size of the place and the number of prisoners it could hold and eventually exterminate.

Again, wishing to destroy any evidence of their crimes against humanity, the Germans ordered the destruction of several of their rather noticeable facilities. The first among them were the crematoriums themselves. As the explosives blew down the walls of several of the vile buildings the remaining prisoners, those who still had the strength, let out a great cheer. However, in their haste, all of the crematoriums were not completely destroyed. Many of the barracks were set on fire in the misguided attempt to hide their existence and what had been done there.

Those still imprisoned in Birkenau could hear faint, muffled sounds in the far off distance. It was the sound of heavy artillery. It was the sound of the Soviets moving forward, forward to rescue them and hopefully restore their freedom. Many of the men still remaining did not have the energy to respond. They just hoped that they'd arrive at the camp sooner rather than later. It was clear to virtually everyone that the Germans had finally lost the war they had begun. The prisoners would look at each other and repeatedly say, "lost cause." However, the "lost cause" this time seemed to actually be for the Germans and not for themselves.

News of the destruction occurring in Birkenau and the approaching Soviets reached the main camp and the rumors began to circulate.

It was mid-January in 1945 and the camp was in chaos. Guards and SS men seemed to be in a hurry, scurrying in all directions with no real clear purpose in mind. Moniek and the other prisoners stayed inside and watched through the front door and windows, trying to glean any concept as to what was happening.

The block senior entered the barrack and when questioned could offer no information, just more unsubstantiated rumors from other block seniors. Like the balance of the prisoners, they hadn't been told anything either. Whispers circulated with possibilities, none of which seemed realistic.

"They're going to release us," one man quietly offered with a controlled degree of optimism.

"We're finally going to be rescued," another one said with a sigh.

Most of the others were still too physically weak to add much if anything to the conversation. They sat in silence and just listened, wondering and hoping if any of this could possibly be true.

There were controlled smiles in the room until one of them finally replied, "What's the matter with you people? They're going to kill us. Don't you know that by now? They're going to kill us all." The room was even more silent as the probable reality erased any hopeful thoughts which had been previously shared. The Third Reich, the Nazis, the SS, and all of Germany who followed Hitler's madness had lost all sense of integrity, conscience, or principle. One man's anger and unbridled hatred had found willing ears and hands and bodies who bullied and cajoled others into following their mad course. These vile souls transformed a once remarkably civilized country into a land in which mass murder was most simply an accepted matter-of-fact.

The soup that night tasted exactly the same as it did each and every night. When the lights were extinguished there were soft sounds of whimpering and prayers. It was difficult for Moniek to tell the difference between the two.

The next morning, as always, the bell shattered the stillness of the pitch black sky but this particular morning the block senior stood in front of the room with two, burly assistants at his side. "This morning there will be a count," he announced with authority. "Everyone outside! Now!" The prisoners did as instructed and stood in their carefully formed lines at attention. Snow had fallen during the night which made it even colder than usual. On the majority of mornings this winter and this one in particular Moniek was extremely thankful for the two cement bags surrounding his chest on the inside of his shirt and the strips covering his feet.

The SS man appeared, clipboard in hand, and counted the prisoners. Then he counted them again. He whispered something to the block senior and left into the darkness of the early morning. The block senior indicated for everyone to go back inside and they followed his instructions without question. Once inside he said, "The morning coffee will be here in a short time. If you wish, go to the latrine now. I'd suggest you do." His delivery was flat. It was clear that he knew something he was not sharing with the others, which only led to more confusion among those who still had the strength or the will to care about anything.

This particular morning brought an unexpected and very special surprise. Instead of the normal slice or crust of bread each man was given a half a loaf. The block senior moved to the front of the room and announced without explanation, "This bread should be eaten very carefully..."

The men didn't know what he meant but he continued, "We're leaving this morning. The camp is being evacuated. I don't know where we're going but this may be all the food you'll have for a few days. Eat as little as you can at one time, small portions."

"You say you have no idea where we're going?" one of the men cautiously asked.

"No. Only that we're leaving in a half an hour. The entire camp. You can do whatever you want for a half an hour, then you have to be back here. I assure you the guards will find anyone who doesn't return and shoot you on the spot."

Prisoners began to mill about, continuing to wonder about their fate. Some of them left the barracks and joined many others on the camp roads. Several made their way to the kitchen, which they broke into, and stole as much food as they could carry. Others broke into the laundry facility and stole extra clothing which would hopefully protect them from the cold which they were certainly going to experience as the day, and more importantly the night, progressed.

The prisoners nearly all congregated back at the barracks at the appointed hour. A few did not return but found hiding places, hoping they would somehow not be detected and avoid whatever lay in store. When the order was given to report outside several of the men who were too ill or frail found it literally impossible to leave their bunks. While it was very unusual, an SS man actually entered the barracks and gave the remaining few a cursory glance. As always, with typical Nazi nonemotion, he told the block senior, "Leave them. They're going to die anyway."

Once outside the building the column began to move forward. They were joined by other groups from other barracks. They walked under the "Work Will Make You Free" sign and past the now empty bandstand where the orchestra used to play on a daily basis, keeping a steady tempo and cadence of doom as thousands and thousands of others marched to their personal destruction.

It was cold, very cold. Those who had not taken precautions and obtained additional clothing or blankets or coverings of any sort were the first to feel the biting pain of the mid-January temperature. The column grew along the way as they were joined by prisoners from Birkenau. All told it is estimated that fifty-six thousand men left the confines of Auschwitz and began what was to tragically become known and forever referred to as the infamous "Death March."

The column was well-guarded by heavily armed SS men walking on either side of the prisoners. Many of them were shivering from the cold. Others who had stolen food from the kitchen now wished they had obtained additional clothing instead. The morning was brutal. And they just kept on walking. When someone got physically sick and moved to the side of the road they were shot by the guards. And the column just kept on walking. In time the snow covering the side of the road ran red with blood. And the column just kept on walking.

The sun finally appeared but offered little relief. There was no rest break. Men relieved themselves as they walked. While the urine provided an initial sense of warmth it was quickly replaced by extensive pain as the urine froze. Minds were a blur. Why were they doing this? What on earth was the point? The Red Army was closing in at a rapid pace and countless soldiers who could have been used to protect their precious Fatherland were marching thousands of starving and freezing prisoners to an unknown destination.

While it was clearly unknown to the vast majority, that destination was back in Germany where all of the survivors could effectively be murdered. Hitler had required children and elderly people to join the army and they were forced to fight the real battle to protect Germany while thousands of trained military personnel were being used to guard at least fifty-six thousand prisoners, the vast majority of them Jews, to march them to their eventual death. This bizarre exercise was a result of the mindless hatred that the Nazis fostered in their hearts and institutionalized; this hatred had quickly become an evil, self-destructive obsession. They had failed to take over the world, failed to be glorious and, now, they would not be cheated of being able to kill these last few pitiful victims.

Hitler's dream was not to be denied at any cost. It was clear that he and his followers were willing to let his entire country be completely destroyed in order to further serve his concept of Aryan Supremacy. All Jews, all "subhumans" were to be exterminated. The mindset of Adolf Hitler and others in the hierarchy of the Third Reich will never be completely known or understood. What is known and understood is his unfailing will to eliminate Europe and eventually the entire world of all Jews, Communists, Gypsies…and on and on. The Nazi mindset could only feed off of hatred — eventually, had they been triumphant, they would have had to feed on themselves.

A man walking beside Moniek stumbled and slipped on the frozen road. Moniek grabbed his arm and helped him back up. "You're going to be fine," Moniek whispered. "You're going to make it."

"I can't go on," the man replied, out of breath, nearly out of life.

"Yes you can," Moniek whispered. "We're all going to make it."

And just as Moniek spoke the words another man dropped on the side of the road. As he vomited in a ditch an SS man shot him in the head. More crimson covered the once pure white snow. Moniek remembered the words he'd heard so many times from each new block senior, "There is no escape from this place."

At midday they were allowed a fifteen minute break and men scrambled and searched for any place to sit down and rest. Some leaned against nearby trees but most just collapsed on the freezing ground. No food was provided. Some eagerly ate the balance of the bread they had been given that morning which would prove in short time to be a grave mistake. Others, emaciated, near starvation, dug through the snow until they found tufts of grass which they ripped up and devoured. This as well, while momentarily filling, in essence provided a death sentence only hours or at the most, days away.

Some of the men became violently ill and couldn't continue the march. And for them, the march was over. They were shot where they lay on the side of the road. The nonstop murder was horrendous and continued throughout the day. When a German shot a prisoner there was no more emotion in the execution than if he were swatting a fly. Life wasn't just cheap, it was irrelevant.

They were marched until nightfall and then long after that. More men fell along the side of the road. More men were shot. The "Death March" became a moving killing field and unlike their previous attempts the Germans had no way of disposing of the carnage they were creating. The bodies were left to a frozen, open coffin in which come summer they would decompose or in all probability be eaten by wild animals.

When they finally stopped, it was in the middle of nowhere, not a building in sight. It mattered little. The prisoners were told that this was where they would be spending the night. They were forced to the side of the road and surrounded by the armed guards who built fires to keep themselves warm but certainly none of the others. The snow covered ground provided only additional pain. Those who had not taken the precaution of obtaining extra clothing were particularly devastated as the temperature fell well below the freezing mark. More grass was dug out of the dirt and eaten. More men became violently ill. There were gunshots throughout the entire night, presumably signaling the demise of prisoners trying to escape. And again the words rang so clearly, "There is no escape from this place."

Very little sleep was possible during the bone-chilling evening. In the morning, as always well before sunrise, the prisoners who were able to catch a small amount of rest were awakened not by the familiar bell but this time by the burst of machine gun fire. "Everyone up! Back on the road!" Those not following instructions quickly enough were beaten. It was apparent that the madness this particular day would not cease.

As the prisoners continued their march up the frozen road, the Soviets were liberating the ghetto at Warsaw and two days later the ghetto at Lodz. Where once two hundred fifty thousand Jews had resided less than nine hundred remained to be liberated. The balance of them had all been sent to various camps throughout Poland and Germany to their destruction.

Moniek's day, like the one before, was filled with sameness. They continued to march without rest or food. Those who stumbled or became ill were shot and left on the side of the road. Strangely enough, cold-blooded murder bizarrely became a way of life. It was just a simple matter of fact that was accepted by most. The Third Reich had brainwashed the majority of an entire population, they had created callousness that unfortunately hadn't dissipated or softened. This horrible inhumanity was the legacy of the Thousand Year Reich. All too many of their captives were the innocent victims of this legacy.

Following yet another pain and agony filled day the prisoners were finally allowed to stop. For the most part they expected, from their previous night's experience, that whatever rest they might receive would be limited at best. They stopped at a deserted farm and naturally the soldiers occupied the farmhouse leaving the majority of the troops outside to build fires and guard the prisoners in the surrounding area. Moniek, fortunately, was among those who were directed into the barn. While forced at gunpoint into the enclosure he found it ironic, thinking wistfully and fondly back to the time that he and his family hid out in a barn, hiding from the same Germans who now pointed loaded weapons at him. Somehow irony doesn't work all that well when there's a machine gun pointed directly in your face.

The barn, while considerably warmer than the outside clime, where many of the others were forced to fend for themselves, was absolutely packed to the walls and rafters with people. It was reminiscent of the last train ride he experienced where people slept while standing straight up, relieved themselves where they stood, and some died during the horrendous process.

The prisoners were forced into the enclosure until there was literally no further room for any more bodies. Moniek eased his way past and through the sea of people until he finally discovered a large pile of hay on the far side of the building. Remembering days and nights past and securing some degree of warmth he fell to his knees and burrowed his way into the bottom of the pile of hay while others prepared to sleep on top of it.

It was reasonably quiet with a modicum degree of warmth and even relative security if for only a fleeting moment. Many men senselessly lost their lives during the last two days. Many more had also lost their lives on several other forced marches as various camps were evacuated and the prisoners walked toward Germany. During the final roll call on January 17th, just prior to their leaving the camp, it was reported that 10,030 prisoners were in Auschwitz I, 11,576 prisoners were in Auschwitz II-Birkenau, and 33,045 were in Auschwitz III (the I.G. Farben facility). In total the entire camp population had been reduced to 54,651. And now, as a result of the severity of the march they were experiencing, that number had greatly diminished.

Those who were still fortunate enough to be alive all needed to find and hold strongly in their hearts a sense of meaning if they were to survive. For Moniek that sense of meaning was that soon this terrible experience would all be over and that he'd eventually be reunited with his family. That was the only thing which kept him going and kept him alive.

With that thought in mind he finally fell asleep.

THIRTY

THE DOORS OF THE barn burst open. "Out! Out! Everybody out!" The German soldiers were screaming, as was their normal demeanor. Prisoners shuffled from their sleeping positions, stiff, without decent rest, still freezing cold. It was going to be another pain-filled and arduous day on the road. A day without food, rest, and in all probability a day many others would die.

"Faster! Faster!" The men moved outside into the darkness and the freezing chill of the morning. The column was formed and began to move forward. They were not even allowed the opportunity of relieving themselves. Moniek began to stir and started to leave the relative warmth of the pile of hay when a hand softly touched his leg and an unfamiliar voice whispered, "Stay where you are. Stay quiet. Don't move."

The voice was both confident and authoritative and Moniek followed the instructions. More prisoners were leaving the barn and the soldiers continued to scream. One of the men, apparently not moving fast enough for the guards, was shot. The report from the blast inside the building created a lingering echo and caused pain in the ears. And as he was told, Moniek stayed perfectly still. He could feel people walking on top of him, on top of the pile of hay. There was another gunshot which was followed by the remaining stragglers leaving the barn. Then it was quiet, very quiet.

Moniek, who like the majority of the others, had slept very little the last two nights, listened cautiously for a few precious moments. The silence continued and remarkably he managed to fall back asleep. In time, and no one had any real concept of time, the same hand he'd felt earlier gently nudged his leg. "They're gone," the voice whispered. "I think it's safe for us to come out now."

Slowly, with enormous caution, the two men left the safety of the pile of hay. Moniek didn't know the man. He'd never seen him before. He looked into the eyes of the total stranger who in all probability had just saved his life and they nodded at one another. Without speaking they moved to the door of the barn and carefully looked outside.

The sun was full in the sky and for an unexplainable and strange reason they each felt a degree of warmth. Perhaps it was the feeling that at least for the time being they were no longer under the heel or the control of the incredibly brutal and vicious Nazis. It was an unusual feeling, one neither one of them had experienced in a very long time. The road outside was empty. The column of their once fellow prisoners was gone. They were alone.

A bird flew past the barn and landed in a nearby tree, his sweet song drifting softly across the mid-morning breeze. It seemed like it had been a lifetime since Moniek had even seen a bird or heard their gentle songs of freedom. Moniek and the stranger looked at each other and smiled a smile of unbelievable relief. Moniek, now sixteen, warmly shook hands with his benefactor. "Thanks," was all he could muster.

"We're not out of this yet," the man replied. "I have no idea where we are or where we're going."

"I know where I'm going. I'm going to Nowy Wisnicz," Moniek said.

The man smiled again. It was a different feeling, a different emotion. Neither of them had really smiled since their incarceration began and they were forced to experience and witness such remarkable cruelty and unimaginable inhumanity. "I guess that's where you're from," he said.

"Yes sir. My family is there and I'm going back home to find them."

The man looked down at the floor and frowned. He looked at Moniek a long time before he spoke. When he did speak his voice was sad. "They may not be there. With everything the Germans have done over the years…well…you shouldn't get your hopes up…you just never know."

Moniek's response was passionate. "I know. They're there. When I go back home, they'll all be there waiting for me, my mother and father and brothers."

The man nodded. "I hope you're right. I really do."

Introductions followed. The man's name was Erich Richter, a Hungarian Jew who had also been in the camp system for nearly three years. Together they determined that it would be much safer for them to wait until dark before they began their travels. While not in sight they assumed that Germans were still nearby. Being captured at this stage would mean instant execution. They'd both seen enough of that and they waited impatiently for the sun to set.

They had two immediate priorities that needed to be met. The first, obviously, was to obtain some food. The second was to exchange their striped prisoner uniforms for something that would be less obvious as they traveled cross country. Wearing civilian clothing they could travel during the day, something which would be impossible wearing the stripes.

As soon as the sun set the two of them left the barn and began their quest. A mile or two down the road they came to a small farm and approached the house. They were greeted by two, large, snarling dogs and wisely decided to continue their trek. Moniek went into nearby fields and attempted to find something growing in the ground that might be edible. Unfortunately, the moving column of prisoners ahead of them had picked the fields clean of whatever was there.

Further down the road they came upon another farm and this time were considerably more cautious. The lights were still on in the farmhouse and fortunately there were no dogs to greet them. Erich was very concerned and after they had decided the place was reasonably safe said, "I think it'd be better and much safer if we waited until morning before we let anyone know we were here. Showing up on their porch in striped uniforms might surprise whoever's inside and cause them to do something dangerous."

Moniek agreed and together they silently entered the barn. There were a few milk cows standing in stalls that paid them no attention but did provide a degree of warmth in the small enclosure. In one corner there was a fair sized pile of hay, obviously used to feed the animals. Moniek and Erich looked at the hay, then at each other, and then smiled. And then, as they had both done the previous night, they burrowed into the warmth of the hay and fell asleep, actually experiencing the breath of freedom for the first time in several years. Moniek dreamed of playing soccer with his brothers in front of their house in Nowy Wicnisz.

"Get up! Both of you! I know you're hiding in there!" It was the man who owned the farm, carrying a rifle, pointing it at the pile of hay, prepared to shoot either one of them. "I saw you both come in last night and just wanted to wait till I could see your faces. You're German prisoners and you belong to them. They'll be back soon and then you'll both be gone."

Moniek and Erich slowly exited the pile, wiping hay from their striped uniforms, wiping sleep from their eyes. The farmer was extremely nervous, waving the gun from side to side, training it on both of them, one to the other, back and forth. It was a very dangerous situation. Moniek was the first to speak and he did so very softly, very slowly. "If you turn us in to the Germans we'll have to tell them that you were willing to hide us here. Do you know what will happen to you and whoever else lives here if we tell them that?"

The man didn't move. He seemed to be frozen in his tracks by the words spoken by the youngster. He knew with a certainty what would happen. It would be a death sentence without the benefit of a trial or the possibility of any rebuttal. He hesitated a moment and then finally lowered his rifle. "What do you want?" he quietly asked.

"We'd like some food," Erich replied. "We haven't eaten in several days. Give us some food and we'll leave you alone."

The owner of the farm rapidly contemplated his options, slowly shook his head in complete frustration, and then backed out of the barn toward the house. Moniek and Erich looked at each other and shrugged. They had no idea what the farmer was going to do. What they did know was that they had the relative protection of the barn and the fact that it would be extremely dangerous to try and move down the road wearing the stripes. They waited. They were both very experienced and very good at that. They'd been doing that for years.

Shortly after their brief encounter the farmer returned to the barn carrying two plates of food, real cooked food. There was chicken and a potato and even some beans. The farmer presented it to them without conversation and moved to the cows in the stalls where he milked them. Moniek and Erich ate heartily, silently in that it had been so very long since either of them had experienced such a feast. The food was warm, cooked through and through. In reality they both felt as if they had entered a new world, a world which for them was only a far-away memory.

As the farmer left the barn he gave them a cursory glance and finally said, "I gave you the food you asked for. Now leave." And with that he retrieved the empty plates and returned to the main house. Moniek and his new-found friend once again looked at one another and shrugged. It was still too light for them to be on the road and while their stomachs were delightfully filled they had no idea when they might eat again. So, like so many other times, they waited.

The farmer returned to the barn later that evening to milk the cows again and was very surprised to find both of them still there. At first he was speechless but finally said, "I thought you said you were going to leave after I gave you some food."

"We can't leave," Moniek replied.

"Why not?"

"Look at us. We can't go anywhere wearing these striped uniforms."

"I don't understand." The farmer replied.

Moniek was extremely cautious with his next proposal. "Give us some clothes we can wear and we'll leave."

Silence. Then finally, "That's what you said about the food."

"Some clothes we can wear and then we'll leave and never see you again."

The farmer slowly nodded and returned to his house. Less than ten minutes later he reappeared carrying an armload of clothing. Moniek and Erich sorted through the items, selecting that which they could wear and they were quickly adorned. They had shirts, jackets and pants. Moniek wisely kept wearing the two layers of cement bags protecting his chest from the winter elements.

With full stomachs and new clothing they left the barn and proceeded down the road. They were now at least an entire day behind the marching column which was most certainly destined for death. As they walked they saw several bodies lying in the ditches on either side, men who had been callously murdered because they were ill or just physically spent. There was no valid reason. The only explanation was that the victims were Jews.

Finally Erich said, "I think we might be better off if we walked through the forest, just to be safe." Moniek nodded and followed him as they moved into the cover of the nearby trees. The ground had a frozen crust to it and made walking extremely difficult. However, that additional burden was of little concern compared to the possibility of being recaptured and executed. While the civilian clothing was an enormous help they did not have in their possession any official papers that identified who they were, why they were where they were, or where they were going.

Late that afternoon as they closely followed the tree line beside the road Moniek noticed several sets of human tracks imprinted in the frozen snow. At first he gave it little thought, logically assuming that the footprints were from the prisoners ahead of them. But there were far less footprints than one would have expected. Something didn't ring true but he couldn't quite put his finger on it.

"Stop!" a voice hissed. "Stop or die!" Six men dressed in heavy winter coats appeared from behind trees. They each had rifles pointed at the two men who had recently found their freedom. Now that delightful dream seemed to have instantly dissipated. They did as they were told and without instruction raised their hands in the air. "Show us your papers," the middle-aged man who seemed to be their leader said.

"We have no papers," Erich quietly replied.

"Who are you? Why are you here?"

Both men took a deep breath and finally Moniek said, "We just escaped from a German concentration camp."

"Which one?" The man asked. "There are many such places." It was clear that he was not impressed in the least.

"Auschwitz," was all Moniek could say. And now the man and the others with him were indeed impressed. They lowered their guns.

"How did you escape?"

"During the march."

"We've seen the march. They went past here just yesterday. They left many bodies in ditches along the way. Many dead men for no reason. The two of you are very fortunate."

"We know."

"What will you do now?" The man asked with a degree of sincerity and concern. "Where will you go? The Germans are still very much here. They know they've lost the war but they're prepared to fight to the death."

"I'm going to Nowy Wisnicz," Moniek replied, staring directly into the man's face and showing no fear at all. "My family is there waiting for me."

"It's a long way from here. What if they're not there?"

"It doesn't matter. I'm going home."

There was a long moment of silence after the man finally said, "You both look like you're hungry. Have you had anything to eat?"

"It's been quite awhile," Erich answered.

The man, the apparent leader of the small group, looked at the others with him and they all nodded in agreement. "You come with me. My farm is not far from here. I'll see that you have something to eat and that you'll be safe, at least for awhile."

As they moved through the forest composed mostly of pine trees Moniek discovered that the leaders name was Guenther Oberski and that he and the others were members of the Polish Partisans. This information put both Moniek and Erich on alert because they had heard rumors that some of the Partisans had the capacity of being as cruel and vicious to the Jews as the Germans. As a result they each reported that they were Polish citizens but left out the most important fact that they were Jewish.

As a Partisan it was not uncommon for Guenther to spend days away from home doing whatever he and his small band of men could to fend off and defeat the Germans. They hid and slept and ate in the forests, attacking small groups of German soldiers in random guerilla warfare, killing as many as possible. They never took any prisoners. They were vicious and unrelenting in their efforts to protect their country. They were most certainly not men who should be taken lightly.

When they reached the farm at dusk, Guenther's wife Celia ran into the barnyard to greet him. She was a warm and pleasant woman and remarkably brave in her own right. She welcomed Moniek and Erich and was personally thrilled that they had escaped from the Nazis. After introductions they all moved inside the warm house where Celia and her two daughters hurriedly prepared a dinner for all.

They had a daughter named Helen who had dark hair and dark eyes and was very attractive. She appeared to be in her mid-teens and was quiet, shy, and very reserved. For reasons unknown to Moniek, Guenther seemed to take an unusually special liking to him. When dinner was completed the partisan offered him a drink of strong liquor, made from potatoes. Having never tasted spirits of any kind Moniek politely declined.

As the men, with the exception of Moniek, drank their after dinner liquor, Celia and her two daughters cleared the table. During this process the dark-haired Helen stole a glance at Moniek and for a fleeting instant they made eye contact. She smiled then quickly turned away, embarrassed. It was a shy and very reserved smile that did not go unnoticed by the other men seated at the table. A very unusual emotion stirred within him. He was sixteen years old. He'd never been with a girl. He'd never even kissed a girl. He didn't remember the last time he'd been near a girl. And Moniek was having feelings deep inside which he didn't understand at all.

"I think I see a little spark there," one of the men said with a large smile. "Moniek, you should talk to her. She'd be a fine catch for any young man."

Guenther silenced him with a cursory glance and softly but forcefully said, "I'll decide when and who my daughter talks with. Not you."

"Sorry," was all the seasoned warrior could say as he hung his head. He knew he'd spoken out of turn.

Moniek and Erich were invited to stay at the farm until they both figured out exactly what it was they were going to do. The opportunity of a warm bed and delicious food for a few days was too difficult to refuse and they politely accepted. Helen moved into the room with her sister and their new guests shared the other one. There was no pile of hay, no frozen ground. They were sleeping in a warm bed with a thick comforter that had a distinct and pleasant fragrance.

The aroma was lingering and try as he might Moniek couldn't get it out of his mind. He remembered that his mother used to wear perfume on nearly a daily basis and this smell certainly had to be the same. Except it wasn't the same. This was the perfume that Helen wore. Even basking in the warmth and the comfort they were experiencing he had difficulty sleeping. In truth he lay there with his eyes wide open, knowing that others were sleeping on frozen ground or in barns and before daybreak would once again begin their march. Then he thought about Helen, and the eye contact they'd made during dinner.

The following day when he and Erich awoke they discovered that Guenther was already gone from the house. His wife didn't know if he would be back that evening or not. There were Germans in the area and they were looking for them. If they found them, in all probability, there would be fewer Germans in the area. Celia fixed a hearty breakfast of eggs and some type of meat which he didn't recognize but whatever it was, it truly tasted wonderful. Moniek and Erich ate in the dining room and Celia and her daughters ate in the kitchen. Even so, Moniek could still smell the sweet aroma of Helen's perfume.

After breakfast the two of them volunteered to help clean off the table and take the dishes to the kitchen but Celia would have none of it. Moniek let out a sigh and replied, "You have been so kind to us, please let us do something to help you."

She offered a kind smile and replied, "The animals in the barn need to be fed." Moniek returned the smile, grabbed his jacket, and without saying a word walked across the barnyard, into the barn, and completed the chores. Later that afternoon he assisted in the kitchen with the peeling of potatoes. The process was remarkably new to him but he did his very best and provided great entertainment for all the women in the house.

"I'm sorry I'm not better at this," he said. Then he gave them all a smile and added, "Actually, I've never ever done this before."

"You're doing just fine," Celia said.

"I think so too," Helen offered, then quickly left the room, her face flushed with embarrassment. Celia noticed and smiled at the youngster. "She's a good girl. Not much in the ways of the world. She doesn't really understand what you've been through."

Moniek turned very serious. "Very few people would understand what I've been through."

She nodded and finally said, "You're doing a fine job with the potatoes."

Guenther and the others arrived at the farm just as the sun went down. There didn't ever seem to be any conversation about the work they did during the day. Celia was thrilled each night when he returned home safe. While the men washed themselves Guenther nodded at Moniek and indicated that he wanted him to follow him outside. Guenther and Celia glanced at each other and she nodded her approval.

They walked into the barn where a few of the animals stirred at the interruption. "I have a feeling you fed them today," he said with calmness.

"Yes sir. I want to do whatever we can to help. You and your family have been very kind."

"You like our family?"

"Yes, sir. Very much."

Guenther cleared his throat and eventually said, "You've noticed my daughter Helen. She likes you. As do I. I would like very much if you would stay here and marry my daughter. She'll be a fine wife and will give you many fine children."

Moniek was taken aback, speechless. "I've never even spoken with her," he finally said.

"Marriages are arranged. Young people don't need to speak to each other. You can do all the speaking you want after you're married."

Moniek rubbed his chin, biding his time, totally confused. Finally, "You just met me in the forest two days ago. How can you possibly figure that I'd be a good husband for your daughter?"

"There are very few young men left. The Germans have seen to that. They've either been mostly been killed or they're in the army against their will. I think you'd be a fine addition to our family."

"I don't know what to say."

"Say that you'll stay here and marry my daughter and be my son-in-law."

After a long hesitation Moniek finally whispered, "Let us talk again in the morning." Guenther nodded acceptance and the two of them returned to the house.

The dinner prepared by the three women was a feast. But Moniek couldn't eat a bite. He excused himself before the others were finished and retired to his room. Once there, experiencing the warmth so many others were not, sleep was elusive. The aroma illuminating from the comforter was disconcerting, enormously troubling. Until this very moment in his young life he had experienced very few opportunities to make any meaningful decisions for himself. Erich entered the bedroom and Moniek pretended he was asleep.

He was awake well before dawn, waiting in the kitchen for Guenther to arrive. They shared a cup of coffee without conversation and Guenther finally said, "Why don't we go for a walk." They put on their jackets and moved outside.

"Would you like me to feed the animals?" Moniek asked.

"The animals can wait," he firmly replied. After a few more steps, "Have you given any thought to our conversation yesterday?"

"Yes sir. A great deal of thought."

"And…?"

"I need to go home and find my family."

"Perhaps someday you'll come back here and see us again?"

"Perhaps, but first I need to find my family. I know they're waiting for me. They have to be worried about me as well."

They walked in silence for nearly a full minute and Guenther finally said, "I understand. I think I have news for you that may be beneficial. Yesterday my men and I saw Soviet troops on the road. They're here. The Germans are retreating as fast as they can. They're going back to Germany and once they're there they'll be defeated as well. I think the roads are reasonably safe."

"Thank you. And as we just said, perhaps someday I'll return."

Erich decided to stay and then in a few days go his own way. Celia provided a great deal of food for Moniek to take with him for his long journey. He stood at the back door of the house, thanking them for all they had done. He shook hands with Helen, the first and only time they had ever touched. Then he left and walked toward the road. He was finally going home. His family was there. He would find them all in Nowy Wisnicz.

Thirty-One

Moniek's return journey to Nowy Wisnicz was mostly made on foot. While the temperature was still well below freezing his heart was enormously warm. He was finally on his way home and could not have been happier. Occasionally a cart would come down the road and he'd hitch a short ride, exchanging what little information he and the driver had and just pleasantly enjoying the company of another person. During one such occurrence he rode on the back of a wagon filled with manure. While the smell was certainly not pleasant his greatest disappointment was that the aroma which he had enjoyed so very much from the comforter he'd been sleeping with had now been erased and no longer captivated him the way it had for the past few days.

It took him more than forty-eight hours to reach Krakow. Along the way a friendly and understanding farmer welcomed him into his meager home, offered him a hot meal and a warm place to sleep. Once in Krakow he found a few other survivors who were also headed in various directions. They were staying in a deserted apartment, all sharing a similar fate over the last few years, and they allowed him to sleep on the floor in the living room. That night before he fell asleep, he wondered what his brothers were doing. Were they sleeping in their rooms, reading, talking? His mother and father, he knew, must be so worried about him. Soon, he thought as he drifted off, he would be with them.

Early the following morning, long before the break of dawn, he was on his way again. He had been told that it would probably be another two-day hike to reach his destination. From all that he'd been through, two days was just a drop in the bucket. He quickened his pace, catching a ride when he could, stopping only that evening for a bite of food and permission to sleep in a barn.

As he walked through Bochnia he all too vividly remembered the crowded apartment where they stayed with the other two families, the shortages of food, the near escape that his own family made, when the first selection occurred. He remembered the Nazis viciously taking people away to Belzek and other camps. He also painfully recalled the fateful day when he entered the rear of a truck expecting to go to work and ended up as a prisoner in Plaszow. That tragic day was the last time he had seen his family.

As he walked through the nearly deserted streets of what had been the ghetto, he wondered how long his family stayed there before being taken to one of the camps. It was possible, he thought, that they had hidden in the woods as they had before. Perhaps they escaped the selections and when the Nazis withdrew, went back home to wait for him. He passed a building that looked like the one that had the overheated attic room they had first stayed in. Without conscious thought, he found that he had come to the place where he was picked up. He looked around at the cracked sidewalk and remembered how he had picked up rocks and thrown them idly, waiting for the truck that would bring him to work. *I was still innocent then,* he thought. *I was a little boy proud that I had found work and could help my family. I hadn't been to hell yet.* And now he had come back and hoping that he could resume his old life.

Moniek walked around the corner and into the bakery storeroom that had sheltered his family. It all seemed as if it had happened only yesterday. In his mind he could still see the faces of his father, mother, and brothers. The last day they were together his father left and as he patted him on the head told him to have a good day. His mother was the last family member he'd seen. She smiled, gave him a tender kiss, and told him to be careful. So very much had transpired over the years since that last pleasant moment. He looked into the corner where he last saw her — how he longed to see her again. But there was nothing there but dust.

Soon that blessed reunion would finally take place. Based on what he'd seen and experienced over the years, a part of his brain realized that there was little chance of Tata, Mother, Abraham, Zishe, and Nuta still being there, in the home where he grew up. Still, deep in his young heart, in a place still untouched by the horrors he'd witnessed, he held the dream that in a matter of hours they'd all be together again.

Moniek's heart began to pound as he first saw Nowy Wisnicz in the distance. The first thing he saw was the towering Castle Wisnicz where he had played so often as a child and spent time listening to conversations spoken in other languages from people from other parts of the world. Over the past three years he'd had the unfortunate opportunity to hear many other languages spoken by people from many different parts of the world. But now that was behind him. Those days were thankfully over. The only voices he wanted to hear were those of his family.

Then he saw it on down the road, his home, and literally stopped in his tracks. The street where he used to play so often was nearly deserted and even though dusk was approaching and it was late January there were only a few chimneys with smoke coming out. The thought didn't really register because he had only one pressing thing consuming his mind.

Even though snow covered the ground, the shrubs and the grass surrounding the house were overgrown and it was obvious they had been unattended for a considerable amount of time. That as well mattered little. What he did notice as he approached the house was that there were no lights coming from within and all of the windows appeared to be open. He cautiously but excitedly walked up the steps of the front porch, opened the door and ran in — home at long last. His heart wanted to find his entire family seated around their dining room table.

But it was nearly dark inside and no one was there. It was cold and empty. Frantically, Moniek went from room to room calling out the names of each of his family members over and over. But he received no response. It couldn't be! They were supposed to be there. What was he going to do? He felt lost, worse almost, than when he was in the camps.

In addition, the house was completely empty, every stick of their fine furniture was gone. As he traveled through the house he closed all the windows, doing whatever he could to keep the cold outside. He tried not to think about what it all meant.

The last room he entered was the kitchen, the one where he'd had so many memorable and unforgettable moments with his mother. Many of them flashed back fondly but were now diminished. Like the rest of the house, everything was gone from the kitchen: the stove, the table where he used to sit and do his homework, even the furnace that kept them so pleasantly warm on bitter evenings like this.

He looked out the window, remembering with great pain the last time he'd stood in this place, and then remembered something else. Moniek moved into the backyard and went methodically from area to area where his father had carefully buried the family possessions. He discovered a series of holes. The holes were all empty. He envisioned momentarily that his father had somehow returned from the ghetto in Bochnia and retrieved the items himself. But that was far too much to hope for and he knew better. Someone else had stolen all of their precious family heirlooms.

Back inside the house it remained very cold and growing darker by the minute. Lonely, he momentarily thought about visiting some of the neighbors he used to know but all those houses seemed to be dark as well. Besides, he was aching and tired, and despite his disappointment, wanted to stay in the house he'd dreamed of so often. He'd slept in the cold and he'd certainly done without food for a very long time. Obviously one more night wouldn't make that much difference.

Deciding safety was still a valid consideration he climbed carefully into the attic which the Ebner family had used as a storage area. To his surprise he found it to be undisturbed. There were many trunks filled with clothing and other assorted items. The one containing the most had a vast assortment of women's apparel. He recognized many of them and pleasant thoughts returned. Some still held the lingering aroma of the perfume his mother was so fond of wearing.

Two more trunks were filled with clothing which had been worn by the four brothers. At first Moniek thought some of the clothing might be wearable but the suits and jackets were all much too small to replace the clothing the farmer had given him just a little more than a week ago. Physically spent from his excursion on the road and mentally drained, he decided that the attic would be the best place to sleep.

Taking several suits and jackets from the trunks he created a workable mattress, certainly more comfortable than many others he'd experienced. Others were used as blankets and provided a modicum of warmth against the chilling temperatures. Heartbroken, he added his mother's clothes to the pile and the wonderful smell comforted him. As tired as he was, sleep came with difficulty. He was flooded with memories, most of them pleasant. He was also obsessed with finding his family no matter where they were because he still believed them to be alive.

As Moniek tossed and turned, trying to find any degree of rest, the Soviet army was in the process of liberating Auschwitz and Birkenau. The few remaining prisoners that the soldiers in the Red Army found were in many cases far too emaciated and ill to eat solid food. Some of those who did eat died a painful death because it had been such a very long time since anything but the disgusting turnip soup had entered their stomachs along with an occasional slice of bread.

Moniek awoke the following morning, fully prepared to renew and continue his quest. He visited several nearby houses where friends once lived. They were either deserted or occupied by strangers who could offer no helpful information and wanted nothing to do with him. He couldn't find anyone who had previously lived in the area when he was growing up.

Since their family home was in what most people often referred to as the non-Jewish section of town, he decided to venture to the other side of town and search for anyone who might be able to provide some help or assistance. He had to find his family. With few other people in sight he made his way down Grunwaldzka Street and past the town square. The majority of the stores and businesses in the square were still closed, many of them boarded up. For the most part these had been Jewish establishments. Moniek wondered where they had all gone but, most sadly, felt he already knew the answer.

He passed the Catholic church where he and his brothers had shoveled snow so many times and helped tend their garden during the summer months. An elderly nun stood on the front steps, cleaning them with an aged broom that had long since seen its better days. Moniek couldn't believe his eyes.

He spoke very quietly so as to not frighten her. "Hello, Sister." She turned around without offering words or any expression. "Don't you remember me? I'm Moniek Ebner. My brothers and I used to help you around here."

She stared for a moment and finally said, "You're that little Jewish boy from up the street, aren't you?"

"Yes, ma'am," he replied with a smile.

The nun stared blankly for another few seconds. Then without another word she opened the door and returned to the inside of the church. Moniek was crushed. He looked around, thinking perhaps she was dismissing someone else. But he was alone, completely alone.

When he got to the Jewish side of town, it was deserted. It was almost as if it were a ghost town. In truth, that's exactly what it was. While walking past the empty houses he noticed a man in his backyard who was working on a harness of some sort. Moniek cautiously approached, like earlier with the nun, not wishing to frighten him. "Excuse me, sir," he politely said.

The man spun around, clearly frightened. "What do you want? I don't have anything. You've already taken everything." He was probably in his mid-fifties, very thin, with dark brown teeth. He stared at the youngster standing in his backyard.

"All I want is some information. I've come a very long way just to find some information about my family."

"You a Jew?" The question was delivered with caution.

"Yes, sir," he replied. "I used to live here."

"I don't recognize you."

"I've been gone a very long time. I've finally come home. My name is Moniek Ebner."

"Your father was in the trading business? Animals and grain and things like that?"

"Yes, sir."

"We used to attend the same synagogue. Until the Nazis came and closed it down." Then he said with great regret, "Never reopened." After a pause, "I remember your father. He was a good man. Why don't we go inside where it's a little warmer?"

Once inside the man apologized for having very little but did offer Moniek a slice of cake and a weak cup of coffee. The room was sparse, two tables and a rickety wooden table. Moniek's first and most logical question was, "Where are all the people? Where have they gone?"

"You say you've been away for a long time?"

"Yes, sir."

"Were you in a camp?"

"Several."

"That's where they've gone. To camps, several camps. Only a handful of all who used to live here came back. The few who did mostly feel like they still need to be in hiding from the Germans."

"But where are the Germans?"

"They've been gone for awhile. As you can clearly see, in addition to the people they took most of everything else. I go into the forest and bring back wood for my small stove and occasionally find some food on a deserted farm."

Moniek took a sip of coffee and explained, "I just stopped at the church up the street and saw a nun I used to do some work for. She recognized me but wouldn't talk to me. Why would she be that way?"

"The Gentiles don't talk all that much to the few Jews who are left. They avoid us, walk the other way, pretend like we don't even exist."

Moniek shook his head, saddened by the information. "How did you survive? How did you manage to escape being captured?"

"Hiding in the woods, traveling by night and sleeping by day, occasionally staying in barns where people were sympathetic to our survival. You had to have help and assistance if you were going to make it to the end."

Moniek knew all too well from personal experience exactly what the man was talking about. "Is your family still with you?" He asked the question softly.

The man sadly shook his head. "They're all gone, my wife, two sons, and two daughters, all gone. I went to the forest one night to look for some food for us and when I returned the Germans had taken them away."

Moniek was understandably sympathetic. "Perhaps they'll return."

And again the man shook his head. "I hope someday they will but I know deep in my heart they won't." Then the room was quiet for a very long time.

Finally Moniek asked if the man had any information about his parents or brothers. The man told him that as far as he was aware, no one who entered the Bochnia ghetto had ever returned. He had heard from several others that all the people taken there were transported elsewhere.

Moniek thanked the man for his hospitality and continued his search. He was convinced there would be no one left in the sparsely occupied Jewish section of town who could offer any help. Suddenly he remembered his grandfather's farm. Quickly, he set off on a five-mile hike into the rural countryside. That's where they went, he thought. He would find his parents and brothers at his grandfather's farm.

Upon his arrival he discovered four second cousins and their mother who had managed to miraculously survive the horror of the Nazi ordeal. He was disappointed again, but happy to find some of his family. They had all changed over the years. Moniek was now sixteen and the others were between twenty and thirty years old. Initially it was a grand reunion until they each began to count off the number of family members who had been taken away at gunpoint while they were in hiding. None of the people taken away were ever heard from again. This included Moniek's grandfather.

Anna, his aunt, and cousins Yagga, Zisha, Sholoma, and Hella welcomed Moniek into the house since it was certainly as much his now as it was theirs. Over a filling dinner the six of them reflected on times past, times when the entire family would gather for celebrations, experience great feasts, and all the children would play together while the adults whispered quietly in the living room. The children were not aware, at the time, that the candid conversations centered around the Jewish persecution which was occurring in Germany and the meteoric rise to power of a stranger named Adolf Hitler.

The men played cards and Moniek helped the women with the dishes, an expression of gratitude which they greatly appreciated. "I just want to do whatever I can to help," Moniek said. They all nodded their thanks. He was very pleased with his acceptance into the group. While not exactly what he was expecting or looking for, at least he'd found some members of his family who had not perished. That alone gave him a great sense of encouragement toward the potential survival of his immediate family.

He looked through the kitchen window and fondly remembered the times he and the others had played wonderful games in the back-yard, assisted their grandfather with the livestock, and gone into the fields to do a weekend of farmhand work, all of which they truly enjoyed and looked forward to. But mostly he remembered the times he'd gone fishing with his father, especially the last time when he was told he was a fine young man and would someday join the family business. As far-fetched as that now seemed he still held that dream dear in his heart. As impossible as it was, he wanted to see his father again, to tell him how much he missed him, to tell him how much he loved him. He would do that with his mother and brothers as well, when he saw them again.

While Moniek felt welcome to a degree he never felt he was a part of the group at the farm. Perhaps this was because he was younger than the rest of them. He didn't know. It was just a feeling. The group seemed to have no particular plan in mind as to what they were going to do. It was assumed they would wait until spring and the warmer weather and then they would move on toward another location, in all probability another country. There was little left for any Jew in Poland.

There was no livestock left on the farm so the majority of the food they ate consisted mostly of vegetables, some nuts and berries, and occasionally a small animal that had been trapped and would provide a fine stew. Moniek was with them for nearly two months and, over time, felt less and less that he was truly a member of the group. He was excluded from conversations. He was occasionally treated as if he was still the child they used to play with in the backyard.

Even though his experiences had been related to them, they seemed to matter little to his aunt or his cousins. While nothing was ever said, it seemed to have no particular effect on them that their younger cousin, unlike millions of other people, had managed to survive the persecution he found while a prisoner in four different concentration camps and among them the two most notorious of them all. Also, they had no idea where his family could be, and had little inclination to help him search.

Upon the arrival of spring, without any consultation or discussion with Moniek, the group of six left their grandparents' farm and began yet another journey. They each carried as much food as they could accumulate and moved down the road, first back toward Bochnia and then a left turn toward Krakow. The cousins, even while seemingly avoiding him on a regular basis, had at least been kind enough to give Moniek some new clothing for the trip, a gesture for which he was most grateful.

As had been the case for at least the past month, the five of them spoke in whispers, excluding Moniek from their conversation. He began to feel that something was about to happen. When they arrived in Krakow three days later, he discovered what they had been whispering about. The group walked to a nondescript building and entered. While it didn't particularly register Moniek noticed that the hallways in the building seemed to be filled with children who for the most part were his own age.

They entered a barren office where a kindly looking middle-aged woman wearing thick eyeglasses was seated behind a scratched-up wooden desk. It was at this moment that Moniek discovered that for reasons he would never understand his aunt and cousins were abandoning him. They were leaving him at an orphanage. They said it would be the best thing for them all. Then the five of them disappeared into the hallway and he never saw them again.

And like so many times in the past, Moniek was once again completely alone. Alone, but still hoping, against all odds, that he would be reunited with his mother, father, and brothers. Since they had not been there waiting for him, he knew they would come back looking for him.

Thirty-Two

Moniek tried desperately to explain to the woman behind the desk that he didn't belong in this place. He most definitely was not an orphan. He was absolutely convinced that his parents were still alive and they were going to come back and find him. The woman was very kind and tremendously understanding. She offered a warm smile and words that were not all that comforting, "Many of our children feel that way. But no parents have returned."

"Mine will." The youngster was adamant and convinced he would be proved correct.

"Perhaps they will," she softly countered. "But until they do, you're more than welcome to stay here with us. You'll have a place to sleep, and food, and others to talk with." She hesitated for a moment. "How does that sound?"

Moniek slowly nodded. At the time he had no other options and accepted her generous offer. The room he was assigned to was warm with four comfortable beds and roommates who were all certainly nice enough. While they had been separated from their own parents for at least three years as well, their families seemed to be little more than a vague memory to them. But the memories in Moniek's mind were clear. Crystal clear and etched into his mind forever. As days passed he became more and more convinced that his own parents would return.

And, as those same days wore on, he grew increasingly bored just sitting around the orphanage with others with whom, for all practical purposes, he had nothing in common. He had no restrictions concerning staying within the confines of the orphanage and was able to go and do whatever he wished. One day, as if drawn by a moth to a flame, he walked to the outskirts of Krakow and looked over the remains of Plaszow. It was long deserted by now and much of it had been demolished — the Germans' final wish to convince the world that the place of horrendous death had never existed. But Moniek knew better.

As he aimlessly traveled the streets of Krakow, he met a small group of people who befriended him. They lived in a house near the orphanage and invited Moniek to join them. They had established a small business manufacturing brushes and brooms. In exchange for room and board Moniek agreed to help them in their endeavor.

Every day during his lunch break Moniek would visit the local Jewish Center, the nearest synagogue, and the orphanage. These were all places where people would post their names if they were still alive, had survived the Nazi atrocities, and were looking for friends or family members. Each day he left all three of the facilities with his head hung low, finding no names, finding no hope. But through the weeks and the following months he continued to believe that his parents were still alive and would return to Krakow to somehow miraculously find him. His faith never wavered or waned.

Each time he visited the orphanage he was told by workers that the longer the time passed, the less chance there was that his parents were alive. There was no encouragement in the least and each time he looked for his parents' names on a list he became more and more disappointed. But still he continued to believe. His belief had kept him going through terrible times; it would keep him going now.

Since Krakow had been liberated, the news, limited as it was, flowed into the city and to its residents. The majority of the other children had no real concept of what was happening but world events were no longer lost on Moniek. He was aware that on May 2nd Soviet troops had effectively captured Berlin and that Adolf Hitler, two days earlier, had taken his own life in a hidden bunker buried well beneath the earth.

Again Moniek revisited the site of Plaszow, looking over the area where so many had died for no reason at all, and reflected on Hitler and what he had done. What tragic consequences he had perpetrated on so many individuals and families and after being one of the greatest mass murderers in history he did not possess the bravery or the honor to stand up and be accountable for his actions. In his death he proved himself to be little more than a sniveling coward.

Moniek looked over the killing field where he'd seen so many others die during the year he spent there. He sadly shook his head at the travesty. He rolled up his sleeve and looked at the number on his forearm, the one which he was told would only go away when he died, and for the first time, in a very long time, tears returned.

On May 7th the Germans officially surrendered and the war in Europe was finally and thankfully over. It was over for the millions and millions of people who had perished at the hands of the Germans but unfortunately it was not over for the Jewish survivors. While they didn't expect to receive flowers or candy now that their persecution was finally at an end; they did, unrealistically, expect civility. However, as had been the case for the Jews for the majority of their entire existence, civility was not to come.

Tragic events called pogroms began erupting throughout the Polish countryside. Partisans were hunting down Jews and killing them at random. It was a bizarre continuation of the war and no one was truly safe, whether in the countryside, a city, or even an orphanage. Moniek and his new friends decided that their fate was better served if they were to leave Poland and with that thought in mind they packed their few things, managed to make passage on a train, and headed toward Germany. The decision seemed sound in that Germany was now under both Soviet and American control and their luck there would most certainly be better than it was where they were.

The trains were now under the complete control of the Russians and traveled on regular schedules where tracks still existed. Others which had been bombed and were unserviceable were a priority and work crews throughout the country worked diligently to repair them. Moniek and his friends were riding comfortably in a compartment when a Russian soldier appeared and asked for their papers. Of course none of them possessed any and their immediate future was suddenly in peril.

Moniek's traveling companions, as well as himself, were all Poles. However, he was the only Jew. As such, as was so often the case, he was singled out and forced to leave the train. At the next stop, with a soldier accompanying him, he was taken to a newly established Soviet jail and placed into a holding cell for several hours, understandably frightened and clearly uncertain about his future.

A guard finally released him late that night, escorted him to a nearby hotel, gave him a railway ticket for early the next morning and told him he must return to Poland. Moniek ate a small meal, slept in a reasonably comfortable bed, and awoke at the appointed hour. However he wasn't really quite fully awake. He made his way to the train station, still groggy from the hours he spent in the holding cell of the jail. Once on the train he immediately fell asleep and as such no one ever bothered to look at or check his ticket.

In his sleepless and confused state Moniek had gotten on the wrong train and instead of returning to Poland as he had been instructed he was actually on his way to Germany, his original destination. He didn't know anyone there or even exactly where he was going but somehow, based on the life he had experienced, he knew that somehow he was going to make it.

Moniek got off the train in Landsburg, Germany, a bit confused and disoriented. Fortunately an American soldier found him wandering aimlessly and asked who he was and where he was going. He answered the first question but could offer no response to the second.

"Where's your family?" the soldier asked.

"I don't know," he sadly replied. "I'm looking for them."

The soldier clearly knew the improbability of a reunion and felt compassion for the young man. "Why don't you come with me," he said softly. "I think I know some people who might be able to help you." Together they walked several blocks during which Moniek related the experiences he'd encountered. The soldier shook his head, noticeably disturbed. After awhile they reached a small river with a bridge going across it. There was a guardhouse at the end of the bridge and an armed sentry appeared.

"Papers," the sentry said without emotion.

"He's with me, Sergeant. I'm taking him to the camp."

The sentry stepped back, offered a smart salute, and raised the gate allowing them to pass through. Moniek's heart felt as if it were about to break when he heard the word "camp." He'd been in so many camps for so many years and seen so much tragedy that he really wasn't quite sure if he could endure another one. But he was being escorted by a soldier wearing a pistol on his hip and this was not something he was unfamiliar with. In the past he'd seen what happened when people tried to run, tried to get away. And so, after a deep sigh, he followed the soldier across the bridge and under a sign which was written in a language he didn't understand.

There were many people in the "camp" and they all seemed to be going about their merry way without any organized supervision. There were children his own age playing soccer and adults talking in small groups and, most important of all, not one single guard was in sight. "Where are we?" Moniek finally asked.

"This is a Displaced Persons Camp. You'll be safe here and in time they'll help you find a safer place to go. These are good people."

He found the words somewhat difficult to believe but also realized that his eyes did not deceive him. He watched all the people around him; they were exercising freedom and enjoying it as well. They walked across a large open area surrounded by many buildings, all of which were very well maintained. The entire facility was well-kept and clean. Sadly, it reminded him of Auschwitz.

The two of them entered what was identified as the Administration Building and the soldier led Moniek into an office where a clerk listened politely as the soldier told her about how he had found the youngster on the street. The woman behind the desk smiled at Moniek and asked his name. Following that, she filled out a brief form and asked that they wait for a few minutes until a counselor was available. True to her word, a few minutes later they were ushered into a well-appointed office where another woman, this one considerably older, greeted Moniek and the soldier and welcomed him to the camp.

Her name was Mrs. Mendelsohn and she appeared to be genuinely pleased to see the young man. During the initial interview she assigned Moniek a room which he would share with others and gave him access to the cafeteria where three meals each day were available. Mrs. Mendelsohn informed him that he would be provided with new clothing. It would actually be used clothing but certainly new to him.

The next thing she said was what really captured his attention. "We have several schools here to teach people a trade. I expect you'll be wanting to go to another country and they in turn will expect that you can do something to earn a living. The first few days you're here just take your time and visit some of the schools and decide which one you like and feel most comfortable with."

Moniek couldn't believe his own ears. Food, shelter, clothing, the possibility of learning a trade. He smiled warmly at Mrs. Mendelsohn and it was delightfully returned. She buzzed an intercom, a device Moniek had never seen before, and asked that a person named Aaron join them. Within seconds a boy Moniek's age entered the room and they were introduced.

"Aaron will take you to your dormitory, help you get some new clothing, and show you where the cafeteria is." She stood up and everyone else followed her lead. "When you feel like you're ready, look in on some of the classes offered, and see if any of them seem like something you'd like to do. And another thing," and this was spoken with great sincerity, "if you ever need anything please don't hesitate to come and see me again. My door will always be open to you."

Moniek thanked the soldier for his assistance and bid him a farewell. But not before the soldier said, "Good luck, young man. I hope you find your parents."

"Thank you, sir, I will." Moniek and Aaron left the office and walked across the open area into a nearby building which he would be calling home for awhile. The rooms were clean, the beds were soft, and every single person he met seemed to be genuinely pleased to meet him. This was something Moniek would grow to understand in the coming months. The cafeteria was quite large and filled with an abundance of sweet smells. One thing he found quite interesting was that the majority of the workers in the camp were all reasonably young.

Next, Aaron took him to get new clothing: shirt, jacket, pants, shoes, and, for the first time in a very long time, underwear. He was deeply touched and turned away so that Aaron wouldn't see the emotion welling up in his face. "It's all right," Aaron said softly. "Most of us have been in the same position and most of us have shared the same feeling."

Dinner that evening was a truly delightful event. It was served family style with many people seated around a large table and an abundance of food. Everyone Moniek met seemed to be genuine in their offer to do anything they could to assist him. The experience reminded him of days past, days spent with his family. Some of those happy memories were sadly diminished by his aunt and second cousins who deserted him in Krakow.

Moniek's roommates, also survivors of the Nazi travesty, were very helpful the following morning and directed him toward various classes where experienced instructors were teaching trades. He visited several classes and actually monitored those which most captured his interest. After a few days, more in-depth conversations with other survivors, and more good food, he went to see Mrs. Mendelsohn.

"Ma'am," he meekly asked. "I've looked at several of the classes you have available..."

"Yes, Moniek," she replied.

"Would it be possible for me to attend two of the classes?"

"You don't think that would be too much to take on at one time?" she replied with a raised eyebrow.

"No, ma'am. I'm a very good student and I learn very quickly."

Mrs. Mendelsohn smiled, nodded, pulled out two registration forms and replied, "I'm sure you are, young man. I'm sure you are."

Moniek enrolled in two classes which gave him little time for anything else. While others engaged in a variety of sporting activities held on a regular basis throughout the camp, and even political organizations, he spent the entirety of his day going from one class to the other.

Following dinner he would retire to his room for a full evening of homework concerning that which he had done that day and preparing for the next.

Within a few months he was reasonably proficient as both an auto mechanic and a welder. These were both trades that the majority of countries accepting refugees would gladly acknowledge and welcome. Mrs. Mendelsohn continued to be Moniek's primary contact, mentor, and greatest supporter. She was actually an employee of the United Nations Relief and Rehabilitation Administration, or UNRA. After many conversations Moniek decided that he wanted to go to Palestine. After what he'd been through he wanted to be a part of a new and burgeoning society.

But Mrs. Mendelsohn explained to him that the quota system for Palestine was quite stringent and the wait could take a very long time. He was not to be deterred. While others played games and participated in political rallies, he continued his studies and became an excellent tradesman in both of his selected areas. Because of his newfound skills he would be a valued addition to any country involved in a rebuilding process.

Each day Moniek carefully checked the message board in the main center, hoping and always expecting to find his parents' or brothers' names. Each day he left the center he was filled with disappointment. He was not alone. Many others also made the daily excursion to the board and, like Moniek, they left without satisfaction. The counselors tried their very best to provide consolation but little was realistically available. The children were alone in the world, without parents or family of any kind. Their parents and their families were all gone. Gone to the gas chambers and the crematoriums. Gone to the burning pits. Gone to senseless deaths on the side of some nondescript road during death marches across Poland.

Thirty-Three

There was a knock at the door of Moniek's room which was very unusual in that it was late in the evening. He awoke, opened it, and to his enormous surprise discovered Mark Sellinger standing in the doorway. Mark was a first cousin from Nowy Wisnicz and Moniek couldn't believe his sleepy eyes. For a second he felt he was having a dream.

They briefly embraced and so as to not disturb his roommates Moniek quickly dressed and they went outside for a walk. They hadn't seen each other for nearly five years and both had certainly changed over that period of time. They'd grown up beyond their years and were now truly young adults. Mark had been in a series of camps as well and the two of them exchanged horror stories. He as well had lost his entire immediate family.

"What are you going to do?" Mark asked.

"I'm going to Palestine. I'm waiting to hear when I can go."

"You know the waiting list is very long and they're allowing very few people to go there."

"Yes, but what other choice do I have? I can't stay here."

"Why don't you go to America? That's where I'm going." Mark spoke the words with a degree of pride.

"I don't know anyone in America. Who would sponsor me?"

"The UNRA can help. Ask them for assistance."

"But what would I do even if I could get there?"

"What classes are you taking?"

Moniek shrugged and replied, "Auto mechanics and welding."

"America is a huge country and growing. You won't have any trouble at all finding work, making a living, starting a new life." Moniek pondered the words. Perhaps Mark was right. If he did indeed go to America he could always go to Palestine later as an American citizen. All things considered, it made a great deal of sense.

The following morning he went to see Mrs. Mendelsohn and inquired about the possibility of going to America. She smiled broadly and explained that the wait would be considerably less than that for Palestine. She also explained that because of his training he wouldn't have any difficulty finding employment. She further explained that she would go to work immediately to find him a sponsor in America.

Having a willing sponsor was a prerequisite in order to go to another country. The sponsor was responsible for paying the passage of the newcomer to the assigned destination and also for guaranteeing that they would not be a financial burden in any way on the host country. It was also normal for the sponsor to provide room and board until the new arrival was on his feet financially and prepared to take care of himself.

Less than a month later, Mrs. Mendelsohn summoned Moniek to her office and happily informed him that her efforts had proven successful. She had obtained a sponsor in New York which was the principal destination for the majority of the refugees from Europe. He was told that within the next couple of weeks he would be transferred to an orphanage in Munich where he would have a short wait and then board a ship to begin his new life.

Moniek was thrilled with the news but still enormously disappointed that he had been unsuccessful in locating his parents or any of his brothers. The sense of isolation and aloneness had plagued him for so long. Not a day went by that he didn't think about his family and the possibility that someday they would all be reunited. He vowed to himself that wherever he ended up he would never give up his search.

Several more weeks passed and word finally came that it was time for him to leave. He packed a small valise with one change of clothes and visited the auto mechanic and the welding schools where the instructors had been so beneficial in his learning process. He thanked them both for their generosity and kindness. After heartfelt handshakes, he made his way across the main area for his final goodbye.

Mrs. Mendelsohn was very proud of Moniek and what he had accomplished and told him so in a manner which reminded him very much of his own mother. He felt an authentic affinity toward her and she returned the feeling. They were both on the verge of tears when she saved each of them by looking at her watch and saying softly, "My goodness, young man. You'd better hurry or you'll miss your train." Moniek nodded, smiled a last smile, turned, and left the building.

The two-day train ride was uneventful. The cars were mostly filled with refugees on their way to safety in other countries. Many people felt that with the fall of Germany and the fact that the country had now been divided between the Soviet Union, Great Britain, and the United States, that it would be a long time before any degree of real security would occur. Many of them felt that living anywhere else was a viable option.

A guide met Moniek at the train station and transported him to the Munich orphanage. While expecting the same living experience he was familiar with in Krakow, he was delightfully pleased with what he discovered upon his arrival. His dormitory was actually more of a clubhouse overlooking a pristine lake. There were rooms around the outside of the facility and an open area in the center which served as the location where everyone ate. The people there, like himself, were mostly awaiting passage to other countries. While they had all experienced the travesties of war and the painful loss of most or all of their families, they were looking forward to beginning life anew in a foreign land where they could finally be free.

Moniek checked with the Administration Building on a daily basis and his American sponsor had still not satisfied all of the requirements necessary to accommodate his passage. And so, he waited. But the wait was not all that unpleasant. The food was plentiful, the people for the most part were congenial and optimistic concerning their future, and the setting was more than delightful. He would walk around the lake watching several varieties of birds flying to and fro, exercising their own freedom. Moniek could relate to the birds and looked forward to beginning his new life.

And then the hammer fell. The United States government determined that Moniek's sponsor was not financially strong enough to fulfill the commitments they required. Moniek was crushed. Again alone, in a new strange place, without hope, he retreated to his room and once again questioned what on earth he was possibly going to do.

A counselor approached and told him that all hope had not been lost. They had other avenues they could pursue and intended to do just that. It took more than three months but they finally obtained another sponsor: the United States government itself. Moniek qualified for government sponsorship in that he was both an orphan and a survivor. While somewhat disturbed by being described as an orphan, since he truly did not believe that he was, he took the news to heart and prepared for his trip.

Within a week he and about twenty other youngsters were taken to the seaport of Bremenhaven and Moniek saw the largest thing he had ever observed in his life. It was a huge gray ship. During the war it was used as a troop and supply transport ship. The name on its bow read *Marine Perch*. This was to be the place where Moniek would spend the next two weeks of his life.

While much of his life had been spent in abject misery, the next fourteen days would prove to be equally miserable. When the giant ship left port, literally packed with people going to America, the sea was calm. The bunks were shared. Some slept while others spent time on deck or in the mess hall. The first day was an exciting adventure. And then came the first night.

A storm raged. Large waves surged, splashing water across the bow of the ship. Many people became ill, violently ill. They ran to the rails of the ship and began to throw up all that they had eaten. Moniek had never been on a boat before, let alone a large ship, and he truly didn't understand what was happening to all these people. He went to the mess hall which was virtually empty and had a fine meal by himself. He even enjoyed seconds, wondering what on earth was causing all these others to be so amazingly ill.

On the next morning at sea Moniek discovered for himself what so many others had already experienced. His chest hurt. His sides ached. Then his stomach began to churn violently and he knew without question he was going to be sick. Leaping out of his bunk he ran to the small bathroom only to find it filled with people who were already there, throwing up. He controlled his gagging as he ran to the deck and along with countless others threw up over the side of the ship. The experience was painful and one which he hoped would not return.

His hopes were unheeded. The passengers ate as little as possible, mostly a bland liquid diet, and even so the vast majority of that also found its way into the ocean. The open sea proved to be unkind for fourteen straight days and nights. There was little sleep and even less comfort. Great mounds of food in the ships galley went uneaten, much of it spoiled. Only a few of the passengers were able to eat anything. This was most certainly not the trip Moniek had envisioned.

And then miraculously the sea finally calmed, the thick gray clouds dissipated, and up ahead he could see it: New York City. It was astonishing in its size and grew more so as the ship sailed into the harbor. The buildings, the skyscrapers, were truly incredible, unlike anything Moniek could even begin to imagine. There were many other large ships pulling into and out of port, all filled with people going to places Moniek never conceived he would ever see.

With the calming of the ocean the seasickness fortunately subsided and stomachs returned to normal. He was still very hungry but knew better than to try and eat anything. Instead he stood at the rail and witnessed the most wondrous thing he'd ever seen: the New York City skyline.

Unlike most refugee ships coming to the United States, the *Marine Perch* went directly to the port in the Bronx borough of the city. Moniek didn't know anything about where they were going or what he was going to do when he got there but that mattered little. At this moment he was transfixed with the skyline as they grew closer to their mooring, the amazing number of people everywhere, and — the best part of all — they were all experiencing the joys of freedom.

The ship docked and the passengers departed, many greeted by family members or sponsors. Moniek and the other orphans and survivors from the ship finally noticed a man holding a sign with the name, "Munich Orphanage" printed on it. The children eased their way down the gangplank and made their way toward the stranger.

Moniek had finally reached American soil. He was actually a free man for the first time in a very long time. As he followed the others to a nearby waiting bus he looked around at the new world he had entered and recommitted the vow in his heart that he would never give up his eternal quest to find his parents and his brothers.

THIRTY-FOUR

MONIEK WAS TAKEN WITH the others to an orphanage on Caldwell Avenue in the Bronx. He was treated well, fed well, and provided with new clothing. And he was still alone with nowhere to go. He spent the majority of his time in the recreation center playing ping-pong and most carefully exploring the streets of New York. One day in the recreation center he noticed a number of thick books on top of a filing cabinet and his inherent curiosity once again took center stage.

The thick books proved to be telephone books and upon closer examination he found several listings for the name "Ebner." He took the books to the Director of Placement at the orphanage, Mrs. Lotte Marcuse, and politely suggested the possibility that some of these people might be relatives of his.

Based on his accidental discovery, Mrs. Marcuse contacted all of the people listed in the phone book. The majority failed to respond, most of those who did responded negatively, but one provided a slight ray of hope. The return letter, while not a relative of Moniek's, suggested that a person in Springfield, Ohio, might possibly be of assistance.

Following numerous communications it was determined that Harry Goldburg was indeed a distant relative. He and his wife Frieda agreed to take Moniek in and give him a home. Another overnight train trip took Moniek to Dayton, Ohio, where they met him and at last he had family members who would care for him and provide him a future.

Moniek enrolled in school, legally changed his first name to Murray, took special instructions from a tutor in English, and became proficient in the language of his newly adopted country. At the age of eighteen, he moved to Columbus, Ohio, to live with another distant cousin, Ann Maybruck and her husband Harry. He enrolled in South High School and proved to be an excellent student, surpassing most of the children who had lived here all of their lives.

He worked at numerous part-time jobs while attending school as a result of insisting on paying rent for his lodging and providing his own spending money. In 1950 he was drafted into the United States Army and expected to see action in the Korean War. After spending four months in basic training with the 101st Airborne at Camp Breckenridge in Kentucky he was offered the opportunity to transfer to Intelligence School at Arlington Farms in Virginia. He opted against this in that it would have called for another two years in the service.

Ironically, instead of being sent to Korea, he was actually deployed to Germany where he served with the 14th Armored Calvary, a tank battalion assigned the task of patrolling the border and protecting the country from intruders. In the year and a half he spent there not a day passed when he didn't recall what Germany had done to him and his family and now he was here protecting them.

Returning to Columbus, Ohio, after his deployment he became an American citizen in 1953. He met Sylvia, the woman who became his wife, and began raising a family.

With great resolve and effort which had been gleaned over the years, he began his own company, Ebner Properties, which builds, owns, and manages apartment units and commercial buildings. He and his wife are the proud parents of three children and six grandchildren.

Thirty-Five

In the summer of 2000, Murray and his family made a heartrending return trip to Poland, specifically to revisit Nowy Wisnicz, the town of his birth, and they planned to visit Auschwitz, the dreaded death camp.

In so many ways, this trip was difficult for Murray Ebner. It would open up all the wounds he had tried so hard to cover with hard calluses. All the terror and pain had been put behind him...but he knew he had to face his past, bring his new family to the places he knew with his old family — to bring the two families together. And he knew he would have to face the ghosts of the camps.

As they drove though the little town of Nowy Wisnicz, Murray recognized so many places, his recall nearly perfect — the castle where he played as a boy, farms, homes, and shops. "I can't believe I'm really here," Murray exclaimed more than once. Finally, down a large avenue, around a sharp curve, into a dead end street...and there it was. Sitting on a little hill, a little worse for wear it seemed, but just as he'd described it.

"There it is!" Moniek, now Murray, was finally home.

He got out of the car slowly, savoring the moment that he had so long denied himself. His wife and children didn't quite know what to expect, weren't sure what his reaction would be. They very quickly saw that the thick skin their father had layered over his past and his painful memories was washing away. His past had always been his own, now he was sharing it with Sylvia, Mark, Lisa, and Cindy.

Murray stood for a moment breathing in the breath of his old life. A thousand memories flooded back to him; he was filled with great emotion. He took it all in, not missing a single detail. Then he walked up to the door and knocked five times. Just for a moment, before the door was opened, he wondered if he would find his mother and father and brothers...but, of course, that was not to be. His home, the building where he was born, had now been converted into four apartments. It was rented to professors of a nearby art school and was in some disrepair. No one in the building remembered anything about the past but they allowed him to walk around.

Excited to be exploring his home again, the memories began to flood back. "Here's the kitchen!" It was a journey through time and space. Though he was able to walk into the room that had been his parent's bedroom for the first time in sixty years, his happiness was bittersweet. The home of his beautiful memories was a little foreign, a little sterile.

Still, he was able to lovingly run his fingers in the carvings on the wall outside his parent's bedroom, as he had sixty years before. And he found pieces of the green tile that once adorned the fireplace, now a treasure more valuable, he thinks, than any of the jewels stolen from his father's hiding places in the garden.

In the house next door, Murray had a joyful reunion with two childhood friends who had married. After hours of reminiscing, Murray was able to leave, knowing he'd reclaimed his memories and brought himself closer to his family and childhood.

"I found nobody," he said. But he found real closure. He got back into the car and never looked back.

The family's next stop was the farm in the country where he used to go with his family as a boy, the farm once owned by his grandfather, the farm where he found the aunts and cousins who left him in the orphanage when they left Poland.

And then, they came to the camps. They came in the August heat, shivering from the memories, awed by the awful cruelty, by the fact that anyone could survive. And Murray began to cry, for himself, for his family and friends and relatives, for everyone who had ever suffered in any of the camps. The trip and the knowledge and closure it would bring demanded a price—Murray would cry himself to sleep every night of the trip. He relived the horrors and the suffering of Auschwitz, Birkenau, and Plaszow. He lost the tough skin he had dedicated his life to developing.

His wife and children had never seen him cry like that. They were in awe of the deep sadness in his eyes. There was no longer fear there, for Eichmann, Frank, Goeth, and their like were gone to infamy and disgrace. But the memories were hard; the absence of loved ones even harder to bear.

In Auschwitz, once the busiest train station in the world, he relived the pain and suffering that he and millions of others had endured. Bone thin faces and violent, tragic events flashed through his mind, as he stood before the cold furnaces, surrounded by the green fields, numb from the horrors he'd witnessed and endured. With reverence he and his family lit candles of remembrance for the millions who had perished. They stood under the blue skies, looking down the tracks that flew off into the horizon. They saw monuments where once the Nazis tried to exterminate the Jews, where the Nazi bureaucrats and their stooges beat and gassed the innocent, tortured and did medical experiments on human beings, shot women and children, and burned the bodies when they were done. How could this perversion happen?

Murray was bent under the weight of these memories, his family's loving hands, touching him always, holding his hands, the only thing that could support him. He had left a lonely little boy and returned a successful man to confront his demons, defeat them, and send them on their way.

Plaszow was especially emotional for Murray. He was so young, and it was the first time he'd ever been away from his family. He hadn't developed that thick, protective layer yet. Also, he was guilty because he knew his disappearance must have caused his parents tremendous pain. When he returned to Plaszow in 2000, it all came back.

At the Birkenau death factory, abandoned, manicured, and empty of victims, the Ebners wandered, numb from exposure to so much casual evil. It was a miracle their father had survived when so many had perished. Murray knew he could no longer be silent about what had happened. He knew that his life would be different after this trip.

Their last stop would be Bochnia. Murray hoped that he would be able to find out something about his family at the last place he had seen them, but he thought it unlikely.

No longer the ruined, empty city it was when Murray was last there, Bochnia also no longer had a ghetto. Murray and his family came into the town expecting to spend little time there; they were unprepared for the bombshell that was to be dropped on them.

So much was different in Bochnia that Murray had trouble orienting himself. Soon, however, he got them into what had once been the Jewish ghetto and the place where he had been picked up by the truck and taken to Plaszow. Once again Murray's memory was proved accurate. "This is where it happened." He pointed to a place on Leonardo Street, much like any street in the town. It seemed such an ordinary spot for so momentous an occurrence that changed so many lives forever.

One hundred and fifty feet away was the bakery storage room. Murray and his family explained who they were and asked to see the bakery storage room where he lived with his father and mother and brothers. It was a twenty-by-twenty room that was shared by three families, ten people. Murray stood there holding his wife, surrounded by his loved ones, all of whom had their hands on his arms, his back, and his shoulders. As Murray looked out the dusty window, he could almost see himself, a thirteen-year-old boy running to show his parents and his brothers the bread he earned.

Without expecting much, he asked the bakery owner if there was anyone who might remember a family who lived in the storage room during the war.

"Yes," he said. "My mother worked here then, perhaps she remembers. I'll go get her."

Murray and his family looked at each other, wondering and waiting.

When the woman came, she explained that her family, who was not Jewish, had been given special permission to have the bakery in the ghetto. She remembered the Ebner family and described them.

Murray cautiously asked the woman if she knew anything at all about his family and what became of them. The woman lowered her eyes to the ground and spoke slowly, sadly. "One of your brothers, I think it was the youngest one—"

"Yes," Murray exclaimed, "Nuta, my brother, Nuta."

"He...he was outside, not really doing anything in particular, and he went too close to the wooden wall which had been built around the neighborhood." She hesitated, wondering if she should continue. Finally she said, "A German guard appeared and shot him. Your father fell to his knees. Crying and mourning." She wiped her eyes. "I'm so sorry."

This news, after all the years of hope, hit Murray like a thunderbolt. Finally, he had news of his family, but it brought him great pain. He cried like his heart would break. All the Ebners cried, holding each other in the dim, dusty room, mourning the murder of a little boy.

They discovered, later, that the woman died just three months after their visit.

Thirty-Six

Despite his experiences, Murray Ebner has little hate or anger. He has tried to move forward, to be a good person. To live his life so his parents and his brothers would be proud of him if they ever met. And he has succeeded.

After years of silence, refusing to speak about the horrors of the war or his experiences, Murray decided his story must be told if the revulsion of what the Germans had done was to be remembered by following generations. He began speaking at civic groups, various organizations, and equally important, at schools. He closes each of his powerful presentations with this: "It is my responsibility to tell those who didn't know the truth what really happened during those tragic years. To testify. Those of us who are survivors must now speak for the dead. I promise from the bottom of my heart that I will never forget those who perished."

The survivors must speak, or the world will forget; others with small hearts and minds will attempt to take the truth and mask it, twist it. Murray Ebner remembers: "It is my responsibility to bear witness. This is why God saved me."

Epilogue

Hitler, Goebbels, Himmler, Bormann, Heydrich...they are all gone. Suicides and failures to the very end, they live on in disgrace, as examples of what human beings should not be. Their failure was obvious to the entire world, long before their end. Millions had to die so they could ignore the simple fact of their own failure. They did everything they could, moved heaven and earth to destroy the Jews and the other objects of their sick hatred, to erase their very memory from men's minds. They expended a huge part of their considerable resources, right up to the end of the war, in destroying the Jews, root and branch. They nearly succeeded.

The Jews live on, all over the world. At a horrifying cost in lives, they survived and have gone on with life as they had so many times before. The incredible Nazi death machine, an engine of the darkest night in men's hearts, with its meticulous records, its pounding weapons, its senseless ideals and useless hatreds, and its pathetically small heart was no match for the Jews.

Murray Ebner has outlived the thousand-year Reich.

So this is what you need to know: Murray Ebner's two families are now one family.

Moniek Ebner will search evermore for his home and his mother and father and brothers, never giving up hope.

Murray Ebner is home, sitting at *Seder* surrounded by his family — loved, content...and victorious.

EUROPEAN-JEWISH CHILDREN'S AID, Inc.
(formerly, GERMAN-JEWISH CHILDREN'S AID, Inc.)

15 PARK ROW
NEW YORK 7, N. Y.

Telephone COrtlandt 7-8700

HERMAN W. BLOCK, Chairman
JOSEPH C. HYMAN, Vice-Chairman
PAUL FELIX WARBURG, Treasurer
ETHEL H. WISE, Secretary

LOTTE MARCUSE, Director of Placements

RECEPTION CENTER: 681 Cauldwell venue
Bronx 55, N.Y

March 7, 1947

Mrs. Anne Maybruck
944 South 18th street
Columbus, Ohio

Dear Mrs. Maybruck:

I am writing you on behalf of a young polish boy who arrived recently from abroad. He came here on an organization affidavit and will receive help from the organization in accordance with government regulations. He is a survivor of several concentration camps, who now wants to start life anew in a new world.He had only known of one relative in this country and had thought he could live in that family. When he came and found out that these plans could not possibly materialise, he became much disturbed and rejected. You can readily see how this would disappoint him.

He was told that you are a relative of his also. Could you trace this relationship and let us know whether you are at all interested? If you are, we would have to ask an organization in Columbus to discuss with you the particulars of the project and how the organization would work matters out with you. If you are not related just let us know. If you are related but cannot offer him a home, let us know right away. He does not know that we are writing to you, for he hesitates to ask for anything. He will let us work out plans for him elsewhere as we do for so many of the boys and girls coming here, once he knows that neither you nor other relatives can give him a home in which to start again.

The boy is Moschek or Moishe EBNER, born 9-15-1929 in Wisznicz Newy, Poland, son of Hirsch Ebner and Feigel, born Sellinger. The father was in buisness. The parents and three of their four children perished during the war in various camps and only Moschek was able to save his life. He is a fine boy, eager to work and learn english. Perhaps you can identify the relationship if I tell you that he is related to a Mr. Joseph Ebner of Springfield, Ohio and Miss Surick, of Brooklyn, N.Y.

I shall be waiting for your reply.

Sincerely,

Lotte Marcuse

Lotte Marcuse,
Director of Placements.

The orphanage caseworker sent this letter to the Maybrucks in search of potential links to family members.

RESIDENT ALIEN'S BORDER
CROSSING IDENTIFICATION CARD

A. R. No. 6563254
NAME EBNER: MOSES SCHYA
ADDRESS 944 So. 18th St.
AT TIME OF ISSUE Columbus, Ohio
DATE OF BIRTH Sept. 20, 1928
PLACE OF BIRTH Wisnicz,Nowy,Poland
SEX Male NATIONALITY Poland
HEIGHT: FT. 5 IN. 10 WEIGHT 154 LBS.
COMP. Dark HAIR Dk.Br. EYES Brown
VISIBLE MARKS OR PECULIARITIES Tattoo, left forearm

SIGNATURE OF HOLDER

No. 656062

Military Border Crossing Identification card.

Murray sitting at the front of a boat with other boys from one of the orphanages he lived in.

Murray at the age of 17 while in one of the three orphanages he lived in during 1946–1947.

Basic training, 101st Airborne.

Basic training, 1951, at Camp Breckenridge, Kentucky.

U.S. Military Identification card.

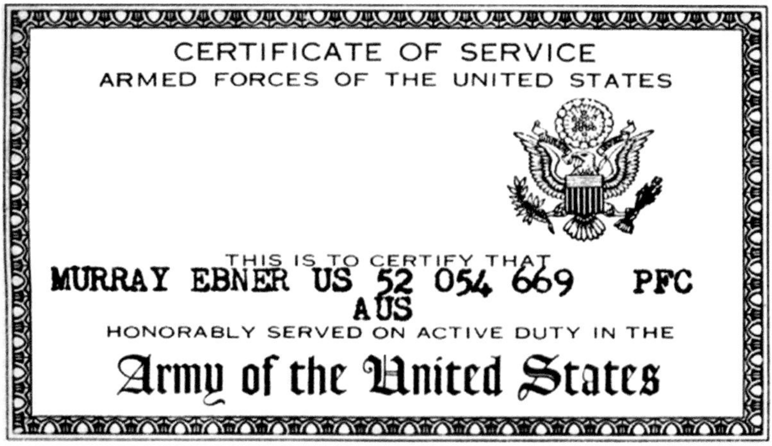

CERTIFICATE OF SERVICE
ARMED FORCES OF THE UNITED STATES

THIS IS TO CERTIFY THAT
MURRAY EBNER US 52 054 669 PFC
AUS
HONORABLY SERVED ON ACTIVE DUTY IN THE
Army of the United States

Certificate of U.S. Military Service, 1950–1952.

Murray on military patrol.

Leisure time with platoon buddies.

THE UNITED STATES OF AMERICA

ORIGINAL
TO BE GIVEN TO
THE PERSON NATURALIZED

No. 7151410

CERTIFICATE OF NATURALIZATION

Petition No. 7298

Personal description of holder as of date of naturalization: Date of birth September 20, 1928 sex Male
complexion Medium color of eyes Brown color of hair Brown height 5 feet 10 inches
weight 155 pounds; visible distinctive marks Tatoo on left forearm "B-2992"
Marital status Single former nationality Polish
I certify that the description above given is true, and that the photograph affixed hereto is a likeness of me.

Murray Ebner
(Complete and true signature of holder)

United States of America
Southern District of Ohio } ss.
Be it known, that at a term of the District Court of United States
held pursuant to law at Columbus, Ohio
on June 29, 1953 the Court having found that MURRAY EBNER
then residing at 944 S. 18th St., Columbus, Ohio

Certificate of citizenship, June 29, 1953, at the age of 25.

Visiting the state capitol while on leave while being stationed at Arlington Farms, Virginia.

Sylvia, Murray's wife-to-be, engagement picture, 1953.

Wedding picture, November 26, 1953.

Miami Beach in the 1950s.

Fun at home in the 1970s.

The front of Murray Ebner's childhood home.

Murray Ebner with family members standing in front of his childhood home in Poland.

Murray Ebner standing in front of his childhood home in Poland.

Murray Ebner standing in the backyard of his childhood home.

Searching for items Murray's father told his family he buried in the backyard of their home at the outbreak of the war.

Family standing in the backyard of the Ebner residence in Poland.

Murray Ebner embraces a neighbor he hadn't seen in over 60 years.

Murray with the original purchaser of his grandfather's farm.

Murray Ebner with bakery owner.

Exterior of the room Murray Ebner lived in with his family and another family in the Ghetto.

Murray Ebner with his children and daughter-in-law inside the room his family and another family lived in inside the Bochnia Ghetto.

Leonardo St. where Murray Ebner was picked up in the Bochnia Ghetto, never to see his family again.

Murray Ebner reflecting on what he remembers to be nearly the very spot he stood when he was picked up in the Bochnia Ghetto by a Nazi truck and taken to the Plazow work camp.

Murray Ebner at Plazow, the first camp where he was imprisoned.

Murray standing in front of the memorial monument at Plazow.

Murray Ebner with his son Mark on the railroad tracks in Auschwitz.

Murray Ebner reflecting as he walks the fence line at the Auschwitz prison camp.

Murray Ebner lighting a candle and reflecting on the moment on the railroad tracks in Auschwitz.

Murray Ebner standing with family members on the railroad tracks in Auschwitz.

The gas chambers at Auschwitz.

The latrine at Auschwitz.

The Barracks at Auschwitz.

Filming in Auschwitz prison camp for the Emmy award winning documentary of Murray Ebner, entitled "Survivor's Journey."

Family standing in front of the gas chamber ruins in Auschwitz.

Murray standing on the railroad tracks in the Auschwitz prison camp.

Murray Ebner's family, top row from left: Lisa Ebner Rosen, Gayle Rosen, Zachary Ebner, Nicole Ebner, Mark Ebner, Aaron Rosen, Cindy Ebner. Front row from left: Sabrina Ebner, Murray Ebner, Sylvia Ebner, Julian Ebner, Jared Rosen.

Murray Ebner, circa 2001.

ThisWeek in Pickerington — Page 3

Eighth-graders learn about Holocaust

By SUSAN PAVILKEY
ThisWeek Staff Writer

By Chris Putman/ThisWeek

Murray Ebner shows students the monthly check he received from the German government.

Some Pickerington Junior High School eighth-grade students got a first-hand account of life in a concentration camp last week, thanks to a man who spent some of his teen years under Nazi control in World War II.

Columbus resident Murray Ebner, whose entire family — with the exception of a few cousins — died in the Nazi Holocaust, told 125 students of his experiences at Auschwitz and other concentration camps during World War II.

Many of the students were noticeably affected by his recounting.

A Jew born in Poland, Ebner told the students he "had a wonderful life" before the Nazi invasion of his country.

"I only survived, not because I was smarter than any of the other prisoners, but because God wanted me to survive so I could let everyone know what terrible things happened in the camps," he told the students.

Ebner was 13 years old when his life fell apart.

"A government like Germany organized and systematically planned the murder of millions of people. You can imagine the evil," he said.

Ebner said Jews made up approximately 10 percent of the Polish population and nearly all those Jews died during the Holocaust.

"My father was in World War I and we'd heard all his stories, so when World War II started, I was excited. I was just a kid. I thought that we could beat the Germans any time," he said.

Ebner said his bravado soon disappeared once the Germans took control of Poland and confiscated all his family's belongings, making it nearly impossible to even purchase food, and then forced all Jews into ghettos.

"My family managed to hide in the woods for a while, but that got miserable with the weather and the bugs. We had to steal food from nearby farms and be very careful, because if the Nazis discovered us, we would be shot. At first, we thought we'd be able to go home in a few days, but we soon realized we'd never be able to go home again," he said.

The family eventually wound up in one of the ghettos, where living conditions were deplorable, Ebner said.

"People were depressed, hungry. The Germans would come every day to 're-settle' people and they went with them, thinking they could get food. They didn't realize they were being taken to concentration camps," Ebner said.

He described a ghastly incident that happened to one of his female cousins.

"One German soldier demanded that she give him her child and she refused. The soldier grabbed the child from her and smashed him up against a wall, killing the boy," he said.

Ebner ended up in a concentration camp after naively accepting a German guard's offer of a truck ride.

"I thought I was going to get some work. I was taken to Krakow, to a cemetery where they were building a concentration camp. My parents never knew what happened to me," he said.

In Krakow, the 13-year-old Ebner saw wheelbarrows full of dead bodies.

"It was the first time I had ever been away from my family. I cried," he said.

Ebner said he narrowly escaped death on several occasions.

"One night, I slept in a different bunk, even though we weren't supposed to. During the night, a German officer came in to look for me, but couldn't find me. I found out the next morning that some people were missing from the roll call and so three people were to be hung as punishment. I was supposed to be one of them," he said.

Ebner said the straw mattresses and barracks where he lived were infested with lice.

"We used to play with the lice for entertainment," he said, drawing groans from many of the students.

Ebner eventually ended up in Auschwitz, where he witnessed prisoners regularly being herded into gas chambers.

Ebner, who admitted that he still has flashbacks of his experiences, said time has been a "big healer."

"I have no desire to return to Poland, although many others have. It was a happy place, but since my family is gone, there is no reason to return," he said.

This article is just one of the hundreds of newspaper articles describing Ebner's featured speaking engagements to tens of thousands of students in middle schools, high schools, and universities in communities all over.

Ebner Holocaust Building, designed, donated, and built by Murray and Sylvia Ebner as a lasting tribute to Ebner and all Columbus survivors.

Ebner Holocaust Building Exhibit—Interactive Area, where the public can listen to any of the dozens of Columbus survivor testimonials at no charge.

Ebner Holocaust Building Exhibit—Family Photos.